PRIZE WINNERS

PRIZE WINNERS

*Recipes and Menu Ideas
from Award-Winning
Foodservice Personalities*

Raymond B. Peddersen

CBI Publishing Company, Inc.
Russia Wharf
286 Congress Street
Boston, MA 02210

Cover design: Kredlow & Gonzalez

Library of Congress Cataloging in Publication Data
Main entry under title:
Prize winners.

   1. Cookery.   2. Quantity cookery.
3. Food service I. Peddersen, Raymond B.
TX715.P942277 1983   641   82-12911
ISBN 0-8436-2253-9

Copyright © 1983 by CBI Publishing Company, Inc.
All rights reserved. This book may not be reproduced by any means without written permission from the publisher.

Printed in the United States of America.

Printing (last digit): 9 8 7 6 5 4 3 2 1

For Shaari Ann,
the pickle on the great hamburger of life

Contents

Preface xxi

Foodservice Operation 1

    Chapter 1 Service of Food 3

    Chapter 2 Special Topics 9

    Chapter 3 Food Purchasing and Inventory Control 16

    Chapter 4 Nonfood Purchasing 47

    Chapter 5 Sanitation 55

    Chapter 6 Recipe Standardization 62

Contributors and Recipes 69

Appendix 295

Contributors

Anton Aigner   Inhilco, Inc.   70
Gertrude Applebaum   Corpus Christi Independent School District   74
Lysle and Albert Aschaffenburg   The Pontchartrain Hotel   76
Arthur C. Avery   Purdue University   80
Jerome Berkman   Cedars-Sinai Medical Center   82
Jerome Berns   The "21" Club   84
John C. Birchfield   Birchfield Foodsystems   88
Vincent J. Bommarito   Tony's Restaurants, Inc.   90
Jack L. Bowman   Saint Joseph's Medical Center   92
Jack F. Braun   The Lemon Tree   94
Dieter H. Buehler   Idle Wild Farm, Inc.   98
Byron L. Byron   American Foodservice Enterprises, Inc.   102
Frances W. Cloyd   Lynchburg College   104
Stuart G. Cross   The Roof, Hotel Utah   108
Ann M. Crowley   Health Care Services Ltd.   110
Edgar L. Davis   Independent restaurateur   112
Paul B. Deignan   United and Children's Hospitals   114
Stanley Demos   The Coach House Restaurant   118
Don A. Dianda   Doros Restaurant   122
S. Kent Dohrman   University of Illinois at Urbana-Champaign   124
Fred W. Dollar   Texas A & M University   128
Charles J. Doulos   Jimmy's Harborside Restaurant, Inc.   130
Paul R. Doyon   West Jersey Hospital System   132
Peter Gust Economou   The Park Lane Manor House   134
Richard N. Frank   Lawry's Foods, Inc., Lawry's Restaurants, Inc.   136
Charles F. Frederiksen   Iowa State University   138
John C. Friese   USDA Food and Nutrition Service   142
Vincenzo Gabriele   Casa Grisanti   150
Angelo Gagliano   Memorial Sloan-Kettering Cancer Center   144

CONTRIBUTORS

Peter Goldman   Hyatt Regency, San Francisco   146
Roland and Victor Gotti   Ernie's   148
Michael Grisanti   Casa Grisanti   150
Kenneth F. Hansen   Scandia   152
Sister Mary Kateri Harkins   Mercy Hospital   154
G. "Jim" Hasslocher   Frontier Enterprises, Inc.   156
Keith Hazeltine   Sam Houston State University   158
Samuel L. Huff   Washington State University   160
Barry B. Hutchings   Swedish Medical Center, Craig Hospital   164
Paul Hysen   Hysen & Associates, Inc.   166
Tony Jaeger   Movenpick Enterprises   170
Faisal A. Kaud   University of Wisconsin Medical Center   172
John H. Koniares   Kernwood at Lynnfield   174
George Lang   The George Lang Corporation   176
Stuart Levin   Top of the Park Restaurant   180
Leon Lianides   The Coach House   182
G. E. Livingston   Food Science Associates, Inc.   184
Garrett Dawson "Sonny" Look   Look's Sir-Loin House, Inc.   186
Beverly M. Lowe   Hampton City Schools   190
Kenneth T. G. Lum   Princes Pauahi Coffee Shop Restaurant   192
Tom G. Margittai   The Four Seasons Restaurant   194
Ella Brennan Martin   Commander's Palace   196
Dan H. Mathews, Jr.   ARA Services, Inc.   198
Frances E. McGlone   Oakland Unified School District   200
Alan McLaren   Community Hospital of Indianapolis   204
Michael Lewis Minor   L. J. Minor Corporation   206
Dearl Morris   Caterpillar Tractor Company   210
Otto E. Mueller   Pennsylvania State University   214
James A. Nassikas   The Stanford Court   218
Robert H. Nelson   Capitol Professional Chef's Association   222
Mary Nix   Cob County Public Schools   224
W. J. O'Sullivan   Ford Motor Company   226
Raymond B. Peddersen   LDS Hospital   230
G. William Peffers   Ingalls Memorial Hospital   234
Michael S. Pinkert   Mental Health Management, Inc.   236
Harry A. Pope   H. A. Pope and Sons, Inc.   238
Lawrence S. Procopio   Palms Restaurant   240
Ruby P. Puckett   Shands Teaching Hospital and Clinics, Inc.   242
Gerald Ramsey   Southern Methodist University   246
Clinton L. Rappole   Hilton College of Hotel and Restaurant Management   248

Karl A. Ratzsch, Jr.   Karl Ratzsch's Restaurant   252
Douglas H. Richie   California State College at Long Beach   254
Willy O. Rossel   Braniff Airways, Inc.   256
Don Roth   Don Roth's Blackhawk Restaurant   260
Winston J. Schuler   Win Schuler's, Inc.   264
Ted L. Smith   Michigan State University   266
Lloyd and Les Stephenson   The Old Apple Farm, Stephenson's Restaurants, Inc.   268
Louis I. Szathmary II   The Bakery Restaurant, Louis Szathmary Associates   270
Jay Treadwell   United States Senate   274
Milton Vallen   Moss Rehabilitation Hospital   276
Jane Young Wallace   *Restaurants & Institutions* magazine   278
Frank George Wangeman   Hilton Hotels Corporation, Hotel Waldorf-Astoria Corporation   280
Paul Craig Weisman   University of Washington Hospital   282
Charles H. Wilson   University of Northern Colorado   284
Ted Wright   The Cloister Hotel   286
Herman E. Zaccarelli   Restaurant, Hotel, and Institutional Management Institute, Purdue University   288

Recipes

APPETIZERS AND HORS D'OEUVRES

    Asparagus Tart (Aigner)   71
    Avocado Lime Salad (Zaccarelli)   289
    Blackhawk Salad (Roth)   261
    Cardinal Salad (Zaccarelli)   289
    Crab Demos (Demos)   119
    Crabmeat Lorenzo (Rossel)   257
    Hot and Cold Salad (Hutchings)   165
    Kippered Salmon Salad Plate (Weisman)   282
    Swedish Meatballs (Huff)   161
    Tiny Smoked Salmon Sandwiches in Black Bread (Levin)   181

SOUPS

    Austrian Green Bean Soup (Minor)   207
    Cabbage Soup (McGlone)   201
    Cheese and Leek Soup (Hysen)   167
    Cheese Soup (Demos)   119
    Cold Cucumber Soup (Treadwell)   274
    Crab and Corn Bisque (Martin)   197
    Cream of Artichoke Soup with Crushed Hazelnuts (Nassikas)   219
    Cream of Kohlrabi Soup (Szathmary)   271
    Cream of Tomato Soup (Minor)   208
    Gazpacho I (Cross)   109
    Gazpacho II (Cross)   109
    Iowa State Bean Soup (Frederiksen)   139
    Karl Ratzsch's Lentil Soup (Ratzsch)   252
    Lima Bean and Bacon Soup (Richie)   254

xiv RECIPES

    Navy Bean Soup (Deignan)　　115
    Oyster Broth (Aschaffenburg)　　77
    Potée Paysanne (Lang)　　178
    Sopa de Calabaza Fria (Rossel)　　257
    Southern Gumbo (Puckett)　　243
    Swiss Onion Soup (Schuler)　　265
    Vegetarian Vegetable Soup (Deigan)　　116
    Vichyssoise (Berns)　　85

ENTREES AND SAUCES

    Baked Liver with Onion Gravy (Morris)　　211
    Baked Red Snapper and Scallop Tartare (Margittai)　　194
    Barbecued Shrimp (Look)　　187
    Béarnaise Sauce (Hansen)　　152
    Beef and Noodle Fiesta (Morris)　　211
    Beef Burgundy (Peddersen)　　231
    Beef Kabob (Bowman)　　92
    Beef Stroganoff (Deignan)　　117
    Blackhawk au Jus for Prime Ribs of Beef (Roth)　　262
    Braised Beef Stew with Vegetables (Morris)　　212
    Cheese Soufflé (Kaud)　　173
    Cheese Strata (Dohrman)　　125
    Chicken Breast New England (Buehler)　　99
    Chicken Cacciatora alla "Palms" (Procopio)　　240
    Chicken Cynthia à la Champagne (Gotti)　　149
    Chicken Velvet (Mueller)　　215
    Chili (Bowman)　　93
    The Coach House Seafood à la Méditerranée (Lianides)　　182
    Cottage Cheese Croquettes (Birchfield)　　89
    Crab Demos (Demos)　　119
    Crab Legs Bercy (Nassikas)　　219
    Crabmeat Imperial à la Citronier (Braun)　　95
    Crabmeat Remick (Aschaffenburg)　　78
    Creamed Pork Tips (Morris)　　213
    Dover Sole My Way (Demos)　　120
    Easy Beef Stroganoff (Wallace)　　279
    Enchilada Verde Casserole (Hasslocher)　　157
    Escalopes de Veau Charleroi (Berns)　　86
    Fettucine con Pesto (Grisanti and Gabriele)　　151
    Golden Mushroom "Sir-Loin" Beef Tips (Look)　　187

Health Sandwich No. 3 (Richie)   255
Hot Chicken Salad (Nix)   225
Jimmy's Baked Stuffed Fillet of Sole with Lobster Newburg Sauce (Doulos)   131
Kalvfilet Oscar (Hansen)   153
Karl Ratzsch's Braised Lamb Shanks Gemüse (Ratzsch)   253
Krautburgers (Wilson)   284
Lamb Chops Stroganoff (O'Sullivan)   226
Lasagna (Peddersen)   232
Lasagna with Vegetable Protein (Dohrman)   126
Lobster Thermidor (Minor)   209
Moussaka (Economou)   135
Mousseline of Salmon (Goldman)   146
Mostaccioli (Mueller)   216
Mushroom-Cheese Bake (Cloyd)   105
Mushrooms à la Chef Robert (Nelson)   222
Nottingham Bird (Braun)   96
Pancakes Oscar (Goldman)   147
Pancit Guisado (Weisman)   283
Pasta con Pesce (Bommarito)   91
Paupiette de Coeur de Filet with Shallot Sauce (Treadwell)   275
"Pepikalua" Hawaiian Beef Marinade (Peffers)   234
Pizza Meatloaf Pie (Frederiksen)   140
Plantation Spareribs (Wilson)   285
Poached Salmon with Sauce Mousseline "Belle Polonaise" (Livingston)   185
Pork Chops Supreme (Hazeltine)   158
Poulet Farci Bon Vivant (Gagliano)   145
Richard Frank's Famous Leftover Hash (Frank)   137
River Trout (Truites de Rivière) (Wangeman)   281
Roast Prime Ribs of Beef (Roth)   263
Saltimbocca alla Romana (Nassikas)   220
San Francisco Cioppino (Byron)   103
Sauce Espagnole (Braun)   97
Sauce Louis (Szathmary)   272
Sauce Supreme (Buehler)   100
Scampi Miracle (Jaeger)   171
Scottish Mince 'n Tatties (McLaren)   205
Seafood Casserole (Cloyd)   106
Selle d'Agneau en Feuilletage (Aigner)   72
Sesame Fried Chicken (Berkman)   82

RECIPES

Shangri-la Sauce (Peffers)   234
Shrimp Cocktail Sauce (Huff)   162
Shrimp Victoria (Dollar)   129
Smothered Pheasant à la G.W.P. (Peffers)   235
Spaghetti Carbonara (Koniares)   175
Spaghetti Meat Sauce (Applebaum)   75
Spanish Sauce for Shrimp (Ramsey)   247
Spareribs à la Vallen (Vallen)   277
Spinach Lasagna (Smith)   267
Sunset Salad with Lorenzo Dressing (Berns)   87
Supreme of Chicken with Wine in White Sauce (Mathews)   199
Sweet and Sour Pork Cubes (Huff)   163
Sweetbreads Sauté au Beurre Noisette (Demos)   121
"Texas" Chili Recipe (Look)   188
Tudie's Chicken Dinner (Look)   189
Veal Cloister (Wright)   287
Veal Michelangelo (Grisanti and Gabriele)   151
Veal Scaloppine alla Doros (Dianda)   123
White Clam Sauce with Spaghetti (Procopio)   241

VEGETABLES

Baked Fennel Parmesan (Margittai)   195
Broccoli Soufflé (Berkman)   83
Carrots Provençal (Rappole)   249
Creamed Spinach (Roth)   263
Escalloped Potatoes (Peddersen)   233
Escalloped Sweet Potatoes (Stephenson)   269
Green Bean Casserole (Cloyd)   106
Green Rice (O'Sullivan)   227
Mushrooms à la Daum (Berns)   87
Ratatouille (Buehler)   101
Ratatouille (Hysen)   168
Rice Mangalais with Curry Sauce (O'Sullivan)   228
Squash Medley (Nix)   225
Tabbuli (Hazeltine)   159

DESSERTS

Apricot-Sour Cream Pie (Zaccarelli)   290
Black Walnut Cake (Cloyd)   107

Butter Pecan Dream Pie (Zaccarelli)   291
Carrot Cake (Avery)   81
Carrot Cake with Cream Cheese Frosting (Frederiksen)   141
Chocolate Chip Cookies (Harkins)   155
Chocolate Mousse (Hysen)   169
Chocolate Silk Pie (Hazeltine)   159
The Coach House Bread and Butter Pudding (Lianides)   183
Crème Renversée (Doyon)   133
Crepes Soufflé (Aschaffenburg)   79
Crepes Carioca (Rossel)   258
Date Dream Dessert (McGlone)   201
Depression Dessert (Friese)   143
Golden Lemon Tart (Aigner)   73
Graham Cracker Torte (McGlone)   202
Guava con Queso (Rossel)   259
Homemade Praline-Pecan Ice Cream (Puckett)   244
Hot Fruit Compote (Applebaum)   74
Irish Coffee Pie (Davis)   113
Lemon Cheese Cake (O'Sullivan)   229
Lemon Meringue Pie (Bowman)   93
Meringue Glacée (Puckett)   245
Midnight Cakes (Mueller)   217
Mocha Cream-Filled Cake (McGlone)   203
Nut Torte (Pope)   239
Pecan Pie (Lowe)   191
Pineapple Flambé (Lum)   193
Praline Ice Cream Pie (Nassikas)   221
Raisin Streusel Pie (Rappole)   250

MISCELLANEOUS

Bran Muffins (Crowley)   111
Bread and Butter Pickles (Nelson)   223
Chinese-Style Relish (Zaccarelli)   292
Curried Fruit Relish (Zaccarelli)   292
Peach-Wine Relish (Zaccarelli)   293
Spoon Bread (Lowe)   191
Waffles Grand Marnier (Pinkert)   237

Appendix

Table of Equivalents 296
Approximate Ingredient Substitutions 297
Fractional Equivalents 298
Common Container Sizes 298
Reconstitution Guide 299
Preheat Guide 299
Timetable for Braising Meats 300
Timetable for Simmering Meats 301
Timetable for Broiling Meats 302
Temperature and Timetable for Roasting Meat 303
Deep Fat Frying Temperatures 304
Timetable for Cooking Vegetables 305
Incorrect Oven Temperatures 306
Temperature Conversion Chart 306
Spice Chart 307
U.S. Grade Standards for Nuts 308
Portion Yields of Cereals, Mixes, and Bakery Products 309
Can Equivalents 310
Case Equivalents 310
Milk Equivalents 310
Canned Fruit Weight Chart 311
Approximate % Yields of Fresh Fruits 312
Approximate % Yields of Vegetables 313
Canned Vegetable Weight Chart 314
Sizes and Weights of Fresh Eggs 315
Egg Products Needed to Replace a Specific Number of Whole Eggs, Egg Yolks, or Egg Whites 315
Pan Sizes to Fit 19⅞ × 11⅞ Openings 316
Dippers and Ladles 316

Preface

The idea behind this book was to gather recipes that are the personal favorites of some of the best restaurant and foodservice professionals in the country. To achieve that end, I approached those people in our industry whose work I respect most. Most of them have received confirmation of their excellence in the form of peer recognition, such as association presidencies, the prestigious IFMA Gold and/or Silver Plate Awards, and *Institutions* Ivy Award of Distinction. All of the contributors have been most generous with their help on this project.

I have a penchant for learning the history of our industry. Therefore, I have included biographies of the contributors so that you, too, can appreciate the industry's history as it is represented by these people. Enjoy!

This book is intended to be more than a basic recipe book or cookbook. Between these covers there are brief chapters on the service of food, inventory control, sanitation, recipe standardization, and the purchase of food and non-food items. A chapter on special topics covers some preparation tips, special diets, and taste panels.

The recipes included are the contributors' *personal* favorites—some originated in their homes and some in their businesses. All recipes and preparation instructions appear as given by the contributor. Wherever possible I have converted the quantities specified to a uniform six-portion yield so that these dishes may grace the family table as well as those of the foodservice operation. I take sole responsibility for the accuracy of the recipe conversions; please let me know of any errors, and they will be corrected for subsequent reprintings of this book.

My deep appreciation is extended to the contributors, to *Institutions* for the use of some material I prepared for their "1980 Foodservice Buying and Specifying Guide," to *The Cornell Hotel and Restaurant Quarterly* for allowing the use of Ericson's recipe calculation materials and *The Essentials of Good Table Service*, to CBI Publishing for the use of some of Dahmer's *The Waiter and Waitress Training Manual*, to the National Institute for the Foodservice Industry for material from *Applied Foodservice Sanitation*, and to the National Restaurant Association for charts. Thanks also to Mike, Norm, and, especially,

Phil for being so patient when I missed the deadline, to Jane Hoover for a fine job of editing, to Jane Wescott and the marketing staff, to my ever-faithful manuscript typist, Diane Halford, to Peggy for her support and help, and to Ed Sanders, D.B.A., and Paul Hysen for inspiration and encouragement over the years.

Raymond B. Peddersen
Salt Lake City, Utah

FOODSERVICE OPERATION

1 Service of Food

This chapter briefly discusses the four types of service of food—American, French, Russian, and English. Diagrams illustrate the correct cover arrangements for the American service. *The Waiter and Waitress Training Manual* by Sondra J. Dahmer and Kurt W. Kahl is the source of much of the following information. It is recommended as an excellent text for professional waiter or waitress training.

AMERICAN SERVICE

American service is less formal than French, Russian, or English service and is the style most commonly used in restaurants in this country. American service is distinguished by the fact that the food is dished onto plates in the kitchen. Except for the salad and the bread and butter, the food is placed on the entree plate. Only one waiter or waitress serves the meal. Food is served from the left of the diner; beverages are served and soiled dishes are cleared from the right.

The table setting for breakfast and lunch differs from the setting for dinner. Breakfast and lunch are less elaborate meals with fewer courses and thus require less serviceware than does dinner. Serviceware used for the American breakfast and lunch cover includes fork, knife, teaspoon, napkin, bread and butter plate, butter spreader (optional), and water glass. The breakfast and lunch cover is placed approximately one inch from the edge of the table. The napkin is in the center of the cover. To the left of the napkin is the fork. To the right of the napkin is the knife, with the cutting edge turned toward the napkin. The teaspoon is to the right of the knife. The water glass is placed directly above the tip of the knife. The bread and butter plate is centered above the tines of the fork. Traditionally, a small butter spreader should be laid across the rim of the bread and butter plate, but today this is done by very few restaurants. (See Figure 1–1.) When coffee or tea is served, the cup and saucer are placed to the right of the teaspoon. Breakfast toast or luncheon salad is placed to the left of the fork. The entrée plate is placed in the center of the cover after the guest has removed the napkin. When side dishes and accompaniments are served, they are placed in convenient locations on the table. (See Figure 1–2.)

Serviceware used for the American dinner cover includes two dinner forks, dinner knife, butter spreader, two teaspoons, service plate (optional), napkin, bread and butter plate, and water glass. The dinner cover is placed approximately one inch from the edge of the table. The napkin is placed in the center of the cover, either on a service plate or by itself. The two dinner forks are to the left of the napkin. The dinner knife is to the immediate right of the napkin; to the right of the knife, in order, are the butter spreader and the two teaspoons. The cutting edges of the knives are turned toward the napkin. The water glass is placed directly above the tip of the butter spreader. The bread and butter plate is centered above the forks. (See Figure 1–3.)

When soup or an appetizer is served, it is placed on an underliner and served in the center of the cover. Salad is placed to the left of the forks. When coffee or tea is served, it is put to the right of the spoons. The entrée plate is placed in the center of the cover. Special purpose silverware is brought to the table as needed, for example, a soup spoon with soup. Bread, accompaniments, and side dishes are placed in convenient locations on the table.[1] (See Figure 1–4.)

FRENCH SERVICE

French service is a formal type of service originated for European nobility and presently enjoyed by a few who can afford the time and expense of meals served in this manner. French service is distinguished by the fact that food is cooked or completed at a side table in view of the guests. Food that can be cooked, assembled, or completed in a reasonable amount of time is brought from the kitchen to the dining room on heavy silver platters and placed on a serving cart called a "guéridon." A small spirit stove called a "réchaud" is used to keep the food warm. The food is readied by cooking, deboning, slicing, and/or garnishing, as necessary, and served on heated plates. Typical specialties that are often served in the French style are Caesar salad, tournedos au poivre (pepper steak), and crêpes suzettes.

French service calls for two waiters working together to serve the meal. There may also be a captain to seat the guests and a wine steward to serve the

---

[1] Sondra J. Dahmer and Kurt W. Kahl, *The Waiter and Waitress Training Manual*, 2nd edition (CBI Publishing Company, Inc., 1982), pp. 14–18.

SERVICE OF FOOD 5

The cover includes the following: (1) bread and butter plate, (2) dinner fork, (3) dinner knife, (4) teaspoon, (5) napkin, (6) water glass.

Figure 1-1 Cover for American Breakfast and Lunch Setting

Dishes are added as follows: (1) plate for breakfast toast or lunch salad, (2) entree plate, (3) cup and saucer.

Figure 1-2 Addition of Dishes to American Breakfast and Lunch Setting

CHAPTER ONE

The cover includes the following: (1) dinner fork, (2) dinner fork, (3) dinner knife, (4) butter spreader, (5) teaspoon, (6) teaspoon, (7) napkin, (8) bread and butter plate, (9) water glass.

Figure 1-3   Cover for American Dinner Setting

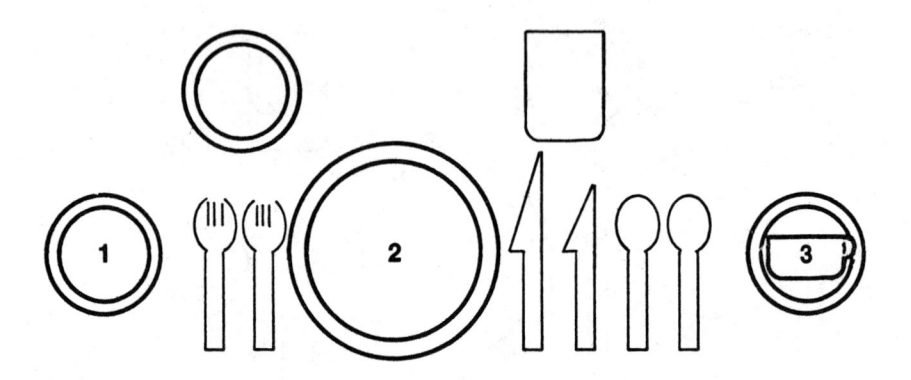

Dishes are added as follows: (1) salad plate, (2) service plate, (3) cup and saucer.

Figure 1-4   Addition of Dishes to American Dinner Setting

wine. The principal waiter is called the "chef de rang" (experienced waiter). The duties are seating the guests when there is no captain, taking the order, serving the drinks, preparing some of the food with flourish, and presenting the check for payment. The second waiter is called the "commis de rang." The duties of this job are taking the order from the chef de rang to the kitchen, picking up the food and carrying it to the dining room, serving the plates dished up by the chef de rang, clearing the dishes, and standing ready to assist whenever necessary. All food is served and cleared from the right of the guest except for butter, bread, and salad, which are served and cleared on the left side of the guest. Finger bowls of warm water with rose petals or lemon slices in them are brought with all finger foods, such as chicken and lobster, and at the end of the meal.[2]

The advantages of French service are that each person is given a great deal of attention and the service is extremely elegant. The disadvantages are that fewer sittings are possible, more space is required for service, many highly trained personnel are required, and service is expensive and time-consuming. As a result, the use of this elegant service is declining both in America and in Europe.

RUSSIAN SERVICE

Russian service is similar in many respects to French service. Both are very formal and elegant, and the guest is given considerable personal attention. Both call for the use of heavy silver serviceware, and the table settings are the same. The two major differences of the Russian service are that only one waiter serves the meal and that the food is fully prepared and attractively arranged on silver platters in the kitchen. The waiter picks up the platters of food and the heated plates and carries them to the dining room on a large tray, which he places on a side stand. Going around the table clockwise, he puts a plate in front of each guest from the right side. Standing to the left and holding the platter of food in his left hand, the waiter shows the food to the guest. Then, using a large spoon and fork, the waiter dishes up the desired portion onto the guest's plate. Service proceeds counterclockwise around the table. The unserved food is returned to the kitchen. As in French service, finger bowls and napkins are provided with the meal, and soiled dishes are cleared when everyone has finished eating.

The advantages of Russian service are that only one waiter is needed and service is as elegant as French service and yet faster and less expensive. Also, no extra space is needed for special equipment, such as the guéridon. The disadvantages are the large investment that must be made in silver serviceware and the number of platters that must be employed when each person selects

---

[2]Dahmer and Kahl, pp. 10–12.

CHAPTER ONE

a different dish. Another disadvantage is that the last one to be served must select from the possibly unappetizing food left by those served previously.[3]

ENGLISH SERVICE

Although English service is used occasionally for a special dinner served in a private dining room of a restaurant, it is more applicable to a meal served by servants in a private home. The food on platters and the heated plates are brought from the kitchen and placed before the host at the head of the table. The host carves, if necessary, and dishes the entrée and vegetable onto the individual plates. He hands the plates to the server standing to the left, who serves them to the hostess, guest of honor, and all the other guests. Dessert may also be served in this manner. All sauces, side dishes, and, in some cases, the vegetables are on the table and are passed around by the guests.[4]

---

[3]This excerpt from *The Essentials of Good Table Service* (pp. 55–58) was originally published by the Cornell University School of Hotel Administration. © 1975.
[4]Dahmer and Kahl, p. 14.

2 Special Topics

Salad dressings should be added to tossed or mixed salads containing soft-textured components (tomato slices) just before they are served, as they should not be allowed to stand for long periods of time. Lettuce and other vegetables for salads should be kept dry to prevent browning and loss of crispness. Ingredients for tossed or mixed salads should be wrapped in plastic film or placed in a covered container and then stored in coolers until used.

Forcing or inducing heating of food with high temperatures or exposed flames will reduce flavor or cause a burnt taste, decrease tenderness, and increase shrinkage. Cooking should always be done at the specified temperature and within the prescribed time span.

Formulations or recipes should be written out clearly and precisely. All quantity measurements should be listed, and the size of the correct measuring utensil, such as ladle or scoop size or number, should be included. Heating cycle and equipment should also be posted.

Holding prepared food in a steam table, cabinet, or under infrared lamps for excessive periods of time will reduce its quality by affecting texture and flavor, increasing shrinkage, or causing loss of nutrients. Foods may become mealy, mushy, soggy, or dry. Overproduction of food should be avoided as much as possible. Coffee should not be held longer than one hour and then only at temperatures of 185° to 190°F. Desserts like cream or custard pies require refrigerated storage to prevent spoilage.

Leftover foods should be packed loosely in shallow pans, labeled, covered, dated, and promptly refrigerated. Foods that are not likely to be reused should be thrown away. Fresh produce should always be washed before serving or using in salads or soups. Washing produce removes soil, dust, insecticides, and surface bacteria.

CONVENIENCE/READY FOODS

Government standards for meat and poultry products are pertinent as guidelines for quality assessment and cost evaluation. To qualify to be classified as a certain product, a food must contain a minimum amount of meat or poultry as prescribed for that product by the USDA. For example, ready-to-serve chicken soup must contain at least 2 percent chicken. Condensed chicken soup must contain at least 4 percent, so that it has at least 2 percent after being diluted with water. But chicken-flavored soup, which is not considered a poultry product, may contain less chicken. While the standards for meat ingredients are usually based on the fresh weight of the product, those for poultry are based on the weight of the cooked, deboned product. Since both meat and poultry shrink during cooking, the standards allow for this fact. For instance, turkey potpie must contain at least 14 percent of cooked turkey. Chicken burgers must be 100 percent chicken; a product containing any fillers must be called chicken patties.

Box 2–1
Recommended Refrigerated Storage Practices

All cooked food or other products removed from original container must be enclosed in clean, sanitized, covered container and identified.

Do not store packaged food in contact with water or undrained ice.

Check refrigerator thermometer regularly. Recommended temperatures:
produce	45°F (7°C) or below
dairy and meat	40°F (4°C) or below
seafood	30°F (−1°C) or below

Store large pieces of meat and all other foods so as to permit free circulation of cool air on all surfaces.

Do not store food directly on floor or base.

Schedule cleaning of equipment and refrigerated storage rooms at regular intervals.

Date all merchandise upon receipt and rotate inventory on a "first-in, first-out" basis.

Check fruits and vegetables daily for spoilage.

Store dairy products separately from strong-odored foods. Store fish apart from other food products.

Establish preventive maintenance program for equipment.

Source: National Restaurant Association.

> Promptly store frozen foods at a temperature of 0°F (−18°C) or below.
>
> Check freezer thermometer frequently.
>
> Cover all food containers.
>
> Wrap all food well to prevent freezer burn.
>
> Defrost as necessary to eliminate excessive frost build-up. If practical, defrost when the least amount of food is in storage.
>
> Plan your opening of the freezer. Get what you need at one time to reduce the loss of cold air.
>
> Remove contents to another freezer when defrosting to permit thorough cleaning and to keep contents dry.
>
> Date all merchandise upon receipt and rotate inventory on a "first-in, first-out" basis.
>
> Keep shelving and floor clean at all times.
>
> Establish preventive maintenance program for equipment.

Source: National Restaurant Association.

Box 2–2 Recommended Frozen Storage Practices

Improper or careless storage techniques downgrade the quality of foods. Poor stock rotation will prolong storing in any of the storage areas (dry, cooler, or freezer) and may lead to flavor and texture changes. Correct storage control procedures will tend to eliminate these problems. (See Box 2–1 and Box 2–2.)

Haphazard food assembly methods, including piling or stacking of food products, spillage and mixing of liquids, such as sauces and gravies, will cause foods to become contaminated by one another and will tend to destroy the inherent character of the food. Spices, condiments, and herbs should be kept according to some neat, orderly system until they are needed for preparation. Sandwich spreads should be refrigerated in tight containers during slack periods. Sandwich meats, fish, and other foods that have a tendency to form a crust or hard surface when exposed to air should be prepared in small quantities or kept covered.

Improper thawing procedures for certain foods will affect quality. Items that are to be heated in a microwave oven may require special thawing techniques to prevent uneven cooking. Foods that are cooked in the frozen state, such as frozen french fries, should not be allowed to thaw, but should be kept in a freezer and cooked only as needed.

Cooking refers to all degrees of food heating (fully or partially), and many factors, such as temperature, timing, formulations, and equipment maintenance, are contributors to the final outcome. For example, a faulty timer on a microwave oven will be responsible for inconsistent quality of foods cooked in that oven. Unfiltered fat used for deep frying will produce low-quality fried products. A loose door or a worn gasket on a steam pressure cooker can cause unsatisfactory cooking. Employment of the proper utensil during food preparation is also essential for consistent quality. Using a 10-gallon container to cook or heat one gallon of a product will result in excessive shrinkage, texture changes, and flavor losses.

SPECIAL DIETS

Noninstitutional foodservice facilities and restaurants are sometimes faced with special dietary requests. It may be helpful to remember the following information on modified diets to meet the special person's need.

Diabetes mellitus is a disease that prevents the body from using sugar normally. This condition requires modifications in both the types and amounts of foods consumed by the afflicted individual. Specific serving sizes from the various food groups must be eaten each day. Therefore, portion size is very important. Usually, a certain caloric level is prescribed, which means that food for a diabetic person must be prepared in a fat-free way. For meats, fish, and poultry, this means broiling, baking, or poaching. Other foods, such as vegetables, may need to be prepared without butter.

Some people who suffer from types of heart disease must follow a cardiac diet. These persons may have to eliminate salt from their diet and will therefore request that food be prepared without the addition of salt. Portion size is also important in many cardiac diets, as is avoidance of saturated fats. Many people can reduce their fat intake by simply removing the skin from chicken or trimming the excess fat from a steak. However, some dishes may require modified cooking methods.

The number of people on reducing diets is increasing every day. The inclusion of a diet platter on the menu will be appreciated by the calorie-conscious. If such an item is offered, fruit for it should be water-packed, *not* packed in syrup. The meat portion should be broiled, baked, or poached, *not* fried. Cottage cheese or yogurt should be lowfat. Skim milk and diet soda are appropriate beverages. Again, the single most important factor is serving size.

HOW TO IMPLEMENT A TASTE PANEL

The purposes of a taste panel or testing committee in a foodservice operation are to help set purchasing specifications according to in-house requirements, to help with buying decisions, and to maintain a continuous program to control costs, quality, taste, and appearance. In order for the taste panel to achieve these purposes, certain basic requirements for its organization and functioning must be followed. Decisions of the taste panel must be accepted by all of its members and must be enforced by management. Good minutes must be kept. A suitable environment must be provided. The panel must meet regularly. Testing procedures must be conducted on a blind basis and in silence. Two or three products of the same range of quality must be available for the committee to test simultaneously; samples must resemble each other as closely as possible and be identified by code numbers or letters. Purveyors must not be informed of the testing.

Who should be included on the taste panel? The composition of the panel varies with the type of foodservice operation, but in general it should include the top decision maker of the operation, the foodservice manager (or counterpart), the purchasing agent or food buyer, the production manager, the dietitian chef, the steward, the catering manager, the dining room manager, the receiving clerk, and the head stockroom clerk. Other recommended members of the panel include the housekeeper, the senior room clerk, the public relations manager, the sous chef, the bell captain, a cook, a pantry person, the butcher, and possibly a guest of the hotel or customer of the restaurant.

The location where the testing procedures are carried out should be permanently established. In a small-to-medium-size operation, it is feasible to combine receiving facilities with a quality-assurance office in which a panel can convene. In any case, the distance between the testing area and the receiving and preparation areas should be as short as possible. An area 8' by 8' is ample space in most cases.

Equipment requirements for testing procedures vary, depending on the type of foodservice operation and the scope of the taste panel's evaluations. Thermometers, a stopwatch or timer, refractometers, hydrometers, scales, sieves, a fat analyzer, and utensils like stainless steel pans, spoons, spatulas, racks, etc., are all likely to be needed. Procedures included in a meaningful testing program are sampling, sensory evaluation (appearance, texture, flavor, evaluation against specs), checking of drained weight, determining the percentage of breading, determining the percentage of fat content, and determining the fill of the container. In order that the results of the procedures can be compiled and interpreted in an efficient and meaningful way, standard forms should be devised to record each panel member's judgments. The following samples are offered as examples of workable formats.

FLAVOR EVALUATION

Name _____ Product _____ Date _____

Check One — Rate Flavor Only — Ignore All Other Differences.

Sample	Better than standard in flavor	Equal to standard in flavor	Below standard in flavor no detectable off-flavor	Slightly off-flavor	Definitely off-flavor not acceptable	Describe off-flavor if possible*
1						
2						
3						
4						
5						
6						
7						
8						
9						
10						
11						
12						
13						
14						
15						

*Suggested words: Bitter   Flat   Metallic   Putrid   Salty   Sweet
                   Burnt   Fragrant   Musty   Puckery   Sour   Woody
                   Earthy   Medicinal Oily   Rancid   Spicy

TASTE PANEL EVALUATION

Name _____ Date _____ Product _____

Check One.

Code	Very good	Good	Fair	Poor	Unaccept-able	Just right	Lacks flavor	Off-flavor	Too flat	Too sweet	Other
						Comments					
1											
2											
3											
4											
5											
6											
7											
8											
9											
10											
11											
12											
13											
14											
15											

3 Food Purchasing and Inventory Control

It is usually indicative of ignorance of the position's tremendous responsibility if a buyer is inconsiderate, harsh, discourteous, or suspicious of sales representatives in general. Most sales representatives are honest, hardworking, and knowledgeable about their products. The majority are educated, trained, and capable. The food buyer should view these men and women as being in a position to help in many ways. There is always the possibility that the salesperson may have a useful purchasing tip or a money-saving proposition. Selling is a highly competitive field, and companies are constantly generating new inducements to increase sales. The advantages of this competition will never be realized unless the buyer's policy is to try to see as many sales representatives as possible. If the buyer fails to capitalize on the competition between companies, the foodservice operation loses financially. Instead of being a buyer, such a person is merely an order giver. In addition, the buyer who capitalizes on competition also avoids the pitfalls of satisfied, one-house, sentiment, and friendship buying.

The more a buyer knows, the more he or she will get for every dollar spent. Price is directly related to quality and quantity. The buyer must keep abreast of current prices for specific grades and quality. It is impossible to study all of the available market reports and government and consumer bulletins, but the buyer should keep some kind of a record, particularly for items purchased frequently, so that he or she can readily compare prices. For items such as equipment that are purchased rarely, the buyer should "shop around" until satisfied with the best available combination of price and service.

The buyer should always strive to purchase stock items in accordance with needs. Before making any purchase, he or she should compute the average consumption of the item in question over a definite time period. The correct amount to order is then apparent.

Buying in quantity will lower costs. A distributor is usually willing to reduce the price per unit in order to get volume business. The cost reduction may total only twenty-five to thirty-five cents per case, but on items ordered in lots of ten, twenty, or more cases even such small savings add up to a considerable amount. Again, a buyer who knows the average consumption of each stock item can lower costs by ordering large quantities of fast-moving items. There is an element of chance in some quantity buying that means that the food buyer must consider several factors before making such a purchase. What is the predicted market supply of the item? If the supply is likely to be above normal, the price is likely to drop after a short time. Conversely, if there is a shortage of an item, the price will no doubt rise as the supply dwindles. An average supply means the price will probably remain stationary, barring unforeseen circumstances. In normal times, many food distributors will contract for future delivery over a period of time. Suppose the buyer orders seventy-five cases of an item. After negotiating the best price for the specified quality, he or she arranges to take delivery in lots of ten, fifteen, or twenty-five cases and to pay on delivery. This process is called "futures"—order it now, take it as needed.

Even modern transportation and frozen-food technology have not completely eliminated seasonal buying. In fact, a buyer can make costly mistakes since many fresh foods cannot be obtained year-round, but only in the regular season. Seasons also directly affect price and quality of canned and frozen foods, so the buyer must be alert and familiar with such terms as "old" and "new" pack.

Fundamentally, the price of all merchandise is controlled by the demand for it. Realizing this relationship, a smart buyer can reap high dividends. Some items, especially perishables, are more affected than others. At times, for instance, excellent buys on wholesale cuts of meat are available. The food buyer is far more likely to be offered these bargains by a jobber than by a packer. When a packer is overstocked on an item, the jobber is offered it at a greatly reduced price. The jobber will then pass this savings along because a quick turnover of inventory is desirable when dealing in perishables.

An experienced buyer knows that you pay not only for merchandise but for service. Service from a supplier includes such things as prompt deliveries, occasional emergency deliveries, exactness in filling orders without padding or substitution, delivery of merchandise in perfect condition, willingness to make adjustments or to allow return for credit, if necessary, obtaining items not carried in stock, error-free billing, and congenial relations. In return, a buyer should make reasonable demands and legitimate complaints. A practical tip to help avoid making unreasonable demands is to be sure to obtain all the facts before lodging a complaint. Even though the vendor may be obligated to remedy the mistake, in the long run reasonableness, patience, and consideration on the part of the buyer will lead to better understanding than will a harsh or threatening attitude.

The responsibility of the buyer does not end when the order has been placed. The buyer should work closely with the receiving clerk to minimize loss. Shortages, breakage, and shipping the wrong merchandise are common errors in transporting foodstuffs. To facilitate routine adjustments of errors, delivery personnel should list discrepancies and sign the receiving slip. This also applies if anything must be picked up for return and credit. If delivery personnel are responsible for errors, this situation must be brought to the attention of management.

LABELING

As the old cliché goes, "the label is the window of the can." Provisions under the Food, Drug, and Cosmetic Act prescribe certain minimum requirements that must be adhered to by all packers and distributors. The provisions for labeling are mandatory for all canned food products shipped in interstate commerce. The law requires that the label contain the following information:

1. The legal name of the product.
2. The common or usual names of all ingredients in descending order of their predominance by weight, unless a standard of identity for the product has been established by the government.
3. The form or style of the vegetable or fruit, unless it is visible through the package.
4. The contents expressed in weight, measure, or numerical count.
5. The names of any artificial flavorings, colorings, or chemical preservatives.
6. The name and address of the manufacturer, packer, or distributor.
7. The variety or color, when applicable.
8. The packing medium, listed near the name of the product.
9. Any special type of treatment.
10. The dietary properties, if important.
11. If the product falls below the quantity or standard of fill established by the act, it must be so stated.
12. All information must be in English, unless an imported product with a foreign language label is distributed solely in an area where that language is predominant.

Four types of open date labeling are as follows:

1. Pack date—date of final packing.
2. Pull date—last recommended date for retail sale.

3. Quality assurance date—date after which the product is not likely to be at peak quality.
4. Expiration date—last day the product should be used for assured quality.

There are no federal regulations on food fortification, but some identity standards prescribe the extent to which foods are to be fortified. A food that uses the same name as a standardized food, but does not meet the standard of identity, must be labeled "imitation." However, it does not have to be labeled "imitation" if it is nutritionally equivalent to the standardized food.

MEAT

Of all the labels, stamps, and codes used in the meat industry, only those of the USDA are to be trusted. State inspection programs use the same criteria as the federal government (for interstate commerce). Military inspection is the same as that of USDA. Religious codes, such as kashruth, certify only that the meat does not violate certain religious laws; they do not guarantee its quality. The inspection stamp or label that says "U.S. Insp'd & P's'd" means that the meat is disease-free, has been prepared in a sanitary plant, and has no added harmful substances. On processed meat products, the label must include, in addition to the inspection stamp, the name and address of the packing plant, the net weight, and a list of ingredients in decreasing order of dominance.

Grading of meat for quality is voluntary. This is performed on about 60 percent of meat sold in the United States. Knowledge of meat-judging indices (see Table 3–1) will enable you to determine quality of ungraded meat. Quality is determined by the kind (class) of animal, the sex, the shape (conformation), the amount of exterior fat (finish), the amount of interior fat (marbling), and the firmness of both the lean and the fat. Conformation has nothing to do with the taste of an animal's meat. The term refers to the animal's shape. The more meat in the higher-priced regions of the body, the better the conformation. An animal with excellent conformation has little meat in such areas as the neck and the shanks, but has thick plump loins, ribs, rounds, and chucks. Finish is the fat covering the animal's carcass and distributed inside the animal and between the muscles. White fat is desirable and is the result of careful breeding and feeding on grain. Heavy, rough fat results from too fast, too heavy, or too long feeding on a feed lot. Good fat is creamy white in appearance and occurs in increasing amounts as the animal ages. Thus, the amount of bovine finish is least on veal, more heavy on calves, and heaviest on beef animals. Lambs are less well finished than yearling muttons; yearling muttons have less finish than muttons. Bovine and ovine fats have a firm to brittle texture, while hog fat is soft. However, very soft hog fat is an indication of slop feeding and is quite undesirable.

Table 3–1 Voluntary Quality Grading

Animal	Prime	Choice	Good	Standard	Commercial	Utility	Cutter	Canner
Steer, Heifer, Bullock	Yes	Yes	Yes	Yes	Yes	Yes	Yes	Yes
Cow	No	Yes	Yes	Yes	Yes	Yes	Yes	Yes
Bull, Stag	No	Yes	Yes	Yes	Yes	Yes	Yes	Yes
Veal	Yes	Yes	Yes	Yes	Yes	Yes	Yes	Yes
Calf	Yes	Yes	Yes	Yes	Yes	Yes	Yes	Yes

	Prime	Choice	Good	Utility	Cull			
Lamb, Yearling, Mutton	Yes	Yes	Yes	Yes	Yes			
Mutton	No	Yes	Yes	Yes	Yes			

	U.S. No. 1	U.S. No. 2	U.S. No. 3	U.S. No. 4	U.S. Utility	Medium	Cull	
Barrows, Gilts	Yes	Yes	Yes	Yes	Yes	No	No	
Sows	Yes	Yes	Yes	No	No	Yes	Yes	

Note: Equivalents are Steer = Barrow, Cow = Sow, Stag = Stag, Heifer = Gilt, Bull = Boar.

How do American beef cattle grade out? 4% Prime, 60% Choice, 25% Good, 11% less than Good.

Source: Raymond B. Peddersen, *Foodservice and Hotel Purchasing*, p. 498. Also published by CBI Publishing Company, Inc. (Boston: 1980).

    The fat appearing in the flesh itself is called marbling. The more numerous the flecks of fat in the meat, the more flavorful, juicy, and tender the meat will be. For that reason, marbling is an important factor in palatability and a prime determinant of grade. On the other hand, the positive food value is in the lean meat. Meat with less finish or yellow finish, or of a lower grade, offers just as much nutritive value per pound as the higher-quality meats do.

    The quality of meat is determined from a combination of factors contributing to the typical, excellent taste (called palatability) of that particular kind. In addition to finish and marbling, other factors for quality grading include the color of the flesh and the age of the animal. When grading veal, calf, ovine, and hogs, the grader determines the grade based on the whole carcass, without seeing a cut surface of the lean. Finish is perhaps the most important of the grading factors. The grader judges not by the amount of external finish, but rather by the fat streaking in the ribs (feathering) and the fat streaking in the inside flank muscles. When grading beef cattle, the carcass is cut at the twelfth rib, so that an evaluation can be made of the degree of ossification (hardening) of the bones and the firmness and marbling of the rib eye muscle. The age or maturity of the animal has much to do with the quality of meat. Age refers to the physiological age of the animal as indicated by the color and texture of the lean, the condition of the bone, and the hardening or ossification of the cartilage, *not* the actual age of the animal. The physiological and actual age are matched only in well-bred, properly raised animals. There is substantial overlap among the different quality factors; therefore, a low rating on some factors may be compensated for by the excellence of others.

In addition to the grading of the quality of meat, there is a grading scale for beef, lamb, and mutton which identifies the yield of trimmed retail cuts that will be achieved. These yield grades are Nos. 1, 2, 3, 4, and 5 and refer in declining order to the amount of yield. Since one objective of meat purchasing is to obtain the most value for the purchasing dollar, a wise meat buyer understands and uses yield grades in meat purchasing.

Meat is usually ordered by weight in pounds or ounces per portion, either raw or cooked weight. Order subprimal cuts by cut name and weight per piece. (See Table 3–2.)

Table 3–2 Portion-cut Products and Weight Ranges

Item no.	Product	3	4	6	8	10	12	14	16	18	20	24
1100	Cubed steaks	X	X	X	X							
1101	Cubed steaks, special	X	X	X	X							
1102	Braising steaks, Swiss		X	X	X							
1103	Rib steaks				X	X	X	X	X	X		
1103A	Rib steaks, boneless		X	X	X	X	X					
1112	Rib eye roll steaks		X	X	X	X	X					
1112A	Rib eye roll, lip-on, steaks	X	X	X	X	X						
1136	Ground beef patties, regular	size as specified										
1136A	Ground beef patties, regular, TVP added	size as specified										
1137	Ground beef patties, special	size as specified										
1167	Knuckle steaks	X	X	X	X	X						
1168	Top (inside) round steaks	X	X	X	X	X	X					
1170	Bottom (gooseneck) round steaks	X	X	X	X	X	X	X	X	X	X	X
1173	Porterhouse steaks					X	X					
1173A	Porterhouse steaks, intermediate						X	X	X	X	X	X
1173B	Porterhouse steaks, short cut						X	X	X	X	X	X	X
1174	T-bone steaks				X	X	X	X	X	X	X	X
1174A	T-bone steaks, intermediate					X	X	X	X	X	X	X

Table 3-2 (Continued)

Item no.	Product	\multicolumn{10}{c}{Portion size (in oz.)}									
		3	4	6	8	10	12	14	16	18	20	24
1174B	T-bone steaks, short cut				X	X	X	X	X	X	X	X
1177	Strip loin steaks, bone-in, intermediate		X	X	X	X	X	X	X	X		
1178	Strip loin steaks, boneless, intermediate				X	X	X	X	X	X	X	X
1179	Strip loin steaks, bone-in, short cut				X	X	X	X	X	X	X	X
1179A	Strip loin steaks, bone-in, extra short cut				X	X	X	X	X	X	X	X
1179B	Strip loin steaks, bone-in, special				X	X	X	X	X	X	X	X
1180	Strip loin steaks, boneless, short cut			X	X	X	X	X	X	X	X	
1180A	Strip loin steaks, boneless, extra short cut		X	X	X	X	X	X	X			
1180B	Strip loin steaks, boneless, special			X	X	X	X	X	X	X	X	
1184	Top sirloin butt steaks		X	X	X	X	X	X	X	X	X	X
1184A	Top sirloin butt steaks, semi-center cut		X	X	X	X	X	X	X			
1184B	Top sirloin butt steaks, center cut		X	X	X	X	X	X	X			
1189	Tenderloin steaks		X	X	X	X	X	X				
1189A	Tenderloin steaks, defatted	X	X	X	X	X	X	X				
1190	Tenderloin steaks, special	X	X	X	X	X	X	X				
1190A	Tenderloin steaks, skinned	X	X	X	X	X	X	X				

Note: Because it is impractical to list all portion weights that purchasers may desire, those identified by the letter "X" are suggested. Other portion weights may be specified if desired.
Source: Raymond B. Peddersen, *Foodservice and Hotel Purchasing*, p. 462. Also published by CBI Publishing Company, Inc. (Boston: 1980).

Veal and Calf   A bovine of an age of up to three months is classified as veal. Veal has a very light pink (actually almost gray-colored) lean meat. The lean and the fat are very soft, smooth, and flexible. The bones are very red, and the rib bones are very narrow.

A calf is a bovine older than tnree months. The lean of a calf is pink to reddish-pink, not as soft and pliable as that of veal, but not nearly as firm as that of beef. The bones are pink and starting to harden. The rib bones are wider than those of veal.

Lamb and Mutton

Lamb is classified according to age. The very young (under weaning age) lamb is often called "hothouse lamb" or "genuine spring lamb." A lamb between two and five months old is called "spring lamb" or, sometimes, "milk lamb" or "milk-fed lamb." Lamb has soft, porous bones, very light pink lean, and creamy white to pink fat, which is soft and pliable. Considered the most reliable indicator of ovine age is the *break joint* of the foreleg. In lamb, these joints break into four well-defined ridges, which are smooth, soft, and blood-red.

Yearling mutton has light red to red flesh, white and fairly firm fat, and fine graining in the flesh. The flesh does not have as little grain as lamb. The break joint in yearling mutton also has four ridges, but the edges are not smooth and the bone is hard and white.

Mutton has medium red to dark red flesh with a grain similar to that of calf or young steer. The fat is quite white and has a brittle consistency. The foreleg of mutton does not break as it does in lamb and yearling mutton. Instead, a hard, shiny, smooth knuckle with two prominent ridges forms.

Pork

Hogs are graded in three stages. The Choice grades are U.S. No. 1, U.S. No. 2, and U.S. No. 3. The differences between these grades have to do with the ratio of lean to fat and with the yield of the loin, the ham, the picnic, and the Boston butt. The U.S. No. 4 (barrows, gilts) and U.S. Medium (sow) grades are at the next level down in the grading scale, which is at the bottom of the consumer grades. U.S. Utility (barrows, gilts) and U.S. Cull grades are not marketed for retail consumption. Sows are graded by a different set of standards than are barrows and gilts.

Some 70 percent of the hog production in this country is further processed before it reaches the retail marketplace. Hogs are raised for a variety of purposes. In the past, they were referred to as Roasting (ten to thirty pits), Shipping (large sows for barrel packing), Meat-Type (fairly lean for bacon and hams), and Fat-Type (hard and skinned hams). Today, hogs that are marketed fall within a very narrow range of weights and carcass lengths. Generally, well-defined grading of pork cuts on the basis of quality is not done; pork is marketed mostly on the basis of weight and the lean-to-fat ratio. When better control of muscular development, amount of finish, evenness of marbling, and uniformity and texture of the lean has been achieved, then accurate quality grading of pork may be possible.

POULTRY

The standards of quality for poultry cover the various factors that determine the grade. These factors include fat covering, fleshing, exposed flesh, discoloration, etc., and are evaluated collectively to determine the grade of the bird. The U.S. Consumer grades for poultry are used for those marketed at the retail level; they are: U.S. Grade A, U.S. Grade B, and U.S. Grade C. The U.S. Procurement grades are intended primarily for institutional use; they are: U.S. Procurement Grade 1 and U.S. Procurement Grade 2. The Procurement grades for poultry place more emphasis on meat yield than on appearance.

Official Identification by Graders Licensed by the USDA

Anyone having a financial interest in a lot of processed poultry may make application to the USDA to have an official grade designation assigned to the lot. This service, which is available throughout the country, is operated on a self-supporting basis. A nominal fee is charged to cover the time and travel expenses of the grader, plus the cost of administering the program.

Many processors utilize full-time resident graders in their plants. This practice enables the plant to apply the U.S. grade mark to each individual package or each individual bird. Many federal, state, county, and city institutions, along with other large-scale buyers, such as the military, steamship lines, independent and chain stores, and private hospitals, make use of the grading system by specifying U.S. grades in their contracts for poultry products.

Classes

Some states provide for a voluntary grading and inspection program. Such programs generally follow the U.S. standards and grades in whole or in part. Producers, as well as processors, often use the government standards of quality as a basis for sorting or selecting birds for market.

"Kind" refers to the different species of poultry, including chickens, turkeys, ducks, geese, guineas, and pigeons. The kinds of poultry are divided into "classes" by grouping according to physical characteristics associated with age and sex. Fryers and hens are examples of classes of chickens. The kinds and classes of live, dressed, and ready-to-cook poultry listed in the U.S. classes, standards, and grades are in general use in all segments of the poultry industry. Poultry should be ordered by desired cut and portion weight; it may be iced, frozen, or cooked, and either tray or bulk-packed.

PROCESSED EGGS

Frozen Eggs

Frozen eggs must be pasteurized, just like milk, to prevent bacterial growth. The market forms are whole eggs, egg whites, egg yolks, and sugared egg yolks. Whole eggs are defined as the entire egg without the shell, cracked, pasteurized, and packaged in 4-lb, 5-lb, 10-lb, or 30-lb containers. Those of the best eating quality have no additives or stabilizers. When comparing the price of eggs in the shell to whole frozen eggs, remember that 11 percent to 12 percent of the weight of eggs is in the shell. The pricing reciprocal is therefore 1.12. Egg whites are defined as the entire egg without the shell and the yolk. The white represents 58 percent of the whole egg. The pricing reciprocal is 1.72. Egg yolks are the entire egg without the shell and the white. The yolk represents

31 percent of the whole egg. The pricing reciprocal is 3.23. Sugared egg yolks are egg yolks, as previously defined, with about 11 percent sugar and up to 5 percent glycerine added to prevent hardening. The different forms of frozen eggs are excellent for use in baking and in making souffles, scrambled eggs, and omelets since no labor has to be expended in shelling eggs or in separating yolks and whites. The buyer should make sure that all frozen eggs have been federally inspected and should try to buy only frozen eggs that are guaranteed to be salmonella-free.

Frozen Roll of Egg. The Ralston-Purina Company markets a frozen, processed roll of egg yielding as many center-cut slices as seventeen hard-cooked eggs. Many foodservice operators have found this product to be most practical for such uses as sliced egg salads and eggs à la Russe. The "Gourm Egg" has food starch and stabilizers added, but these do not noticeably affect the taste.

Hard-cooked Refrigerated Eggs. In some areas of the country, hard-cooked eggs can be purchased already shelled, with a refrigerator shelf-life of up to three weeks.

Dried Eggs

Eggs are dried by either a roller process or a spray process. They are treated with enzymes to remove glucose. There is a high bacteria count in dried eggs; thus the buyer should be sure to buy dried eggs that are guaranteed to be salmonella-free, and the operator should refrigerate such products. Many dried egg nog and custard bases are available that are of high quality. Since there are no federal quality standards covering these products, the buyer must test them for preference.

COFFEE

Coffee is difficult to keep. Oils and other constitutents that provide the flavor and fragrance are easily dissipated or, if exposed to air, are quickly oxidized to other substances with disagreeable odors and tastes. In contrast, coffee brewed from freshly roasted and ground beans and served in an atmosphere where the air is still full of the rich aroma released by the roasting, grinding, and brewing is a rare treat. By the time most roasted and ground coffee reaches the consumer, even if it is protected in a vacuum-packed container, much of its aroma and flavor have been lost. Once the container is opened, this deterioration speeds up. It can be retarded (but not stopped) by keeping the coffee container tightly closed and by storing it in a cool place. Coffee should be purchased in amounts small enough to be used quickly.

The coffee beans that the foodservice operator buys have usually been both roasted and ground. Coffee is usually a blend of more than one variety of coffee bean. Some major varieties (with characteristics and origins) are Armenia, full-bodied (Colombia); Aukola, light, sweet (Sumatra); Blue Mountain, full-bodied (Jamaica); Bogotá, full-bodied (Colombia); Coatepec, full-bodied (Mexico); Excelso, full-bodied (Colombia); Giradot, full-bodied (Colombia); Java, mild, good quality (Java); Liverica, somewhat acrid (Venezuela); Mandhelling, light, sweet (Sumatra); Manizales, full-bodied (Colombia); Maracaibo, light, rich (Venezuela); Medellín, full-bodied (Colombia); Mocha, full-bodied, rich (Arabia); Oaxaca, low-quality (Mexico); Rio, low-quality (Mexico); Robusta, somewhat acrid (Kenya); Sevilla, full-bodied (Colombia); and Santos, somewhat acrid, high-quality (Brazil).

Any grind of coffee contains particles of many sizes. The samples differ only in the proportion of each size of particles they contain. These proportions are measured by shaking the ground coffee through a set of graded screens. A drip (or urn) grind, for example, should contain about 7 percent of particles that will be held back by a 14-mesh screen, 73 percent that will be held back by a 28-mesh screen, and 20 percent that will pass through a 28-mesh screen. (Table 3–3 summarizes the proportions of three common grinds.) Any day-to-day or periodic variations in the consistency of the grind supplied can result in an inconsistent beverage. As the percentage of large particles increases, the brewed coffee will be weaker. As the percentage of fine particles increases, the brew may become bitter. Food operators should know whether their suppliers are actually measuring the grinds and whether consistency of grind is being maintained.

Some things to look for when buying coffee: (1) coloring—the color should be even throughout the bean (the coffee might be dyed); (2) additives—cereals and beans may have been ground into the coffee; (3) glazing—adding of materials during the roasting to improve color and add weight, but not to improve quality.

A specification for purchasing coffee should include: (1) roast, (2) grind, (3) percentage of types desired in blend, and (4) packaging. Since few food-service operators have the purchasing power to specify the types, it is suggested that several blends be ordered "in the bean" for quality evaluation. Customer tasting must be part of the cost/quality evaluation.

Table 3–3 Coffee Grinds

	Regular	*Drip*	*Fine*
14-mesh screen	33 percent	7 percent	None
28-mesh screen	55 percent	73 percent	70 percent
Pan	12 percent	20 percent	30 percent

FATS AND OILS

Commonly used food fats are complex mixtures that do not have a sharp melting point but solidify over a wide temperature range. This fact is demonstrated by the clouding that occurs when oils are refrigerated. Many vegetable oils, particularly salad oils, are "winterized" to prevent this. The process of winterizing oil consists of chilling it to a temperature of 40° to 45°F and removing the precipitated solids by filtration. The resulting oil remains clear at ordinary refrigerator temperatures.

The first recognizable sign of deterioration in fats (such as lard), oils, and shortenings, is the development of rancidity. This is an oxidative change; in vegetable oils it is inhibited by naturally occurring antioxidants. Since animal fats do not contain natural antioxidants to protect them, chemical agents must be added to them to delay the onset of rancidity. The USDA has approved about a dozen antioxidants and specified the amounts that may be used in animal fats.

Shortenings, whether of vegetable origin or mixtures of vegetable oils and animal fats, keep well at room temperatures. Only shortenings containing animal fats are inspected by the USDA. A system of continuous inspection has been developed; the federal inspectors are placed in each plant to supervise the handling of the product at every step. Inspection is concerned with facilities, equipment, sanitation, source and quality of raw materials, acceptable manufacturing practices, laboratory testing, and labeling. Only edible fats from U.S. inspected and passed carcasses may be used in animal fat shortenings.

Shortenings with added emulsifiers have a low smoke point. When fats or oils are heated to a high temperature, some decomposition occurs. Finally, the smoke point is reached; at which visible fumes are given off. The fumes have an unpleasant odor and are irritating to the nose and eyes. Food fried in smoking fats is likely to have an unpleasant flavor. Also, the fat becomes rancid faster than fat which has not been heated to smoke temperatures. Another undesirable effect is that foods absorb more fat when they are cooked in one with a low smoke point. An ideal fat for frying, therefore, is one that has a fairly high smoke point. Most cooking oils and all hydrogenated shortenings (without emulsifiers) have high smoke points. Butter, margarine, and shortenings with emulsifiers have low smoke points and do not make good frying fats. Lards have varying smoke points. Repeated use of fat lowers the smoke point.

FISH AND SHELLFISH

There are approximately 200 varieties of fish marketed in the United States. Vertebrate or fin fish are characterized by a backbone and fins. They are of two types: fat and lean. Fat fish, such as mackerel, salmon, and swordfish, are usually broiled or baked. Lean fish, such as cod, flounder, and haddock, are best for frying. Shellfish have bodies partially or completely covered with a shell. Shellfish are also divided into two classes: crustaceans and mollusks. Crustaceans, such as shrimp and lobster, have hard shells over the back portions of the body and over the claws, and softer shells for protection of the underparts of the body and legs. Mollusks, such as clams, oysters, and scallops, have two shells of the same size and shape, usually hard and ordinarily held tightly closed.

The market forms of fish are defined as follows: (1) round (whole)—as it comes from the water; (2) drawn—eviscerated; (3) dressed—eviscerated with head, tail, and fins off; (4) fillets—half of the fish (backbone to belly) with the head, tail, fins, and skin off; (5) sticks—blocks of fish meat of uniform size; (6) steaks—cross sections of a fish cut from a dressed fish with the skin off. (See Figure 3–1.)

When buying fresh fish, the buyer should look for certain things as evidence of quality. These are bright, shiny skin; no loose scales; bright, bulging, clean eyes; red inside the gills; firm flesh that bounces back when pressed; no strong odors; and no slime. Because fish deteriorates very quickly, it is advisable to buy fresh fish only if it is to be used within forty-eight hours.

All of the most popular varieties of fish are available frozen. Frozen fish should exhibit shiny skin with no discoloration, red inside the gills and no strong odors. A surface glaze of ice (6 percent minimum) is permitted. Avoid "drip" or ice on the packages as they indicate that the product may have been thawed and refrozen. Avoid containers that are not intact.

Fresh shellfish should have clear color, clean odor, clear liquids, no slime or slipperyness of surface, and strong muscle tension. When purchasing shellfish, the buyer should be sure that the produce is alive. Live shellfish will react to being touched or prodded. The only exception to this is shrimp, which should be iced. The shells of crustaceans will turn red when cooked.

Table 3–4 lists common forms in which seafood is purchased along with expected portion yields.

Dressed or Pan-Dressed Fish are scaled and eviscerated, usually with the head, tail, and fins removed. The smaller sizes are ready for cooking as purchased (pan-dressed). The larger sizes of dressed fish may be baked as purchased but frequently are cut into steaks or serving size portions.

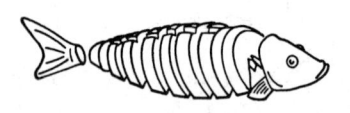

Steaks are cross-sectioned slices of the larger sizes of fish. They are ready to cook as purchased, except for dividing the very largest into serving size portions. A cross section of the backbone is usually the only bone in the steak.

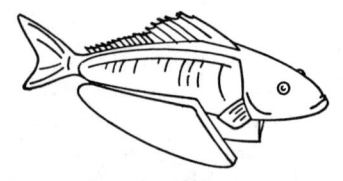

Fillets are the sides of the fish, cut lengthwise away from the backbone. They are practically boneless.

Figure 3–1 Market Forms of Fresh and Frozen Fish

Table 3-4 Forms of Seafood Purchased with Portion Yields

Item	State	Unit purchased	Portion size	No. of portions
Salmon	Canned	16 oz (13 oz)	3 oz	4.3
Salmon	Canned	64 oz (50 oz)	3 oz	16.7
Sardines, Maine	Canned	12 oz (10 oz)	3 oz	1.2
Sardines, Pacific	Canned	15 oz (11.5 oz)	3 oz	3.8
Tuna	Canned	7 oz (6 oz)	3 oz	2.0
Tuna	Canned	66½ oz (58 oz)	3 oz	19.3
Fillets	Fresh; Frozen	1 lb	3 oz	3.4
Steaks	Fresh; Frozen	1 lb	3 oz	3.1
Dressed	Fresh; Frozen	1 lb	3 oz	2.4
Drawn	Fresh; Frozen	1 lb	3 oz	1.7
Whole	Fresh; Frozen	1 lb	3 oz	1.4
Portions, breaded	Frozen	1 lb	2 oz	8
Portions, breaded	Frozen	1 lb	3 oz	5.3
Portions, unbreaded	Frozen	1 lb	2 oz	8
Portions, unbreaded	Frozen	1 lb	3 oz	5.3
Crabmeat	Fresh; Frozen	1 lb	3 oz	5.2
Lobster meat	Fresh; Frozen	1 lb	3 oz	4.8
Scallops	Fresh; Frozen	1 lb	3 oz	3.4
Shrimp, cooked	Fresh; Frozen	1 lb	3 oz	5.3
Shrimp, raw/shell	Fresh; Frozen	1 lb	3 oz	2.7
Shrimp, raw/peeled	Fresh; Frozen	1 lb	3 oz	3.3
Shrimp, breaded	Fresh; Frozen	1 lb	3 oz	4.5

Note: Quantities in parentheses for canned seafood represent the actual weight of contents.
Source: Raymond B. Peddersen, *Foodservice and Hotel Purchasing*, p. 400. Also published by CBI Publishing Company, Inc. (Boston: 1980).

FRUITS AND VEGETABLES

Fresh Fruits

When a buyer specifies a U.S. grade, such as U.S. No. 1, for fresh fruit, the grade has a definite meaning that makes it unnecessary to write out further details. A full set of U.S. grade standards for fresh fruits (and vegetables) can be obtained free by writing to: Fresh Products Standardization Section, Agricultural Marketing Service, Washington, D.C. 20250. However, it should be noted that there can be quite a range of quality within a grade, due to the tolerances provided. Also, although U.S. No. 1 is the highest grade for some commodities, it is a lower grade for others. Higher grades include U.S. Extra Fancy, U.S. Fancy, and U.S. Extra No. 1. The buyer should always stipulate that the fruit be up to the specified grade at delivery, not merely at the time it was shipped.

Figure 3-2 USDA Grade Marks

When the buyer is purchasing fresh fruit intended for special uses, it may be necessary to specify other characteristics than those defined by grade. In almost every instance, it is necessary to specify variety since there are considerable differences making one variety suitable for certain uses and another variety for different ones. Thus, Delicious apples are appropriate for table service or salads but are not suitable for baking.

The intended use will also determine what size of fruit is needed. The medium sizes generally cost more per package than either the very small or very large sizes, because medium sizes are more in demand. However, when whole fruit is to be served, obviously a large size of a fruit will cost more than a much smaller one. Size is usually indicated by the count in a standard container; the lowest counts correspond to the largest sizes.

Quantity should be stated precisely and in terms appropriate to the commodity. Thus, in the case of strawberries, it might be "30 12-pt trays." In the case of watermelons, it might be "12 melons, average 30 lb each." In the case of bananas, it might be "10 40-lb cartons" (also specifying the size of the bananas as small, medium, or large).

It is often advisable to specify brands, because fruits packed under some labels are consistently good. Thorough knowledge of labels comes with experience, but suppliers can sometimes be informative.

A certain fruit from one growing area may be very different from the same fruit from another. In some cases, it is recommended to specify the geographic source of the fruit. For example, as a result of climatic conditions, pears from the far western states are superior to those from eastern ones.

The following is a list of things to avoid in buying fresh fruits.

Apples: overripe, bruised, and decayed areas; scald (tan or brown area of irregular shape).

Apricots: badly bruised or decayed areas.

Bananas: bruised, discolored skin; decay (dull, grayish, aged appearance).

Blackberries, Blueberries: dullness, softness, and mold.

Cantaloupes: torn stems, jagged stem scars, or very green stems (immature); softness of the melons or deep cracks in the rinds (overripe).

Cherries (Sweet): dull appearance, softness, shriveled fruit, or brown stems (overripe).

Cranberries: soft, spongy, or leaky berries.

Grapefruits: rough, ridged, or wrinkled skin; pointed shape (indicates pulpiness, lack of juice).

Grapes: soft or wrinkled fruit, bleached areas around the stems, leaking or decayed fruits.

Lemons: shriveled, hard-skinned, soft, spongy, or brown fruit; discolored sunken areas (indicates aging and deterioration).

Limes: dull, dry skin (indicates aging and loss of acid flavor).

Melons (Honeydew): cuts or punctures through the rind, large bruised areas, decayed areas.

Nectarines: hard, dull, shriveled fruit (indicates immaturity); cracked or punctured skin; softness; overripe or decayed areas.

Oranges: dull, dry skin; spongy texture; weakened areas around the stem ends (indicates aging and deterioration).

Peaches: small, round tan spots of decay.

Pears: shriveling near the stems, hard spots on the surface.

Pineapples: dull, yellowish-green color; sunken or slightly pointed pips; dry appearance.

Plums: skin breaks or punctures; brown discoloration; excessive softness, leaking, or decay.

Raspberries: dull appearance, softness, mold.

Strawberries: soft or moldy berries.

Tangerines: soft spots.

Watermelons: decay penetrating from the stem ends.

Fresh Vegetables

The buyer should specify and insist on freshness of produce. If vegetables are wilted or stale, they should be rejected, regardless of bargain prices. The original characteristics of a vegetable, such as bright color, crispness, good weight for size, good shape, lack of mechanical damage, and absence of decay should be well preserved. Fresh vegetables are living, breathing organisms. Their life processes continue after harvesting until they die and decay. They use oxygen and give off heat and water. Retention of freshness requires keeping their temperature low to retard the life processes and, in most cases but not all, keeping humidity high to conserve moisture. Vegetables that are warm when received should be considered suspect even if visible wilting has not yet occurred. The useful life of most vegetables is drastically shortened if they are allowed to remain warm even for a few hours (exceptions include sweet potatoes, white potatoes, and tomatoes).

If vegetables are bought very early or very late in their season (an exception is sweet corn which is often at its best in early and late periods), they need to be bought with extra care. At those times, they are almost certain to be high in price, but are not therefore necessarily of high quality. Generally, vegetables are lower in price and of better quality and flavor when they are in the peak of season. A precise, detailed guide to the availability and sources of each produce commodity by months is the annual *USDA Report on Fresh Fruit and Vegetable Unload Totals for 41 Cities*. Any buyer who purchases in quantity should have this report handy. It can be obtained for free from: USDA, Washington, D.C. 20250.

The best buyer is not necessarily the one who gets everything for the least money, but, instead, is the one who obtains vegetables best suited to the particular uses to which they are to be put. Experience will prove that the cheapest vegetables may not be the best value. Low price must be balanced against such factors as freshness, tenderness, shape and appearance, size, amount of trim loss, and total amount of waste.

The federal and state standard grades are a handy tool for the buyer. Instead of detailing lengthy specifications, he or she can ask for U.S. No. 1 celery or U.S. No. 1 cauliflower. The buyer should specify that the produce must meet the grade at the time of delivery to the receiving room. A vegetable that met the grade at the time of shipping might be below grade later. The buyer also may want to include any special requirements; for example, he or she may want pascal celery of a particular size from a preferred growing area, or may want film-wrapped cauliflower minus the jacket leaves and ribs. A set of the federal vegetable standards is available for free from: Fruit and Vegetable Division, USDA, Washington, D.C. 20250.

For most vegetables, varietal distinctions are unimportant and are little used in institutional buying. Type, however, is of considerable importance. Thus, pascal celery is not a varietal name, but a type designation. Danish cabbage designates a type, as does domestic round cabbage. Variety is a more important distinction for potatoes, but, even so, type and origin are of more consequence. Even experts have trouble picking out individual varieties from a jumbled pile of many varieties of potatoes.

If the size of the vegetable is crucial for a particular use, as it often is, it should be precisely specified. Terms such as small or large should be used only if they are part of a definition of a standard grade specified in your order. Otherwise, size should be stated exactly with reference to length, diameter, the number of pieces contained in a standard pack, such as 24s of lettuce, or weight, such as 20–25 lb watermelons.

Vegetables are available in many kinds of containers or packages, supplying different net weights and varying degrees of protection. The buyer should specify the container most suitable for the needs of the operation. For example, an institutional kitchen probably wants brussels sprouts packed in a 25-lb drum or carton rather than in pint cups held in a crate or tray. Information on standard containers and their net weights and other data on weights and measures for many produce items are widely available.

The following is a list of things to avoid in buying fresh vegetables.

Asparagus: wilted, flabby spears or mushy tips (indicate aging).

Avocados: dark, sunken spots; deeply cracked or broken skins (indicate decay).

Beans (Green or Wax): wilted or dry beans with enlarged seeds (signs of aging).

Broccoli: soft, slippery, water-soaked irregular brown spots (signs of decay); spreading, wilted, yellow, or enlarged flower buds on the heads (indicates aging).

Brussels Sprouts: soft, open, or wilted sprouts; yellow or discolored leaves; small holes or ragged edges on leaves (signs of worm damage).

Cabbages: faded, yellowed, or wilted outer leaves; heads with decay (indicates worm and insect damage).

Carrots: sunken or mushy spots, mold, flabbiness (indicates aging and poor condition).

Cauliflower: spotted or spreading heads (indicate aging, overmaturity, or disease).

Celery: wilted, flabby branches; yellow leaves; dark streaks inside the branches; coarse central stems; brown to black discoloration of center branches; insect damage.

Corn: underdeveloped ears; depressed or deep-yellow kernels; yellowed, wilted, or dried husks.

Cucumbers: thick cross sections with faded or yellow color (indicates overmaturity), wilted or spongy condition.

Greens (Collards, Kale, Spinach, Turnip, Mustard): tough, fibrous, leaf stems; decayed, yellowed, bruised leaves; soft decay.

Greens (Salad): wilted or yellowed plants.

Lettuce (Head): firm heads showing tan or brownish discoloration of leaf stems at base, leaf tip burn.

Lettuce (Leaf): noticeable wilting, discolored leaves, or spots of soft decay.

Lettuce (Romaine): lack of green color, irregular shape, leaf tip burn, serious discoloration, soft decay.

Okra: long, pale, very firm, or dry pods.

Onions: thick, hollow, woody bulbs; seed items; freshly sprouted.

Parsley: water-soaked, discolored, or slimy leaves.

Peas (Green): whitish-green, yellow, or wilted pods.

Peppers: pale or dull color; lack of firmness; soft, mushy spots; green to black slimy decay around stems.

Potatoes (Sweet): worm holes.

Potatoes (White): excessive sprouts, softness and flabbiness.

Radishes: cuts or gouges.

Squash (Summer): dull surface and tough rind (indicates aging or overmaturity).

Squash (Winter): water-soaked or moldy spots (indicate freezing injury or decay).

Tomatoes: softness; bruises; deep, long cracks in the skins.

Turnips: excessive leaf scars, fibrous roots, deep cuts, or decay.

Partially Prepared Vegetables. Many local produce suppliers offer foodservice buyers a number of fresh vegetables in partially prepared form. Most widely available are peeled potatoes—marketed as peeled, whole; peeled, cut in various sizes and styles for french fries; peeled, sliced for cottage fries; and peeled, cut, blanched for french fries. Other items offered by suppliers include washed, cut, and mixed salad greens; coleslaw mixes; peeled and diced, sliced, or shredded carrots; washed and cut spinach; peeled, sliced, and chopped onions; and peeled and sliced or diced turnips or parsnips. While these partially prepared vegetables are not yet available everywhere, produce dealers are sure to respond if the demand is there.

Canned Fruits and Vegetables

The U.S. grades for canned fruits and vegetables are defined as follows. Grade A (Fancy) is assigned to fruits and vegetables of the highest quality. They have been carefully selected for uniformity in size, color, maturity, and tenderness and are practically free from defects and blemishes. When appearance and flavor must be faultless, this grade should be used. Grade B (Choice for fruits, Extra Standard for vegetables) means produce of fine quality but somewhat lower than Grade A in one or more factors. Grade B products generally offer the best combination of quality and price and are recommended for most uses. Grade C (Standard) means the product is wholesome but fails to meet the exacting standards of Grade B. Where appearance or tenderness is not crucial, Grade C provides good value. For example, tomatoes or green beans to be used in an entree recipe or peaches to be used in a gelatin mold can be Grade C.

Substandard does not mean that canned food is unwholesome. All canned goods must be wholesome under the provisions of the Food, Drug, and Cosmetic Act. Substandard does mean that the canned food has some defect greater than that allowed for in Grade C. For some products, there are Grades A and C, but no Grade B. This is true of applesauce, fruit cocktail, tomato puree, and tomato paste.

A product can achieve an overall score above the minimum required for a grade, but still be assigned the lower grade because one or more factors have failed to meet the minimum level prescribed for the higher grade. This is called the "limiting rule." For example, canned peas have a limiting rule for color; often Grade B peas would have been Grade A except for being adjudged as Grade B in color. For canned tomatoes, the difference between Grade A and Grade B is often only 4.3 oz of drained weight. In that case, if the price difference is less than 6.3 percent, Grade A is the better buy; if more than 6.3 percent, Grade B is the better buy.

Minimum drained weight designates the minimum amount of food contained in a single can. The average drained weight of all cans in a case should exceed the minimum. To check drained weights, drain the contents of a can through a No. 8 or No. 12 sieve (or even a colander if you do not have either sieve) for two minutes, then check the weight of the drained product. Drained weight is not noted on some products, such as peas, Elberta peaches, creamstyle corn, and tomato puree. On these products, the USDA applies a standard of fill. Proper fill is defined as the maximum quantity that can be processed and sealed in a container without crushing or breaking the contents. The usual method of checking the fill is to measure the distance from the top of the opened can to the top of the contents. This "headspace" is a maximum of $^{27}/_{32}$nds of an inch in No. 13 or No. 3 cylinder cans.

Syrup density is not a factor in grading. However, for the best grades, syrup with the greatest amount of sugar is used. "Brix" is a measurement of the sugar content of the syrup in a can. "Brix in" refers to the content at the time of packing; "Brix out" refers to the content fifteen or more days after packing. Each degree(°) of Brix out corresponds to about one percent of sugar.

Writing the Specification. The buyer should use information that conforms to canning industry and U.S. government standards. This makes it possible for all suppliers to quote bids on essentially the same product and permits the buyer to accurately evaluate quotations. (See Table 3–5.) Remember to use only the terminology that applies, for example, there is no such term as Extra Fancy, and Grade C fruits do not come packed in Extra-Heavy Syrup. Copies of the complete requirements for all canned fruits and vegetables can be obtained for a dime each from: U.S. Department of Agriculture, Washington, D.C. 20250.

Table 3–5 Specifications for Canned Goods Bids

Bid description	Fruit example	Vegetable example
Product	Peaches	Green beans
Style	Halves	Cut
Count or sieve	35/40	Sieve 5
Case count/can size	6/No. 10	24/No. 2½
Source	Northwest	Northwest
Variety	Clingstone	Blue Lake
U.S. Grade	B (Choice)	A (Fancy)
Point score	80 or above	90 or above
Packing medium	Heavy syrup (18°+)	Water
Minimum drained weight or can fill	64.0 oz+/can	16.2 oz+/can

Box 3–1 Definition of Terms for Judging Quality

Flavor: Because there is such a great variation in individual likes and dislikes, it is exceedingly difficult to score so elusive a factor as "flavor." In most of the U.S. Standards for grades of foods, the term "normal flavor" is used. In commercial grading, however, "flavor" is the prime factor. If what we eat tastes good, we somehow overlook minor deficiencies.

General Appearance: Our judgment sets the appearance factor very high in the scale of our responses. If a food does not look good, the visual prejudice may very well affect one's opinion of flavor. For this reason, some food experts rate "general appearance" every bit as important as "flavor."

The relative importance of all other factors depends entirely on the product being judged. While no attempt will be made here to score "quality" or "standard" factors for all the available grades, the important factors by which to judge the quality of some of the more popular products are listed here to help food buyers make certain that deliveries conform to purchase specifications.

Color: The factor of "color" is the chief subdivision of "general appearance"; and to receive proper rating, "color" should be typical of the product. Many food experts score "color" on a par with flavor for some items.

Type: By "type" is meant distinctive classifications of a specific product. For example, culturally bleached asparagus is one distinct type, and green asparagus is a separate type.

**Box 3-1
Continued**

Style: When we refer to "style", we think of prevalent ideas of form adaptable to popular food items and generally made available to buyers by canners and processors. For example, two styles of peaches are sliced or halves.

Count: Actual number of pieces found on opening and examining container contents.

Uniformity of Size: The degree of consistency among pieces relative to the spatial dimensions, their freedom from variation or difference in magnitude.

Symmetry: The degree of consistency among pieces relative to harmonious proportions.

Absence of Defects: By "absence of defects" is meant the degree of freedom from grit, from harmless foreign or other extraneous material, and from damage from poor or careless handling or from mechanical, pathological, insect, or other injury.

General Character: Under the factor of "general character," consideration is given to degree of ripeness or maturity, the texture and condition of the flesh, the firmness and tenderness of the product, its tendency to retain its apparent original conformation and size without material disintegration, the wholeness or cut, the consistency or finish, and the clearness of liquor or syrup.

Maturity: This factor refers to the degree of development or the ripeness of the product.

Texture: By "texture" is meant structural composition or character of the product's tissues.

Firmness: This factor refers to the degree of soundness of the product's structure.

Tenderness: This factor refers to the degree of the product's freedom from tough or hard fibers.

Wholeness: By "wholeness" is meant the state of completeness or entirety of the product.

Cut: This factor refers to the character of the division of the product, that is, the effect of the cut on the appearance of the product.

Consistency: In some products, such as fruit butters, this factor refers to viscosity, that is, stickiness or gumminess. In other products, such as tomato catsup and tomato puree, the term is applied to density or specific gravity.

Box 3-1 Continued

> *Finish:* This factor refers to the size and texture of particles in the product, that is, the smoothness, evenness, and uniformity of grain.
>
> *Clearness of Liquor:* This factor requires no elaboration. The degree of sediment and cloudiness materially affects the total score for quality.
>
> *Clearness of Syrup:* Any degree of sediment or cloudiness materially affects the total grading score.
>
> *Syrup Density:* The degree or percentage, by weight, of sugar in the syrup solution, as measured by either the Brix scale or Balling scale on hydrometers or saccharimeters.
>
> *Drained Weight:* The weight of the product after draining the liquor or syrup according to the method prescribed by the National Canners Associaton or the USDA.

Source: Raymond B. Peddersen, *Foodservice and Hotel Purchasing*, pp. 100–101. Also published by CBI Publishing Company, Inc. (Boston: 1980).

Canned and Frozen Fruit. The following is a list of things to avoid when buying canned and frozen fruit.

Apples (Canned): hardness or softness; excess brown, gray, or pink color; pieces of inedible tissue; and excessive skin, bruises, or other defects.

Applesauce: thin consistency; dull, poor, or pink color; off-flavor; particles of seeds; flecks from bruised portions; and pieces of peel or inedible tissue.

Apricots (Canned): pale yellow color covering more than one-half of each apricot; light greenish color covering more than one-fourth of each apricot; brown coloring; excessive numbers of broken or crushed halves; lack of uniformity in size and thickness; loose pits; dirt or grit; excessive damage; and oxidation.

Apricots (Frozen): dark or oxidation discoloration; dull orange to amber color.

Cherries (Red Tart): excessive numbers of pits; loose, soft, tough, or leathery fruit; defects that extend into fruit tissue.

Citrus Fruits: lack of brightness; tinge of amber color; excessive numbers of broken segments; mushy, fibrous segments; prominent presence of seeds and membranes; scorched, bitter, or flat taste.

Cranberry Sauce: presence of stems or pieces of leaf; poor color.

Fruit Cocktail: excessive sediment; poor color; hard or mushy fruit; cap stems on grapes; variability in size of fruit.

Fruit Mixtures: excessive sediment; poor color; pieces of peel; hard, crushed, or frayed fruit.

Peaches: dark or oxidation discoloration; dull orange to amber color.

Peaches (Elberta): off-color or wide color variation; excessive variation in size, symmetry, and thickness; excessive number of soft or hard pieces; crushed or broken pieces; loose pits, stems, and leaves.

Peaches (Yellow Cling): off-color or wide color variation; excessive variation in size, symmetry, and thickness; excessive number of soft or hard pieces; crushed or broken pieces; loose pits, stems, and leaves.

Pears: "dead white" or "chalky" pears; pink or brown cast; mushiness or partly crushed or broken fruit; toughness, hardness, or graininess; poorly peeled and trimmed fruit; interior stems.

Pineapple: off-color or excess light color; white markings; excess number of blemished units; deep eyes; brown spots or bruises; or pieces of peel.

Prunes: mixed varieties and sizes; variable texture and color; scars or scabs; cracked or split units; excessive moisture.

Raisins: grit, sand, or silt; fermented or sugared raisins; undeveloped raisins.

Table 3–6 Number of Servings of Fruit per Can (½-cup servings)

Canned fruit	6 cans/case No. 10 can	24 cans/case No. 2½ can	No. 303 can
Apples (sliced)	24	6.5	4
Applesauce	27	7	4
Apricots (halves)	15–16	3.5–4	4
Bananas (mashed)	29	7	4
Cherries (red tart)	24–26	—	3–4
Cherries (sweet)	27	7	3–4
Cranberry sauce	29	7	4
Fruit cocktail	27	7.5	4–4.5
Grapefruit sections	—	—	4
Peaches (halves or slices)	25	7	3
Pears (halves)	25	7	3
Pineapple (chunks)	27	7.5	—
Raspberries	27	—	4
Strawberries	27	—	4

Source: Raymond B. Peddersen, *Foodservice and Hotel Purchasing*, p. 215. Also published by CBI Publishing Company, Inc. (Boston: 1980).

CHAPTER THREE

Canned Vegetables. The following is a list of things to avoid in buying canned vegetables.

Asparagus: soft, mushy, tough, or fibrous cuts; shattered, open, or flowered heads; off-color (light yellow-green); stringy or frayed edges; excessive grit; too few heads; bitter or undesirable taste.

Beans: cloudy or off-color liquid; spotted beans; large seeds or worm holes; soft or mushy beans; excessive numbers of unsnipped ends; loose stem ends; tough, inedible strings; uneven, ragged, or split units; small pieces of pod.

Beans (Dry): variability in size; cracked seed coats; foreign material; pinholes caused by insect damage.

Corn: dull color in golden varieties, brownish cast in white varieties; irregular or raggedly cut kernels with cob tissues; tough or leathery kernels; clusters of grain; worm-eaten kernels, excessive sweetness or saltiness.

Peas: cloudy liquor and accumulation of sediment; color variation or off-color; spotted, discolored, or broken peas; excessive hardness or mushiness; tough or mealy peas; foreign material such as pods, thistle buds.

Table 3–7 Number of Servings of Vegetables per Can (½-cup servings)

Canned vegetable	6 cans/case No. 10 can	24 cans/case No. 2½ can	No. 303 can
Asparagus (cuts and tips)	20	—	—
Beans (lima)	24	—	4
Beans (snap, green or wax)	21	5.5	3
Beets (sliced)	23	—	3.25
Carrots (sliced)	23	—	3.25
Corn (whole kernel)	23	—	3.5
Okra	20	—	3.5
Onions (small, whole)	20	—	3
Peas (green)	23	—	3
Potatoes (small, whole)	25	—	—
Pumpkin (mashed)	26.5	7	—
Spinach	15	4.5–5	3
Squash (summer)	17.5	—	3
Tomatoes	25.5	7	4
Catsup	111	—	—

Source: Raymond B. Peddersen, *Foodservice and Hotel Purchasing,* p. 301. Also published by CBI Publishing Company, Inc. (Boston: 1980).

> | | |
> |---|---|
> | Fruit Juices: | 18 fluid-ounce can yields 4.5 servings.
46 fluid-ounce can yields 11.50 servings.
96 fluid-ounce can yields 24 servings. |
> | Vegetable Juices: | 23 fluid-ounce can yields 5.75 servings.
46 fluid-ounce can yields 11.50 servings.
96 fluid-ounce can yields 24 servings. |

Box 3–2 Number of Servings of Juices per Can

Source: Raymond B. Peddersen, *Foodservice and Hotel Purchasing*, p. 301. Also published by CBI Publishing Company, Inc. (Boston: 1980).

Tomatoes (Whole or Pieces): pale red, yellow, and green portions; pieces of skin or core material; blemished, watery, or soft pieces; mold; insects; poor flavor.

Tomato Puree: yellowish-red solids; scorched, bitter, salty, or green tomato flavor; excessive number of dark specks; scalelike particles from seeds, peel, or core; thin consistency.

Tomato Products. The degree of concentration of the product is not considered a factor of quality for the purposes of the standards for natural tomato soluble solids, but the following designations of concentration of tomato solids may be used.

Extra heavy concentration: 39.3 percent or more

Heavy concentration: 32 percent or more, but less than 39.3 percent

Medium concentration: 28 percent or more, but less than 32 percent

Light concentration: 24 percent or more, but less than 28 percent

Texture is the degree of fineness or coarseness of the product. Texture is rated after the product is diluted with water to between 8 percent and 9 percent, inclusive, of natural tomato soluble solids. "Fine" texture means a smooth, uniform finish. "Coarse" texture means a coarse, slightly granular finish.

Six grades of frozen vegetables are marketed in the United States: (1) High Grade A, which is not always available; (2) Grade A; (3) Grade AAB, which is A for color, A for lack of defects, and B for maturity, a good steam table pack; (4) Grade B; (5) Grade AAC, which is A for color, A for lack of defects, and C for maturity, looks good but has poor eating quality; and (6) Grade C or better.

Frozen Vegetables

Table 3–8 Number of Servings of Frozen Vegetables (3 ounces cooked)

Frozen vegetable	Yield/lb
Asparagus (cuts and tips)	4.27
Beans (lima)	5.33
Beans (snap, green or wax)	4.85
Broccoli (cut or chopped)	4.53
Carrots (sliced)	5.12
Corn (whole kernel)	5.17
Okra	4.37
Peas (green)	5.12
Potatoes (French fries)	8 (10 pieces)
Spinach	4.27
Squash (summer)	4.64

Source: Raymond B. Peddersen, *Foodservice and Hotel Purchasing*, p. 301. Also published by CBI Publishing Company, Inc. (Boston: 1980).

Frozen vegetable grading factors are color, size, defects, character, maturity, and taste. Color is more important in some products than in others, for example, baby limas versus peas or corn. Size is very important for grading some items, such as peas, but irrelevant in grading others, such as broccoli. Defects are rated from minor to severe, with some, like spinach, critical. Character has to do with product development; this factor is unimportant when grading peas or corn, but critical for cauliflower or spinach. Maturity has to do with tenderness. Taste means that the item when processed must taste like the original produce. Frozen vegetables are packed in 2-, 2½-, 3-, and 20-pound cartons. A clue to the geographical origin of a frozen vegetable is the manufacturer of the boxboard, since boxboard is usually manufactured and printed in the area of the processor.

The following is a list of things to avoid in buying frozen vegetables.

Asparagus: soft, mushy, tough, or fibrous cuts; shattered, open, or flowered heads; off-color (light yellow-green); stringy or frayed edges; excessive grit; too few heads; bitter or undesirable taste.

Beans: off-color; mixed variety; loose stems; small pieces; damaged, blemished, or tough, stringy units; excessive sloughing; off-flavor or odor.

Corn: dull or off-color; crushed, broken, or ragged kernels; pieces of cob, silk, or husk; tough or seriously damaged kernels; off-flavor or odor.

Peas: dull, off-color extraneous material; broken or blemished peas; loose skins; off-flavor or odor.

Potatoes (French Fried): excessive numbers of light-or dark-colored units; excessive number of chips, slivers, or irregularly sized pieces; carbon specks; dark discoloration; excessive oiliness or sogginess after heating; off-flavor or odor.

Potatoes (Hash Browns): excessive number of light- or dark-colored units; excessive number of chips, slivers, or irregularly sized pieces; carbon specks; dark discoloration; excessive oiliness or sogginess after heating; off-flavor or odor.

PICKLES AND RELISHES

Pickles are called either "cured pickles" or "fresh-pack pickles," depending on the method used to pack them. Each type has its own characteristics of flavor and texture. Cured pickles are slightly fermented in a salt brine for several months. They are then desalted and washed. The pickling process is completed in a vinegar solution, which is also a fermentation product. This solution is seasoned to give the desired flavor characteristics. The curing process imparts subtle flavor changes and produces edible acids in the pickles themselves. Cured pickles are usually crisp, dark green, and somewhat translucent. Fresh-pack pickles are relatively new in the marketplace. In the fresh-pack process, the cucumbers are packed directly into the final containers, and then covered with a pickling solution containing vinegars, other acids, flavorings, and other ingredients to give the desired characteristics to the pickles. The containers are then sealed and pasteurized to preserve the contents. Fresh-pack pickles have not been fermented; they retain something of the flavor of fresh cucumbers. They are usually a light yellow-green color and are not as salty or as acid as the cured pickles. Fresh-pack often appears on the label of these pickles.

Pickles belong to a larger family of foods having many of the same characteristics and adding interest and zest to meals. Many fruits and vegetables other than cucumbers are pickled commercially. Some of these are peaches, pears, crabapples, watermelon rind, beets, onions, okra, peppers, tomatoes (ripe or green), and green beans. A wide variety of relishes are also available for foodservice use, such as pepper-onion, tomato-apple chutney, tomato-pear chutney, horseradish, and corn relish.

SUGAR

Sugar is almost pure sucrose if made by evaporating and crystallizing sugar cane or sugar beets. Corn sugar, made by the hydrolysis of the starch of corn, is dextrose. Glucose is dextrose in syrup form. Cellulose is crystallized dextrose. Sugar's fineness of texture is indicated by a number of x's; x is the most coarse and 10x is the finest. Powdered sugar is marked xx or 2x. Confectioner's sugar, which is used for icing, is marked xxxx or 4x. It has 3 percent starch added, as does 6x sugar.

Molasses is uncrystallized sugar. Brown sugar (also called "soft") is a mixture of granulated sugar and molasses. Grades of brown sugar are Nos. 1 through 15, with 15 being the darkest color. Buy No. 8 through No. 10 for light brown, No. 11 through No. 15 for dark brown.

Granulated sugar is available in 100-lb, 50-lb, 25-lb, 10-lb, 5-lb, 2-lb, and 1-lb containers, as well as in cases of 1000 to 3000 individual packets of ⅙ or ¼ oz. Powdered and brown sugars are usually purchased in cases of twenty-four 1-lb boxes.

HOW TO DETERMINE YOUR INVENTORY NEEDS

The important adjective with respect to inventory is *adequate*. If a foodservice operation buys and stores too much, its food costs may increase because of the "using a little bit more because it's there" factor. The secret of maintaining adequate inventory lies in planning ahead. A determination of near-future needs should be based on the following:

1. A *customer participation forecast*. The expected number of customers per meal and per week is determined from a combination of past experience and such concrete factors as head counts (plant employment figures, number of student board contracts, number of patients, etc.), weather conditions, special function preregistrations, and seasonal or holiday trends.
2. A *menu plan*. In choosing menu items, keep known customer preferences in mind. To estimate quantities of raw materials needed, consult your recipe file for a listing of ingredients and amounts for each menu item.
3. A *review of previous food production records*. Past food production records can help predict required product quantities.

Acceptable Inventory Levels

Table 3–9 shows recommended inventory levels for different types of product. The levels are expressed in terms of average weekly usage. Naturally, these levels must be adjusted to suit the individual operation and to take into consideration such local conditions as source of supply, contract terms, weather severity at certain seasons, etc. A foodservice operation should establish the current actual inventory levels for these product categories. Then an attempt can be made to reduce stock on hand gradually until a "reasonable, comfortable" level is reached.

Manager should provide the receiver with complete purchase order information, including the name of the supplier, the name of the delivery agent (if special entrance permission is required by management), approximate time

Table 3-9 Recommended Inventory Levels

Type of product	Acceptable average weeks inventory on hand
Meats, seafood, etc.	0.8 to 1.0
Fresh and frozen	0.4 to 0.6
Groceries	1.5 to 2.0
Other supplies*	2.0 to 3.5

Note: The amount of supplies varies considerably, since it is a function of such factors as the amount of paper used in service in the operation and the extent of cleaning responsibilities.

of delivery, exact quantities of items ordered, product descriptions and specifications for each item ordered, and the unit price of each item ordered. The receiver should also be provided with an alphabetical, expansion, file portfolio for holding purchase orders and daily invoices or delivery tickets. It is also important that the receiver use an adequate receiving scale. Minimum requirements for the scale depend on the size of the operation and the weight of products received. Maximum weight capacity is determined by individual needs; minimum weight gradations should usually be ¼ pound. The accuracy of the scale should be checked periodically by a qualified service representative. Readability of the scale, the height of its platform, the size of its platform pan or cradle, and whether it is equipped with an invoice imprinter are also factors. The scale should be located in the normal flow pattern of received merchandise, near the delivery entrance.

Receivers should have copies of purveyor invoices or delivery tickets. These should state for each item the exact quantity shipped, the exact product description as specified by the order, and the unit price and price extension. Any shortages should be noted and reported. Any overages should be refused or noted and reported to the buyer. The receiver should verify each item or container against the delivery invoice whenever possible. It is especially important to check for (1) short or excessive counts—*count* each item bought by the piece; (2) short or excessive weights—*weigh* each item bought by weight (do not include the weight of the packing medium or the container); (3) short fills or short packs—*examine* the fill of containers or packages, particularly items that are usually repacked (such as fruits and vegetables) and occasionally weigh items like wrapped loaves of bread and check the number of usable slices; and (4) shrinkage, leakage, or breakage. The receiver must inspect the delivered products for specified quality, ingredients as listed on label, order of listed ingredients (ingredients are listed in descending order of predominance), label brands or quality declarations, meat trim or fat cover, USDA inspection stamps and USDA grade shield, wholesomeness, discoloration, odors, mold, spores, bruises, softness due to decay or deterioration, immaturity (green or hard), viscosity, packaging date codes (dates of packing and expiration). Also it is recommended to spot check temperatures of dairy products, 38°–45°F; meat and poultry, 33°–38°F; fish and shellfish, 23°–30°F; frozen foods (meats, fruits, and vegetables), −20°–0°F. The receiver should always verify receiving documents with rubber receiving stamp and signature at the time of receipt. The purveyor's delivery ticket or invoice should be stamped, signed, and attached to the purchase order for accounting. The receiver's last responsibility is to see that the received products are delivered to the proper storage areas.

4 Nonfood Purchasing

TEXTILES

To select the proper linens, the three most important features to consider are durability, laundry costs, and, lastly, purchase price. From these three features, the true cost of an item can be determined.

The original price is only one factor in determining the actual cost of an article during its period of service. The cost per use is obtained by adding the original price of the article to the total laundry cost during its life expectancy and dividing by the life expectancy or the total number of launderings that can be expected for the item. The formula is written as:

$$\text{Cost per use} = \frac{\text{Wt} \times \text{Ldr Cost/lb} \times \text{Life Exp} + \text{Orig Price}}{\text{Life Exp}}$$

The cost per use formula is of invaluable assistance in determining the difference between operating efficiency (and a profit) or incompetency (and a loss). For example, a tablecloth weighing 1.4 lb, which has a life expectancy of 250 launderings and costs $3.50 when new, is processed in a laundry whose laundry cost is $.10 per lb. Cost per use is derived from the formula:

$$\text{Cost per use} = \frac{(1.4)(.10)(250) + 3.50}{250} = \frac{35 + 3.50}{250} = \frac{38.50}{250} = \$.1542$$

It is quite evident from the above cost per use calculation that the original purchase price plays a relatively insignificant part in arriving at the true cost of an item. In the above, note that the foodservice institution invested $35.00

in the laundering of the tablecloth during a period of 250 uses. The investment represented by the original cost of $3.50 is rather insignificant when compared to this investment of $35.00 to process this item through the laundry 250 times. In fact, it is the number of launderings an article can sustain that is the most important factor in determining the true cost of an item or its cost per use. The finesse in purchasing linen, therefore, is the ability to closely approximate the probable additional uses obtainable from an item, weighed against the cost of laundering it and its purchase price.

Construction and Types of Weaves

The durability of a fabric is contingent on the construction of the material. Construction of a woven piece of textile is achieved by the interlacing of yarns woven at right angles to each other. The lengthwise threads are called the warp. The crosswise threads are called filling or weft. The lengthwise sides or edges of a fabric are called the selvages. There are three types of weaves, but we are concerned with only two basic weaves, namely, plain and twill. The plain weave is the most common type of weave. It is accomplished by alternately interlacing the warp and filling threads, one warp over and one warp under the filling throughout the entire extent of the fabric. Both muslin and percale, for example, are made with plain weaves. The twill weave results in diagonal lines on the face of the cloth. Each warp thread does not interlace with each filling thread. Instead, it interlaces with only every second, third, or fourth filling thread, floating over or under the remainder. This creates the illusion of a diagonal weave. Twill weaves are frequently used for heavier cloths, sheets, and work clothes.

The number of threads interlaced together in a square inch constitutes a "thread count." For example, the most commonly used sheet in hotels or hospitals is approximately 180 threads per square inch. It is made with approximately 94 threads per inch running in the warp, that is, lengthwise, direction and 86 threads per inch in the fill, for a total thread count of 180 per square inch.

The weight of the average 180 thread count sheet is approximately 3.6 ounces per square yard. The weight of a fabric is specified in one of two ways— either ounces per square yard or yards per pound. When the weight is specified in yards per pound, it is important that the width of the fabric be defined. Naturally, the wider the fabric, the more it will weigh per lineal yard than narrower fabric of similar construction.

In addition to the thread count and weight of a fabric, it is necessary to be aware of its tensile strength, since this gives a good indication of its potential durability. The tensile strength is determined in a laboratory under conditions of controlled temperature and humidity. It is the number of pounds required to break a strip of fabric or textile that is one inch wide and three inches long. Another important indicator for predetermining the possible durability of a fabric is an abrasion test, which measures the degree to which a fabric resists surface wear. Institutional linens, including apparel for personnel, are very often more subject to surface wear than to strain. The abrasion test determines how many rubs the material can withstand under certain circumstances before the thread weakens.

Tablecloths and Napkins

Tablecloths and napkins of the best quality are made of cotton damask, two layers thick and weighing 10 ounces or more per square yard. This fabric has about 200 threads per square inch and shrinks less than 10 percent. Combed cotton, broadcloth, and momie cloth are also commonly used. The trend in recent years has been to use synthetic fibers because they are wrinkle-resistant and easy to care for. Some of these synthetic fibers also resist absorption of spills. That quality may please the restaurant owner but displease the customer.

Tablecloths and napkins should be ordered preshrunk. If ordering by the cut size, the buyer should remember that shrinkage reduces tablecloth dimensions by as much as four inches (a 72 × 72 cut becomes a 69 × 69 cloth) and napkin dimensions by as much as two inches. The buyer should specify a seam strength of 64 pounds or greater, nonfading or colorfast colors, a breaking strength appropriate to the type of material, and a weight of at least 4 ounces per square yard for single thickness materials.

A napkin is a piece of fabric or paper used to protect clothing and to wipe lips and fingers. A napkin usually measures about 14 to 23 inches square. It may be made of damask, momie cloth, or broadcloth. Fibers used include cotton, rayon, linen, and polyesters. Napkins should be ordered by specifying weave, fiber, and count in dozens.

DINNERWARE

Dishes are made of either ceramics or glass (in the case of Pyroceram, both), or of a plastic called melamine. Ceramics are dense, relatively nonporous substances produced by baking clay. The baking process is called vitrification when done at high temperatures. The types of ceramics are (1) china, which is made of a high-quality clay that may contain some ground bone or calcium phosphate and is vitrified at 2250°F or above; (2) stoneware, which is made of clay not as fine as that used for china and is vitrified at about 2200°F; (3) pottery, which is made of even less refined clay and is baked, but not vitrified, at about 1500°F; (4) terra cotta, which is baked at about 1000°F. Glass dishes are made of glass which is manufactured from boric oxide, soda, and silica (sand). Pyroceram is made of metals, silica, and clay. Melamine dishes are made by casting or pressing heat-softened plastic into dish shapes.

The unfired clay piece of china is called a bisque. The bisque is vitrified and then cleaned. At this point, a decoration and/or a glaze may be applied. The bisque is then baked (or fired) again at a temperature slightly less than 2200°F. Some final decorating in materials that would melt at the vitrifying temperatures, such as silver and gold, is sometimes done after the final firing. This is called overglazing. The glaze is a type of glass that adds a shine and toughness to the china. The glaze should be applied evenly over the surface of the dish. When the glaze has worn through, after as many as 750 uses, the piece of china should be discarded. It is important that the glaze allows water to "sheet" freely from the surface of the dish. Decorations are applied to the bisque by hand or by stencil or decal. The china must be baked separately for each color used in the decoration, so the more colors that are added, the higher the manufacturing expense. Having a custom pattern produced for an operation should add only a fraction of a cent to the cost per use of the china, but it will require placement of large orders and lead time of about six months for delivery.

For foodservice use, china must be strong. The addition of aluminum oxide to the clay instead of the ground quartz usually used will make china as much as twice as tough and will increase its resistance to chipping many times over. Such china is said to have an alumna body. Toughness is also increased by a thicker body, a thicker base (well), and a rolled or scalloped edge. China should be able to withstand rapid temperature changes and impacts to the body and edge. The glaze should withstand moisture and sharp knives.

There are no standard sizes for dishes. Each manufacturer has its own sizes; frequently not all sizes are produced of all the patterns carried. China grades are as follows: (1) selects, (2) firsts, (3) seconds, (4) thirds, and (5) culls or dumps. Selects and firsts are always among those pieces fired around the rim of the kiln.

Dinnerware is ordered by size of piece in inches or ounces of capacity, name of piece, and count. Bowls: from 4⅝ to about 6 inches wide (nappy or side dish or mankey dish or fruit bowl); from 5½ to about 8 inches wide (grapefruit bowl, cereal or oatmeal bowl, salad bowl, soup bowl); from 7½ to about 9 inches wide, with wide rim (soup plate). Cups, without handle: 3⅝ inch or larger, from 6½-ounces to about 8-ounces capacity (bouillon cup); about 3-ounces capacity (oriental or Chinese tea cup). Cups, with handle: from about 5-ounces to 10-ounces capacity (tea cup or coffee cup); from about 2½-ounces to 4½-ounces capacity (demitasse or after-dinner cup). Plates: from about 5 to 6½ inches wide (bread and butter plate); from about 6 to 8½ inches wide (salad or dessert plate); from about 7½ to 9 inches wide (dinner plate).

FLATWARE

Because of the skyrocketing prices of silver in the past decade, stainless steel flatware is used in most restaurants and institutions. Stainless steel flatware costs only 10 to 50 percent as much as silverplate and only 3 to 15 percent as much as sterling silver. It is not difficult to understand the wide acceptance of stainless steel considering raw cost alone; but it popularity is even easier to understand considering the necessity for burnishing and periodic replating of silverplate.

Stainless steel flatware is usually punched out of sheets of stainless steel. The spread in prices of stainless steel flatware is a result of the manufacturing process used. Flatware that is not punched out is made from stainless steel that has been formed to different thicknesses by rollers. This process, known as grading, produces a stronger utensil, which is priced higher. Good stainless steel flatware is at least 12-gage. The best stainless steel flatware is manufactured from 18-8 chrome/nickel alloy. The next best is 17-7 chrome/nickel. Other chrome alloys are known by their numbers, such as 301, 302, 410, or 430, with the higher numbers representing more chrome in the alloy. The chrome content determines the lightness and brightness of the color. These are desirable factors which have to be weighed against the ease with which chrome rusts and pits. The finish given to stainless steel equipment in general is usually No. 4. Stainless steel flatware, however, is usually given the brighter and more reflective No. 2B and No. 7 finishes.

The important consideration when buying teaspoons is the strength of the neck. Hollow handle knives give better balance, but the handle must be welded to the blade. The weld point is usually susceptible to rust and may be hard to sanitize. Forks, especially, should not have any rough edges. Rough edges, scratches, or manufacturing defects of any kind should not be accepted.

Silverplated flatware is used where elegance and class are musts. Silverplated flatware is manufactured by coating copper and nickel "blanks" with silver by electrolysis. The points of greatest wear, for example, the spoon bowl and back and the fork tines, should have an undercoating, or inlay, of silver to prevent wearing through. Silverplate flatware is purchased by the weight of silver in a gross of teaspoons and the weight of the blanks. The silver weight varies from 2½ ounces to 8 ounces per gross, and the blank weight varies from 9 to 11 pounds per gross.

GLASSWARE

Glassware is defined as any drinking utensils without handles, including disposable cups and glass, acrylic, plastic, and metal tumblers and goblets. Glassware does not include mugs (with handles). Order glassware by name, capacity in ounces, and quantity in dozens or hundreds. (See Table 4-1.)

Glass is made by fusing sand (silica) in combination with soda and lime at high temperatures. Addition of metals to this mixture adds strength and beauty. Thus, good crystal contains 24 percent lead. Glassware is usually very fragile. (There is one line of very competitively priced glassware available today that is extremely difficult to break.) To make it stronger manufacturers may add metals or other compounds, cool it slowly, reheat and then recool it (which causes the surfaces to shrink and gain tensile strength), shape it in other than straight or flared shapes, or make it thicker.

Table 4-1 Glassware for Restaurants and Hotels

		Seating capacity	
Item	100	200	300
Coffee shop			
5 oz juice	12 dozen	24 dozen	36 dozen
10 oz water	24 dozen	36 dozen	60 dozen
12 oz ice tea	12 dozen	24 dozen	24 dozen
Dining room			
5 oz juice	12 dozen	24 dozen	30 dozen
12 oz ice tea	12 dozen	24 dozen	24 dozen
10 oz water goblet	24 dozen	30 dozen	42 dozen
5½ oz sherbet	12 dozen	18 dozen	30 dozen
4½ oz fruit cocktail	12 dozen	18 dozen	30 dozen
4½ oz parfait	12 dozen	18 dozen	30 dozen
6½ oz finger bowl	12 dozen	18 dozen	30 dozen
Banquet			
5 oz juice	12 dozen	24 dozen	36 dozen
12 oz ice tea	12 dozen	24 dozen	24 dozen
10 oz water goblet	18 dozen	24 dozen	36 dozen
5½ oz low sherbet	12 dozen	18 dozen	30 dozen
4½ oz fruit cocktail	12 dozen	24 dozen	30 dozen
5½ oz champagne	12 dozen	24 dozen	30 dozen
4½ oz parfait	12 dozen	18 dozen	30 dozen
6½ oz finger bowl	12 dozen	18 dozen	30 dozen
Room service			
8 oz room tumbler	Minimum 2 to a room		
Ash tray	Minimum 2 to a room		

		Seating capacity		
Item	25	50	75	100
Fountain service				
5 oz juice	6 dozen	6 dozen	12 dozen	12 dozen
6⅞ oz beverage	6 dozen	6 dozen	12 dozen	12 dozen
10 oz water	6 dozen	6 dozen	12 dozen	12 dozen
10 oz malted milk	6 dozen	6 dozen	12 dozen	12 dozen
12 oz soda	6 dozen	6 dozen	12 dozen	12 dozen

Source: Courtesy Libbey Glass, Division of Owens-Illinois.

SMALLWARES

Smallwares (hand utensils and equipment) are relatively inexpensive individually, but taken as a whole, they account for a substantial investment in the foodservice operation. Smallwares are the most used of all kitchen equipment. Unlike fixed equipment, they are constantly banged around, dropped, and subjected to abuse. Careless selection of these items can result in unhappy employees, frequent replacement of equipment, and reduction in the efficiency of production. For example, scoops with a weak releasing mechanism make efficient dishing of food nearly impossible. Employees either lose time or switch to a functioning scoop of the wrong size. Knives manufactured of a metal that does not hold a sharp edge may cause loss of time, as well as employee injuries.

When purchasing smallwares, the buyer should consider the following:

1. *Frequency of use.* The strongest, most durable piece available should be selected for frequently used items. Infrequently used items may be of lesser quality.
2. *Safety.* Knives without blade guards, for example, impose an unneeded kitchen hazard.
3. *Sanitation.* Select equipment with easy-to-clean surfaces. Look for the National Sanitation Foundation (NSF) sticker as a guarantee of easy-cleaning design.
4. *Ease of use.* Pick the equipment that is easiest to handle. Why create unnecessary labor?
5. *Terminology.* Knowledge of correct terminology for smallwares is important. The buyer may need a meat turner, but inadvertently order a spatula.

Pots and Pans

Aluminum is a good material for pots and pans because of its good thermal conduction properties, but it also has disadvantages in that it corrodes fairly easily and is damaged by alkaline cleaning compounds. Aluminum pots and pans are generally manufactured in light-, medium-, and heavyweight cast aluminum, and aluminum utensils are made of sheet aluminum. Because aluminum smallwares damage easily, they should only be made of anodized aluminum. Aluminum is inexpensive compared to stainless steel or copper.

Cast iron is inexpensive. Cast iron is usually not selected for commercial use, however, because of its tendencies to rust and to break when dropped and its heaviness.

Copper has the best thermal conduction properties of any of the metals used for kitchen equipment, but it is also the most expensive. Before purchasing copper utensils, the buyer should also consider the ease with which copper is scratched and dented and that it readily forms a green rust. Copper's excellent thermal conduction can be obtained at lower cost by purchasing pots and pans with copper bottoms or with copper cores covered with stainless steel.

Stainless steel is often the metal chosen, because it is both attractive and durable. The choice of stainless steel for hand utensils is usually wise. For pots and pans, however, stainless steel has disadvantages. It is a poor thermal conductor, expensive, and rather heavy compared to aluminim. It does clean relatively easily and is resistant to corrosion. Sheet steel is an inexpensive material commonly used for baking and roasting pans. Like cast iron, sheet steel rusts easily.

Tin is often used for pie tins (although the trend is toward disposable aluminum) and for coating sheet steel and copper utensils, such as mixing bowls. Tin is rust-resistant, but it wears through quickly.

Plastics that can withstand temperatures up to 300°F and can take virtually as much abuse as metals have been available in commercial equipment since the early 1970s. They are still relatively expensive, but are finding increasing acceptance due to their very light weight and optical transparency. Enameled porcelain utensils have virtually disappeared from commercial kitchens because of the ease with which they crack, chip, and scratch. They clean easily and are inexpensive, but are not recommended.

5 Sanitation

INTRODUCTION

The purpose of this section is to discuss thoroughly the basic and most essential facts relating directly to the prevention of food-borne illness. The reader will gain a basic understanding of the principles of safe food handling. *Applied Foodservice Sanitation*, published by the National Institute for the Foodservice Industry (NIFI) and developed in collaboration with the National Sanitation Foundation, is the primary source of the information presented in this section.[1]

The National Institute for the Foodservice Industry has a rapidly growing nationwide program that provides to people who are directly or indirectly involved in foodservice careers the opportunity to be certified in foodservice sanitation on completion of a course of study. This program has received approval and endorsements from the National Restaurant Association, the International Food Service Executives Association, and the American Culinary Federation; it represents a major step forward for the foodservice industry in its efforts to maintain and upgrade professional food sanitation standards.

THE BASIC ESSENTIALS OF FOOD SANITATION

The person preparing food seldom thinks in the terms used by technical experts on food. However, since the preparer is the crucial upholder of health standards, he or she should have as a clear-cut primary objective the protection of people from illness caused by contamination of food by harmful organisms

---

[1] National Institute for the Foodservice Industry, *Applied Foodservice Sanitation* (Chicago: National Institute for the Foodservice Industry, 1974), pp. 34–52.

and their toxins or by other poisonous materials. In meeting this responsibility, the person preparing food should be totally committed to two courses of action, which are as follows: (1) keep food free of bacterial contaminants initially; and (2) prevent the growth of any bacteria that may invade food during storage, preparation, or service.

The distinction between contamination and spoilage of food is as follows. In most cases, food that has deteriorated to the point of losing color, texture, flavor, or desirable aroma will not cause illness. On the other hand, food that is contaminated with harmful organisms and their toxins does not always betray this condition by its appearance or taste. Potentially hazardous foods, as defined by the United States Public Health Service, are foods that are capable of supporting rapid and progressive growth of infectious or toxicogenic (poison-producing) microorganisms. Microorganisms in food cause illness in two ways: (1) some bacteria are disease germs—feeding on the nutrients in certain foods, especially those containing milk and eggs and other ingredients of animal origin, multiplying very rapidly at favorable temperatures, using the food as a medium for growth and for transportation to the part of the body which they infect; (2) other bacteria are not themselves infectious, but discharge from their bodies wastes that are toxic to people.

Microorganisms require a moist, warm, nutritious environment to prosper. Their growth can be slowed or stopped by refrigeration, and they can be destroyed by heat. It is that middle range between 45°F and 140°F that is most dangerous. It represents the temperature zone in which bacteria can multiply most rapidly and efficiently. Microorganisms occur in a variety of shapes and sizes. They can live in any conditions in which humans can survive, and in some in which humans can't. Bacteria have little or no means of locomotion, so they depend on someone or something to move them from place to place—water, food, wind, insects, rodents or other animal carriers, or humans. A typical bacterium measures 1/25,000th of an inch (one micron). Bacteria are one-celled, thin-walled living creatures that need food, give off wastes, and reproduce. Their reproduction process is simple—they divide in two. If conditions are favorable, as mentioned previously, this doubling by fission may occur several times in an hour. In this way, a single cell can multiply into millions in a brief time, developing a colony.

The most common types of food-borne illnesses, with their causes and some preventative measures will be covered next.

Staphylococcal Infections. The symptoms of staphylococcal infections are vomiting, diarrhea, and cramps. Onset occurs three to eight hours after ingestion. Duration is from one to two days. The cause is *Staphylococcus aureus*, a type of bacteria commonly present in nose, throat, and skin infections. It releases toxins highly resistant to heat. Foods implicated include moist, heavily handled, high-protein foods that remain for some time at bacteria incubating temperatures, such as milk-egg custards, meat pies, turkey stuffing, chicken salad, tuna salad, potato salad, gravies, sauces, and warmed-over foods. Preventative measures are to store these foods at or below 40°F; to exclude foodhandlers with respiratory illness, pimples, infected cuts, or burns; to minimize contact between hands and food; and to reheat leftovers thoroughly to 165°F or above.

Perfringens Poisoning. The symptoms of perfringens poisoning are nausea, diarrhea, and acute inflammation of stomach and intestines. They first appear from eight to twenty hours after eating contaminated food. Duration is up to twenty-four hours. The cause is *Clostridium perfringens*, a type of spore-forming bacteria found generally in soil, dust, and the intestinal tracts of animals. The spores withstand most cooking temperatures; surviving cells flourish in the absence of air. This microorganism is a natural contaminant of meat. Foods implicated are raw meat, raw vegetables, and partly cooked meat that is slowly cooled and served later or that is served after insufficient reheating. Preventative measures are careful time and temperature control, quick chilling of cooked meat dishes that are to be eaten later, and isolation of raw components that may cross-contaminate cooked items.

Salmonellosis. The symptoms of salmonellosis are headache followed by vomiting, diarrhea, abdominal cramps, and fever. Severe infections cause high fever and may be fatal. Onset occurs twelve to thirty-six hours after exposure. Duration is from two to seven days. The cause of this form of food poisoning is *Salmonella* bacteria, which are widespread in nature and which live and grow in the intestines of humans and animals. Some 800 types cause gastrointestinal illness; one species, *Salmonella typhosa*, causes typhoid fever. Foods implicated include meat and poultry (especially with finely-cut components), egg products, puddings, shellfish, soups, gravies, sauces, and warmed-over food. Preventative measures include strict personal hygiene, avoidance of fecal contamination from unclean foodhandlers and unsafe practices, and the elimination of rodents and flies.

Shigellosis. The symptoms of shigellosis (also known as bacillary dysentery) are mild to severe diarrhea, fever, cramps, chills, lassitude, and dehydration. Onset occurs one to seven days after ingestion. Duration is of indefinite length, depending on treatment. The cause is *Shigella sonnei* and other species that are found in the feces of infected humans, transmitted from person to person or by contaminated food and water. Foods implicated are contaminated milk; beans; potato, tuna, shrimp, turkey, and macaroni salads; apple cider; and other moist mixed foods. Preventative measures are strict, personal hygiene, safe food handling, sanitary food and water sources, insect and vermin control, and sanitary sewage disposal.

Botulism. The symptoms of botulism are vomiting, abdominal pain, headache, double vision, and progressive respiratory paralysis. They appear from two hours to six days after ingestion. Paralysis may persist for months. There is a high fatality rate associated with botulism, 50–65 percent in the United States. The cause is *Clostridium botulinum*, which grows in the absence of air, such as in sealed containers, from spores with a high resistance to heat. The toxins produced are deadly but vulnerable to high temperatures. This bacteria is found in soil, water, and animal intestines. Foods implicated are improperly canned or refrigerated low-acid foods, green beans, corn, beets, spinach, figs, olives, tuna, smoked fish, and fermented foods. Preventative measures are to pressure cook foods at high temperatures when canning, to boil and stir home-canned food for twenty minutes before serving, to keep foods refrigerated, to use plenty of salt when curing foods, and to discard food in swollen cans.

Streptococcal Infections. The symptoms of gastrointestinal streptococcal infections are nausea, vomiting, colic, and diarrhea. Scarlet fever presents septic sore throat symptoms; tonsillitis brings high fever, headache, vomiting, and rash. These infections are caused by *Streptococcus faecalis* and associated species, which are found in soil and manure and which are transmitted by meat animals and workers contaminated by feces, and by *Streptococcus pyogenes*, which are mainly transmitted through the air from the nose and throat of an infected human. Foods implicated are sausages, evaporated milk, meat croquettes, meat pies, poultry, ham, puddings, milk, ice cream, eggs, steamed lobster, potato salad, egg salad, and custard. Preventative measures are to chill foods rapidly in small quantities, to cook food thoroughly, to prevent fecal contamination by food handlers, and to use only pasteurized dairy products. Rapid chilling is stressed.

Infectious Hepatitis. The symptoms of infectious hepatitis are jaundice, fever, nausea, and abdominal discomfort. Onset occurs from ten to fifty days after exposure. Duration is from a few weeks to several months. The cause is a hepatitis virus, which originates in the feces, urine, and blood of infected humans and of human carriers. It is mainly transmitted from person to person, but is also waterborne. Foods implicated are shellfish harvested from polluted waters, milk, orange juice, potato salad, cold cuts, frozen strawberries, glazed doughnuts, and whipped cream. Preventative measures include cooking oysters, clams, etc., thoroughly; disinfecting; heating suspected water or milk; and observing strict personal hygiene.

Trichinosis. The symptoms of trichinosis are vomiting, diarrhea, fever, sweating, muscular pain, chills, skin lesions, and prostration. Incubation takes from four to twenty-eight days. The cause is *Trichinella spiralis*, a delicate roundworm whose larva invade the intestine and later imbed themselves in muscle tissue. The disease is transmitted by infected swine, rats, and certain wild animals. The primary food implicated is raw or uncooked pork from hogs that were fed contaminated swill. The best preventative measure is to cook pork thoroughly at 150°F or above, internal temperature.

Gastrointestinal Illness. The causes of other gastrointestinal illnesses are foods of animal origin contaminated by bacteria (from food handlers) allowed to multiply through lack of refrigeration, undercooking, or insufficient reheating. Foods implicated are poultry and its dressing, meats, gravy, eggs, dairy products, potato or macaroni salads, custards, cream-filled pastry, fish, and shellfish. Preventative measures include time and temperature control, cooking food properly, serving food promptly or holding it at above 145°F or chilling promptly to 45°F or below, good personal hygiene, a clean kitchen, and sanitary equipment and utensils.

Chemical Poisoning. Chemical poisoning is caused by toxic substances in pesticides, cleaning compounds, solvents, polishes, and other nonfood compounds; by metal poisoning from lead, copper, cadmium, and zinc containers and equipment; by misuse of food preservatives, colorants, and other food additives; and by natural poisons, toxic molds, fungi, etc. Preventative actions are to use only approved chemical compounds and to use them only as directed, to maintain a special storage area for such items with proper labeling, and to use equipment only for the purpose for which it is designed.

Rules for Safe Food Handling

During a ten-year period (1960–1970), the United States Center for Disease Control in Atlanta, Georgia, conducted a study of those infractions of procedures of food handling that proved to be definite causes of food-borne illness. As a result of that study, the food handling rules listed below were set forth.[2] Close attention to these rules of good practice should prevent most of the diseases attributed to bacterial poisoning and infection, and a large part of all food-borne disease.

1. Refrigerate food properly.
2. Cook food or heat-process it thoroughly.
3. Relieve infected employees of foodhandling duties.
4. Require strict personal hygiene.
5. Use extreme care in storing and handling food prepared in advance.
6. Give special attention to preparation of raw ingredients that are liable for contamination, especially if they are to be added to food that gets little or no further cooking.
7. Keep food above or below the optimum bacteria incubation temperatures.

[2]Utah State Department of Health, *Foodservice Sanitation Manual* (Salt Lake City: Utah State Department of Health, 1973).

8. Heat leftovers quickly to a temperature that is lethal to bacteria, or cook quickly before storage.
9. Avoid carrying contamination from raw to cooked and ready-to-serve foods via hands, equipment, or utensils.
10. Disinfect storage areas without contaminating the stored food. Clean and sanitize food preparation and serving equipment.

Rules for Personal Hygiene. A good program of personal hygiene for those handling food should include the following points:

1. The hair should be neat, clean, and odorless and kept under control.
2. The hands and nails should always be thoroughly washed after: contact with infected or otherwise unsanitary areas of the body; use of a handkerchief; contact with unclean equipment or work surfaces, soiled clothing, cleaning rags, etc.; handling raw food, particularly meat and poultry; handling money; smoking; clearing away soiled dishes and utensils. *Frequent hand washing is absolutely necessary.*
3. Clothing should always be clean.

Specific Recommendations. The following is a list of specific recommendations concerning those principles of food sanitation practice that are most often violated:

1. Use extra care when handling foods of high protein content, such as cooked and processed meats, meat products, poultry, eggs, gravies, fish, shellfish, custards, and puddings. Such foods readily support the growth of bacteria.
2. Wash fresh fruits and vegetables thoroughly with clean water. They may be heavily contaminated with germs or with chemicals used in insecticides that can produce injurious effects.
3. Allow frozen foods to thaw in the refrigerator if possible; because freezing tends to break down tissues, foods are much more susceptible to bacterial invasion after thawing. It is a good practice to cook such foods immediately. If they are not to be eaten at once, storage under 40°F is recommended. Once foods are thawed, never refreeze them.
4. Refrigerate large batches of foods like potato salad in shallow pans so that the entire mass will cool quickly. When reheating large batches of foods like spaghetti, stir so that heating will be uniform and thorough.
5. Lessen the time between preparation and service as much as possible.
6. Store preparations for hashes, croquettes, salmon cakes, corn fritters, etc., in the refrigerator immediately after mixing, then heat thoroughly just before serving. These types of foods require complete

cooking. If they are merely browned on the outside, bacteria left alive in the warm moist centers will reproduce rapidly.
7. Cook all pork thoroughly until white.
8. Refrigerate ham that is to be served cold immediately after boiling or baking, then slice it just before serving. Careful handling after cooking is very important.
9. Make sure preparation tables and working surfaces are clean and smooth; have no cracks, open seams, or sharp corners; and are constructed of noncorrodible materials.
10. Avoid breathing or talking over food, as it may be contaminated by unseen saliva. For this reason also, once food has been served to a person, never serve it to another person, even though it appears to be untouched and untasted.
11. Cover any food on display to protect it from contamination by flies, dust, coughs, and sneezes.
12. Avoid direct contact between hands and food being dispensed. For example, use a scoop for handling ice and a pair of tongs for handling bread and butter.
13. Keep milk and cream below 45°F. Serve milk in the original container.

6 Recipe Standardization

Standardized recipes and portion control have been much discussed by accountants, food production managers, chefs, and supervisors. Among some, there is not a clear understanding of exactly what is meant by a "standardized" recipe. A "standardized recipe" means more than simply a "well-written" recipe. *Standardized recipes are recipes revised to be practical for a particular operation.*

In food production, standardized recipes are an important tool that can be adapted to every type of feeding operation in order to maintain quality and cost control. A standardized recipe is based on the portion size and yield requirements of the individual operation, and it is especially adapted to the operator's equipment and purchasing procedure.

AIDS PORTION CONTROL

Recipe standardization is the major element of portion control or portion planning. *Portion control is giving a definite quantity of good food for a definite percentage of profit.* When applied to the foodservice industry in its entirety, it provides planning skills comparable to controls that other industries have been using for a long time. Better planning skills have been long overdue in the food industry.

Increased food and labor costs are forcing the volume feeding industry to use portion planning. Because of the work involved in standardizing recipes to achieve portion planning, some busy food operators become discouraged at the outset.

This article by Professor Myrtle H. Ericson was originally published in the May 1960 issue of *The Cornell Hotel and Restaurant Administration Quarterly*, and is reprinted here with the permission of the Cornell University School of Hotel Administration, © 1960.

It is a big job. The person executing the transition from ordinary recipes to standardized, portion-planning recipes must be well qualified, must have high food standards, and, moreover, must have the complete cooperation of the entire staff. Yet, the advantages that can be achieved in planning, production, and especially in cost controls have proved that standardized recipes are worth the effort required to develop them.

ADVANTAGES OF STANDARDIZED RECIPES

Standardized recipes are advantageous to food operators because they

1. Save time for both cook and manager, allowing more time and money for skill in preparing, serving, and merchandising of food.
2. Eliminate guesswork and waste due to poor estimating of quantities and failures in cooking.
3. Eliminate variation in quality and quantity of the product, making frequent sampling and "doctoring" unnecessary.
4. Prevent being dependent upon any one cook or chef.
5. Assist in portion control and food-cost control by providing a means of
    figuring accurate cost of the food used.
    estimating yield to be expected.
    checking losses and making necessary adjustments by use of fewer or cheaper materials.
    maintaining quality and preventing leftovers.

FACTORS INVOLVED IN STANDARDIZATION

To achieve standardized recipes and quality products consistently, (the end result of recipe standardization) the following points need to be considered:

1. Skill of the worker
    a. Good work habits result in efficient service, better relations and superior products.
    b. Orient top management and train supervisors first since training is the key to better work habits and necessary at all levels.
    c. Supervision in the transition to portion-control must do a *show and tell* job. This can only be accomplished by on-the-job training.
    d. Preparation of a training manual may be necessary. This depends on the size of the operation.
2. Menu planning
    a. To plan a menu adequately, it is important to analyze the clientele.
        1. Restaurant, hotel, industrial feeding, schools, etc.
        2. Section of the country, nationality and income.
    b. The menu affects the number of people employed.

      c. The kitchen equipment and kitchen layout including service area affects the menu.

      d. The menu affects the way the food is prepared and the size of the portion served.

3. Purchasing and inventory procedure
    a. Planning through recipe standardization permits purchasing all foods by the portion. Example: recipe set up for a No. 10, No. 5 can, etc.
    b. Whenever possible, store food by the portion and issue food by the portion, according to the recipe or requisition. This permits coordination of purchasing with a portion-planned inventory.
    c. A portion planned inventory system will keep the operator informed of portions on hand at all times.
    d. Set-up purchasing specifications.
    e. Insure adequate receiving controls, weighing and checking.
4. Storage facilities

    A storeroom planned for control should have:
    a. Food stored with tags or crayon marked information visible for easy inventory. All perishable items should be marked and stored in "first in–first out" basis.
    b. Shelves and cabinets designed to hold food in the standard units in which it is purchased.
    c. Food stored by type. Canned vegetables in one section— Canned fruits in another section.
    d. All food checked out by requisition, and the storeroom *must* be locked at all times.
5. Recipes may be obtained from the following sources:
    a. Small quantity recipes which will need to be tested and enlarged (first to 25 servings) which are adapted to each place of business.
    b. Quantity recipe books and trade magazines.
    c. Recipes sent out by firms which have test kitchens set-up to perfect recipes using their products.
    d. State and National Restaurant Association.
    e. State and Federal Institutions.
    f. Prepared mixes.
6. Equipment needed for standardization
    a. Available equipment
        1. Techniques and equipment should be available for weighing.
        2. Pan sizes purchased in relation to yields. Example: 9 or 10 inch pie tins—yield, 8 servings.
        3. Methods and techniques for mixing.
        4. Serving equipment such as ladles and scoops.
    b. New equipment
        1. How much business dictates the amount and size of portioning equipment needed. Low volume operations may get by with

simple, inexpensive devices while larger volume businesses will need more elaborate and perhaps more costly equipment.
2. The following formula is a helpful guide in determining the advisability of adding new equipment.

If:[1] A = Actual savings in labor during life of the equipment.
B = Cost of equipment installed.
C = Operating and maintenance costs during life of the equipment.
D = Interest on investments.

Then:
$$\frac{A}{BCD} = E$$

If E is 1.1 or more, the equipment should more than pay for itself. If it is 1.5 or more—the equipment is a must.

PROCEDURE FOR ENLARGING RECIPES

1. "Factor" method.
2. Percentage method.

PROCEDURE FOR TESTING A QUANTITY RECIPE

1. Select a basic recipe from a reliable source. Evaluate it as to proportions, methods, yield and cost to be sure the recipe is practical and adaptable to your operation.
2. Decide on any modifications necessary or desirable to make the recipe more suitable to your unit or to reduce cost.
3. Have a skilled worker make a recipe for 25 and judge the finished product. Make several tests if necessary.
4. If satisfactory, convert it to the desired yield for your establishment.
5. Make the larger quantity and judge the quality of the finished product by using a standard rating scale and a carefully selected judging panel.
6. Have the departments test the recipe and report results. If the results are satisfactory, incorporate it in your file.

SETTING UP A RECIPE FILE

1. A card index or loose-leaf notebook may be used.
2. If cards are used, use a card no smaller than 3 × 5, 4 × 6, or 5 × 8. The larger size is recommended. Leave sufficient blank space

[1] Dr. Pearl Aldrich, Head, Food Service Laboratory, Michigan State University.

so printing stands out clearly. Use heavy lines to separate groups of ingredients to be handled or added together, light lines to separate ingredients for [sic] each other to facilitate reading amounts for each ingredient without error.
3. Cards should be protected by a cellophane jacket.
4. It is advisable to have a master file in the office containing all the recipes. Duplicate copies of the recipes used in that unit should be on file in the different departments in the kitchen. Any changes made in the recipe should be made on all sets. In addition to the master file, the office should have a copy of each recipe on which cost information can be recorded instead of the method of preparation. This can be set up to show percent food cost in addition to cost per serving, if that information is desired. Check for seasonal changes in cost which might affect the selling price.

PROCEDURE FOR WRITING A RECIPE

Include all information useful in preparing and serving the food, such as:

1. Name of product.
2. Classification (Example: Entree, Fish).
3. Yield (number of servings).
4. Portion serving size (Weight and measure).
5. Total batch weight or volume.
6. Pan size. When necessary for clarity, include depth of pan.
7. Give the temperature and time for oven baking at the heading of the recipe as well as at the end of the recipe.
8. List the ingredients in order of use. Use no abbreviations.
9. Quantity of ingredients
   a. Weights are more accurate than measures except for quantities of less than one ounce.
   b. Edible Portions (E.P.) weights rather than As Purchased (A.P.) weights unless both are included.
   c. Weight or volume expressed in largest unit possible. Example: 1 pound 8 ounces instead of 24 ounces, 1 gallon 2 quarts instead of 6 quarts.
10. Put descriptive terms such as "shredded," "cut," "sifted," or "chopped" before the ingredient if the process is to be carried out before measuring; and after the ingredient if the process is carried out after measuring.
11. When necessary for clarity, specify the type and/or brand name of ingredients to be used, "Kraft's Blue Cheese," "tartrate baking powder," "heavy cream," etc.
12. Use applicable terminology as cream, fold, blend, season, scald. Avoid long descriptive phrases.

13. Do not abbreviate except when necessary to save space.
14. Give amounts of ingredients in the easiest measurements, as ¼ cup instead of 4 tablespoons; but not ⅕ or ⅛ cup.
15. For baking powders, specify type and amount or give one amount which is satisfactory with any type of baking powder.
16. Start and end the entire recipe on one side of a page or card. Variations may be put on the back of the card.
17. In the directions:
    a. Use complete sentences. Make reference to all of the ingredients, indicating how and when they are to be incorporated. Use word pictures such as "chill until syrupy" or "beat until foamy."
    b. It is not necessary to repeat the quantity of the ingredients in the method for combining the recipe.
    c. Directions for handling materials and special precautions.
    d. Mixing speed and length of mixing (approximately).
    e. Scaling weight or measure.
    f. Cooking equipment to be used and pan preparation (greasing, flouring, etc.).
    g. Repeat the temperature and time of baking in the body of the recipe. Try to give both general and specific tests and temperatures. For example: Bake in 350°F (moderate) oven.
18. Directions for serving:
    a. Garnishes and accompaniments.
    b. Serving equipment, size and kind, ladle or ounces.

CONTRIBUTORS AND RECIPES

ANTON AIGNER President, Inhilco, Inc., New York, New York

1978 IFMA SILVER PLATE AWARD

In December, 1978, Anton Aigner assumed the presidency of Inhilco, the wholly owned subsidiary of Hilton International operating the multifaceted restaurant facilities in New York City's World Trade Center.

Prior to this, from 1974, Mr. Aigner served as Director of Food and Beverage Planning and Development for Hilton International, a position with responsibilities involving the more than 400 restaurants and cocktail lounges in 75 Hilton International hotels around the globe. During his tenure in this position, he established and directed Hilton International's innovative Food Research Center at the Queen Elizabeth Hotel in Montreal. This unique facility conducts research into all aspects of food preparation, technique, and service. It functions in an advisory capacity to all Hilton International hotels by means of in-house publications, bulletins, and a sophisticated microfiche system presenting a broad variety of special projects.

Before being named Director of Food and Beverage Planning and Development, Mr. Aigner was Director of Food and Beverage for Hilton International in the United Kingdom and, prior to that, Food and Beverage Manager of the London Hilton. In 1971 and 1972, he was Food and Beverage Manager of the Paris Hilton. Born and educated in Germany, Mr. Aigner served at several fine hotels in Europe before joining Hilton International at the London Hilton in 1964.

Mr. Aigner's professional memberships include the National Restaurant Association; Les Amis d'Escoffier; Food and Beverage Managers Association, United Kingdom, of which he is a founding member; and Confrèrie des Chevaliers du Tastevin.

Asparagus Tart
APPETIZER

Ingredients:	4 portions	6 portions	___ portions
Pie crust dough	150 g	225 g	
Asparagus spears, boiled until al dente and cut into 2 pieces, the tips ⅔ of whole stalk	22 pieces	33 pieces	
Milk	2.5 dl	3.75 dl	
Eggs, whole, mixed well	2.5 dl	3.75 dl	
Salt and pepper	to taste	to taste	

Roll out the pie crust dough and line the bottom of a cake mold, leaving an edge 2 cm high. Bake blind. Place the asparagus tips around the outside of the crust, then lay the smaller ends in the empty space between the tips. Mix the milk with the eggs; stir well, season, and strain to remove the foam. Pour mixture over the asparagus, just covering. Bake the tart at 200°C for approximately 20 minutes.

Notes:

Selle d'Agneau en Feuilletage
ENTREE

Ingredients:	4 portions	6 portions	___ portions
Saddle of lamb, off the bone, trimmed, net wt	600 g	900 g	
Peanut oil	1 cl	1.5 cl	
Butter	10 g	15 g	
Salt and pepper			
Puff pastry	300 g	450 g	

STUFFING

Spinach, blanched	75 g	112.5 g	
Mushrooms, chopped	75 g	112.5 g	
Shallots, diced	15 g	22.5 g	
Lamb's liver, diced	30 g	45 g	
Butter	10 g	15 g	
Peanut oil	1 cl	1.5 cl	
Salt and pepper	to taste	to taste	

Remove fillet from saddle of lamb by cutting down along the center bone and peeling meat away. Remove all traces of fat and sinew. Cut into large and small fillets. Season the fillets and saute "bleu" in peanut oil and butter.

Saute the shallots in butter and oil; add the mushrooms and liver. Saute for 3 minutes, then remove the liver and continue cooking the shallots and mushrooms. Add the blanched spinach and season to taste. Remove from the heat. Return the liver and pass through a cutter set on the fine blade. Season to taste.

Take the large fillet, place stuffing on it and place the small fillet on top of that. Roll out the pastry. Place the stuffed fillets in the middle, brush with egg wash, and wrap the pastry around. Seal well. Refrigerate. Brush with egg wash again before baking in a 200°C oven for 17 minutes until golden brown. Serve with vegetable purée and gratin dauphinois.

Notes:

Golden Lemon Tart
DESSERT

Ingredients:	6–9 portions	___portions
Pie crust dough	170 g	
Lemon juice	1.4 dl	
Water	2.2 dl	
Sugar	70 g	
Cornstarch	40 g	
Egg yolks	175 g (7)	
Butter	30 g	
Macaroons	6	
Whipped cream, 35%	2 dl	
Lemons, very thinly sliced	3	
Fleurons, glazed	to garnish	
Apricot glaze	to garnish	

Roll out pie crust dough and bake blind in a greased pie mold until golden brown.

Dissolve cornstarch with some of the water and mix this with the egg yolks. Boil the lemon juice, the rest of the water, and the sugar. Mix a little of this hot liquid with the egg mixture. Pour into the remaining hot liquid, stirring constantly. Bring to a boil again, add butter, remove from heat, strain, and cool.

Fold whipped cream into lemon cream. Crumble the macaroons and add them to the cream mixture. Fill pie crust with cream mixture and smooth the surface. Place glazed fleurons around the edge. Dip lemon slices into apricot glaze and use them to decorate entire surface of tart.

Notes:

GERTRUDE APPLEBAUM Director of Food Services, Corpus Christi Independent School District, Corpus Christi, Texas

    1982 President, American School Food Service Association
    1977 MAFSI MARKET MOVER AWARD
    1973 IFMA SILVER PLATE AWARD

Gertrude Applebaum, the former chair of the International Gold and Silver Plate Society, has held offices at every level of the American School Food Service Association. Her career of thirty-five years in school food service was preceded by work as a chemist and a hospital dietitian. A member of eight professional associations, Ms. Applebaum has published many articles and has addressed conferences in every part of the United States.

Hot Fruit Compote
DESSERT

Ingredients:	12 portions	___portions
Peach halves, canned	1 can (#2½)	
Apricots, canned	1 can (#2½)	
Pears, canned	1 can (#303)	
Pineapple, sliced, canned	1 can (#303)	
Cherries, pie, pitted	1 can (#303)	
Butter or margarine, melted	¼ c	
Coconut macaroons	18	
Almonds, slivered	½ c	
Brown sugar	¼ c	
Sherry	½ c	

Drain fruit and pat with paper towels until completely dry. Grease large baking dish with butter or margarine and cover bottom with half of macaroons. Layer fruit with macaroons. Sprinkle top with almonds, brown sugar, sherry, and rest of butter or margarine. Bake at 350° for 30 minutes.

This is a delicious meat accompaniment. It will serve approximately 12— ½ c or more per person.

Notes:

Spaghetti Meat Sauce

SAUCE

Ingredients:	10 portions	___portions
Onions, chopped	4	
Garlic	1 clove	
Oil	¼ c	
Ground beef	2 lb	
Tomatoes, canned	1 can (#2)	
Tomato soup, canned	1 can	
Tomato paste	1 can	
Mushrooms, canned	1 small can	
Chili powder	½ t	
Basil	½ t	
Thyme	½ t	
Oregano	½ t	
Bay leaves	2	
Tabasco	to taste	
Salt	2 t	
Pepper	¼ t	
Cayenne pepper	to taste	
Wine	to taste	
Spaghetti sauce mix	1 pkg	
Green stuffed olives	to taste	

Fry onions and garlic in oil; remove from pan. Add meat and cook until crumbly. Add tomatoes and remaining ingredients except olives. Simmer 2 hours. Add olives. This sauce freezes well.

Notes:

LYSLE AND ALBERT ASCHAFFENBURG The Pontchartrain Hotel, New Orleans, Louisiana

>1973   Ivy Award of Distinction
>1969   IFMA Gold Plate Award

In 1948, Lysle Aschaffenburg implemented his theory that one of the most important services a hotel can offer is elegant foodservice. He converted space that had been a parlor into the Caribbean Room. In a very short time, it gained a reputation as a fine dining room. A little later, as a result of its success, the size of the restaurant was tripled by annexing space that had been a patio and garden. Today, the Caribbean Room is rated among the best eating places in New Orleans. It has been a Holiday award winner for the past fifteen years.

Among the specialties of the Caribbean Room are Oyster Broth, Trout Veronique with Hollandaise, and Crêpe Soufflé. One of the most dramatic items on the menu is the Mile High Ice Cream Pie served with a sauceboat of Chocolate Sauce. Faced for the first time with this seemingly unconquerable concoction, one male patron of the Pontchartrain buried his head briefly in his hands. A slim and charming woman at an adjoining table leaned over and said encouragingly, "Go ahead, you can do it. I did." And so did he, finding it delectable to the last bite.

Fine food and fine service are equal assets of the Pontchartrain. Since the death of his father in 1980, Albert Aschaffenburg has continued the approach to service that was presented to the employees. Actually, the high standards set by father and son have become ingrained in their employees, many of whom have been with the hotel for twenty-five years.

Oyster Broth SOUP

Ingredients:	10 portions	6 portions	___portions
Onion, white	1	⅔	
Celery, pieces (not stalk)	2	1¼	
Butter	½ lb	⅓ lb	
Flour	2 oz	1¼ oz	
Water	½ gal	1¼ qt	
Oysters	½ gal	1¼ qt	
Bay leaves	2	1¼	
Salt and pepper	to taste	to taste	
Parsley	garnish	garnish	

Chop onion and celery; saute together with butter (do not brown). Add flour, water, oysters, and seasonings. Bring to boil. Simmer 10 minutes. Strain. Serve garnished with parsley.

Notes:

Crabmeat Remick
ENTREE

Ingredients:	6 portions	___portions
Crabmeat, lump	1 lb	
Bacon, small pieces, cooked	6	
REMICK SAUCE		
Mustard, dry	½ t	
Paprika	½ t	
Celery salt	½ t	
Tabasco	½ t	
Chili sauce	½ c	
Tarragon vinegar	1 T	
Mayonnaise	½ c	

Divide the crabmeat into 6 portions; pile into individual ramekins. Heat in oven. While waiting for crabmeat to heat, make the sauce. Blend together all dry ingredients and Tabasco. Add chili sauce and tarragon vinegar and mix well. Then blend in mayonnaise.

When crabmeat is very hot, remove ramekins from oven and place a piece of crisp bacon in the center of each. Top with Remick Sauce, just enough to cover. Return ramekins to oven for just a few seconds; then serve immediately. (The Remick Sauce will separate if left in the oven too long.)

Notes:

Ingredients:	6 portions	___ portions
CREPES		
Flour	1 c	
Milk	1½ c	
Eggs	2	*Crepes*
Sugar	2 T	*Soufflé*
Oil	1 T	**DESSERT**
Salt	⅓ t	
Egg whites	4	
Sugar, powdered, sifted	1 c	
Orange peel, finely shredded	1½ t	
Dessert crepes, 6-inch	12	
Sugar, granulated	⅓ c	
Cornstarch	2 t	
Mace, ground	¼ t	
Milk	1 c	
Cream, light	½ c	
Egg yolks, beaten	4	
Rum, light	2 T	

 To make crepes, combine flour, milk, eggs, sugar, oil, and salt in a bowl. Beat with rotary beater until blended. Heat a lightly greased 6-inch skillet. Remove from heat. Spoon in 2 T batter; lift and tilt skillet to spread batter. Return to heat; brown on one side. Invert pan over paper towel; remove crepe. Repeat to make 16 to 18 crepes, greasing skillet as needed.

 In a small mixer bowl, beat egg whites to soft peaks. Gradually add powdered sugar, beating until stiff peaks form. Fold in 1 t of the orange peel. Spoon meringue onto one side of each crepe; roll up. Place crepes in lightly greased 13 × 9 × 2-inch baking dish. Bake, uncovered, in 400° oven for 10 minutes.

 While crepes bake, combine granulated sugar, cornstarch, and mace in medium saucepan. Add milk, cream, egg yolks, and ½ t of the orange peel. Cook and stir until thickened; don't boil. Remove from heat and stir in rum. Serve warm over crepes.

Notes:

ARTHUR C. AVERY Ph.D.; F.F.S.R., Professor Emeritus of Restaurant, Hotel, and Institutional Management, Purdue University, West Lafayette, Indiana

- 1980 Mary Matthews Award, Outstanding Teacher in the School of Consumer and Family Sciences, Purdue University
- 1978 Howard B. Meek Award, Hospitality Educator of the Year, Council of Hotel, Restaurant, and Institutional Education
- 1976 Fellow of the Society for the Advancement of Food Service Research
- 1970 Educator of the Year, Food Service Executives of Indiana
- 1965 Trendmaker Award, *Foodservice* magazine
- 1965 Group Accomplishment Award, U.S. Navy Bancroft Hall

Arthur Avery is the author of *Cosmopolitan Fish Cookery for the Philippines* (1949), *Fish Preservation for the Philippines* (1950), *Increasing Productivity in Foodservice* (1973), and *A Modern Guide to Foodservice Equipment* (1980), as well as over 280 magazine and journal articles. He was the editor of *Fish for Food Products*, while serving as a fishery products technologist in the Philippines Program from 1947 to 1950. He was the director of the Food Science and Engineering Division, United States Navy from 1951 to 1966. Mr. Avery was an instructor at the University of Missouri from 1966 to 1968. Then he accepted the position of Professor of Restaurant, Hotel, and Institutional Management at Purdue University, which affiliation has continued to the present.

Mr. Avery's professional achievements include the positions of past president of the Society for the Advancement of Food Service Research, past president of the International Society of Foodservice Consultants, past director of the Council of Hotel, Restaurant, and Institutional Education, and, currently, trustee of the National Sanitation Foundation. He is best known for his work in human engineering for energy conservation, equipment research, food purchasing, and training methods.

Carrot Cake
DESSERT

Ingredients:	12–16 portions	___ portions
Sugar	2 c	
Salad oil	1½ c	
Eggs	4	
Flour	2 c	
Soda	2 t	
Cinnamon	3 t	
Salt	1 t	
Carrots, grated	3 c	
Vanilla	2 t	
ICING AND FILLING		
Margarine	½ c	
Cream cheese	8 oz	
Sugar, powdered	8 oz	
Vanilla	1 t	
Nuts, chopped	1 c	

Beat together sugar, oil, and eggs. Sift together flour, soda, cinnamon, and salt; add to first mixture. Add grated carrots and vanilla. Bake in two 9-inch or three 8-inch pans, well greased and floured. Bake at 325°F for 35–40 minutes.

Have margarine and cream cheese at room temperature; blend. Then add sugar while beating, followed by vanilla. Add nuts.

Notes:

JEROME BERKMAN   R.D., M.B.A., Director of Food Service, Cedars-Sinai Medical Center, Los Angeles, California

    1975 IVY AWARD OF DISTINCTION
    1971 IFMA SILVER PLATE AWARD
    1963 Award for Excellence in Food Service, *Modern Hospitals*

    Combine a tireless, natural desire to build a better mousetrap with a strong dislike for the traditional tray assembly line and the almost inevitable result is Jerome Berkman's approach to foodservice at Cedars-Sinai Medical Center in Los Angeles. Mr. Berkman has developed a system that eliminates the tray line. It not only makes à la carte menus possible, but also enables foodservice department staff to serve food readied in one of the modular kitchens located near patients' rooms on each floor.

    This system requires a large production kitchen where the food is prepared in advance. It is then frozen or chilled and appropriate amounts are transported to each floor. A meal can be reconstituted and available whenever the patient is ready instead of being "a half-hour and three rings away." A second advantage of the system, "hot food hot and cold food cold," is especially appreciated by the hospital's "captive audience."

    Mr. Berkman has always been at the leading edge of technological and humanistic development in the foodservice industry. He is a widely renowned speaker and a member of numerous associations.

Sesame Fried Chicken

ENTREE

Ingredients:	972 portions	6 portions	___portions
Flour	to coat	to coat	
Lawry's Seasoned Salt	8 oz	1 T	
White pepper, ground	1¾ c	½ oz	
MSG	5⅔ c	1½ oz	
Domestic paprika	3 lb	1½ oz	
Sesame seeds, whole	220 oz	7 oz	
Chicken breasts, boneless, split	972	6	
Chicken thighs, boneless	972	6	
Shortening	45 cans	1½ cans	

82

Mix flour, seasonings, and sesame seeds. *Keeping breasts and thighs separate,* dip each piece of chicken in water and then into the flour mixture. Coat only 125–150 pieces at a time. Keep the rest in the refrigerator. Fry chicken in preheated shortening at 350° for 5 minutes until golden brown. Change shortening once during production—when chicken starts to overbrown. Place fried breasts and thighs on separate sheet pans.

While more chicken is frying, put one fried breast and one fried thigh into each entree dish. Put 21 dishes on each sheet pan, cover with sheets of plastic wrap, and send to the packagers or to the blast freezers every 30 minutes. The cooked chicken must not sit at room temperature any longer than that.

Notes:

Broccoli Soufflé

VEGETABLE

Ingredients:	432 portions	6 portions	___portions
Broccoli cuts	30 lb	6⅔ oz	
Bacon ends	18½ lb	4¼ oz	
Onions, raw, peeled	12 lb	3 oz	
Bread, unsliced	4 loaves	2½ oz	
Milk	1 gal	1¾ oz	
Deionized water	3 gal	5½ oz	
Chicken soup base	¾ c	1/10 oz	
Salt	5 T + 1 t	¼ t	
Eggs	20 doz	3–4	
Cream of tartar	5 T + 1 t	¼ t	

Cook broccoli in steam kettle until done and *drain thoroughly.* Cook bacon ends (yield ½ gal of bacon fat) in steam kettle or tilt skillet. Remove bacon pieces from fat. Chop onions fine with vegetable chopper and saute in bacon fat until golden brown. Remove from heat. Use food chopper to make bread crumbs from loaves of bread. To sauteed onions, add bread crumbs, milk, water, chicken soup base, salt, and well-drained broccoli. Mix well.

Separate eggs. Beat egg yolks until creamy and thick and add to the broccoli mixture. Beat egg whites until foamy, then sprinkle the cream of tartar over the top. Continue to beat until stiff but not dry. Fold broccoli mixture into egg whites and send to packaging.

Notes:

H. JEROME "JERRY" BERNS Vice-President and Secretary, The "21" Club, New York, New York

1981	Fine Dining Hall of Fame, *Nation's Restaurant News*
1979	IFMA GOLD PLATE AWARD
1978	Andre Simon Medal, International Food and Wine Society
1977	Restaurateur of the Year, New York
1977	Restaurateur of the Year, NRA
1976	Diplomate, National Institute for the Foodservice Industry
1972	IVY AWARD OF DISTINCTION
1968	Escoffier Award
1968	Chevalier Merite d'Agricole (France)

Proprietor of the world renowned "21" Club, Jerry Berns has a most unusual background. A 1929 graduate of the University of Cincinnati (Honorary Ph.D. in 1962, Outstanding Alumni in 1968), he spent nine years as drama critic and editor for the *Cincinnati Enquirer* before assuming his current position in 1945.

Mr. Berns has deservedly received every award of note the foodservice industry has to bestow. He has served in executive board capacities for the New York City, New York State, and National Restaurant Associations, for the New York Convention and Visitors Bureau, for the Culinary Institute of America, and for several other civic, educational, and industry organizations. Mr. Berns is also a trustee of the Local No. 1 Waiters' Union Pension Fund, a most unusual position for a restaurant owner!

Vichyssoise SOUP

Ingredients:	4–5 portions	___portions
Butter	½ lb	
Onions, medium, peeled and sliced	2	
Potatoes, small, peeled and sliced	5	
Leeks, chopped	4	
Chicken broth	2 qt	
Prosciutto bone (or piece of ham bone)	1	
Salt and pepper	to taste	
Light cream	3½–4 c	
Worcestershire sauce	dash	
Tabasco	dash	
Nutmeg	pinch	
Chives, fresh, chopped	garnish	

Melt the butter in a large heavy saucepan or kettle. Add the onions, potatoes, and leeks; saute for 15–20 minutes. Add the chicken broth and the prosciutto (or ham) bone and simmer, covered, for 2 hours until thick. Season with salt and pepper. Remove the bone and strain soup through a fine sieve. Cool. Slowly add the cream, stirring until the desired consistency is reached. Season with Worcestershire sauce, Tabasco, and nutmeg. Chill. Serve garnished with chopped chives.

Notes:

Escalopes de Veau Charleroi
ENTREE

Ingredients:	6 portions	___portions
Butter, unsalted	8 T	
Onions, medium, chopped	2	
Mushrooms, medium, chopped	12	
Bay leaves	2	
Rosemary	pinch	
Rice, raw, long grain	1 c	
Water	3 c	
Salt and pepper	to taste	
Egg yolks	2	
Whipped cream, unsweetened	2 c	
Parmesan cheese, grated	½ c	
Veal scallops, pounded, 3½-in diameter	8	
Flour	½ c	
Madeira wine	½ c	
Brown sauce	1 c	

Preheat oven to 350°. In a deep casserole, melt 4 T of the butter. Saute the onions and mushrooms over a low flame until softened but not brown (about 10 minutes). Add the bay leaves and rosemary and cook for another 15 minutes, keeping the flame very low. Stirring constantly, add the rice and cook briefly until it is coated with butter. Slowly stir in the water and season with salt and pepper. When the mixture comes to a boil, cover the casserole and bake in the oven for about 25 minutes, or until the rice is tender. After the mixture has cooled, purée it in a food mill. Beat the egg yolks and add them to the purée, stirring well. Carefully fold in the whipped cream and half of the grated cheese. Put the mixture into a pastry bag and set aside.

Lightly coat pounded veal slices with flour, shaking to remove excess. In a large skillet, melt the remaining butter (4 T) and brown the veal slices on both sides over a medium flame, cooking about 10 minutes in all. Arrange the veal on an oven-proof serving dish and preheat the broiler.

Pour the Madeira into the skillet in which the veal was cooked and stir well. Boil over a high flame for a few minutes until the juices are reduced by about half. Mixing thoroughly with a whisk, slowly add the brown sauce and simmer until warmed through. Set aside.

Squeeze the mixture in the pastry bag over the slices of veal, making a crisscross pattern on each piece. Sprinkle the remaining half of the grated cheese over the tops. Place the dish under the broiler until the tops are golden brown. The sauce may be poured onto the serving dish around the veal or served separately.

Notes:

Ingredients:	4 portions	___portions
Cabbage, green	½ head	
Lettuce, iceberg	½ head	
Beef tongue or ham, cooked, thinly sliced	5 slices	
Chicken breast, poached and boned	1	
Chicken thighs, poached and boned	2	
LORENZO DRESSING		
Chili sauce	½ c	
Watercress, chopped	½ c	
"21" French dressing	½ c	

Sunset Salad with Lorenzo Dressing

ENTREE

Cut all salad ingredients into julienne strips. Combine in a large salad bowl.
To make dressing, combine chili sauce and watercress. Add "21" French dressing and blend thoroughly. Chill. To serve, toss salad with Lorenzo Dressing.

Notes:

Ingredients:	4 portions	___portions
Mushrooms, sliced	2 c	
Onions, minced	1 c	
Danish ham and/or tongue, julienned	1 c	
Salt and pepper	to taste	
Butter, unsalted	½ c	
Brown sauce	¼ c	
Parsley, fresh	garnish	

Mushrooms à la Daum

VEGETABLE

In a mixing bowl, combine mushrooms, onions, ham and/or tongue, and seasonings. Melt the butter in a skillet. Saute the mushroom mixture over a medium flame for about 5 minutes, until the mushrooms and onions are soft. Stir in the brown sauce and heat for an additional minute. Serve over toast or prepared artichoke bottoms. Garnish with fresh parsley.

Notes:

JOHN C. BIRCHFIELD   President, Birchfield Foodsystems, East Lansing, Michigan, and Visiting Professor, School of Hotel, Restaurant, and Institutional Management, Michigan State University, East Lansing, Michigan

> 1974   Distinguished Service Award, NACUFS
> 1973   IFMA SILVER PLATE AWARD

Mr. Birchfield is a graduate of the Cornell School of Hotel and Restaurant Administration and received his master's degree at Rutgers University in the field of institutional management. Prior to assuming his present position in September, 1977, he was associated with Westminster College in Princeton, New Jersey, as Vice-President of Business Affairs. His experience in foodservice covers a twelve-year span as Director of Food Services and Housing at the University of Tennessee and as the manager of the undergraduate dining halls at Princeton University. He is past president of the National Association of College and University Food Services. Mr. Birchfield is the author of *Foodservices Operations Manual* (1979) and *Contemporary Quantity Recipe File* (1975).

Mr. Birchfield is now the president of Birchfield Foodsystems of East Lansing, Michigan. His company is involved in operations analysis and in consulting work on the layout and design of foodservice facilities for hotels, hospitals, clubs, restaurants, and colleges and universities. He is currently doing research work on the use of selected equipment for renovations of food facilities to reduce the costs of energy and labor.

Cottage Cheese Croquettes
ENTREE

Ingredients:	31 portions	___ portions
Peppers, dehydrated, diced	.62 oz	
Onions, dehydrated, chopped	.33 oz	
Water, cold	1 c	
Cottage cheese	6 lb	
Bread crumbs	1.5 lb	
Pecans, medium fancy, chopped	.75 lb	
Paprika, ground	1 t	
Salt	1.5 t	
Milk, instant nonfat dry	.50 oz	
Water, cold	.50 oz	
Eggs	2.0 oz	
Flour	3.0 oz	
Bread crumbs	6.0 oz	
Green pea sauce	.50 gal	

Weigh green peppers and onions and reconstitute with cold water for at least 1 hour. Drain. Combine cottage cheese, 1.5 lb of bread crumbs, chopped pecans, drained green peppers, drained onions, paprika, and salt. Mix well. Measure mixture with a No. 10 scoop and shape into cone-shaped croquettes. Refrigerate overnight.

Dissolve dry milk in water; add thawed eggs and mix well. Roll croquettes in flour, dip in egg-milk mixture, and roll in 6 oz of bread crumbs.

Prepare green pea sauce. Fry croquettes in deep fat at 325°F until golden brown, about 3 minutes. Drain well. Place in serving pans. Serve with 2 oz of green pea sauce over each portion. Or, for a variation, try it with parsley or pimiento sauce.

Notes:

VINCENT J. BOMMARITO President, Tony's Restaurants, Inc., St. Louis, Missouri

1971   IVY AWARD OF DISTINCTION

What started out as their father Anthony's spaghetti joint has been turned into one of the finest restaurants in the country by Vincent J. Bommarito and his brother Anthony, Jr. (who also captured a 1980 Ivy award for his restaurant named, of course, Anthony's).

Vince Bommarito has spent a lifetime working with the restaurant but has found time to serve in St. Louis as Chairman of the Beautification Committee, Director of the Zoo Board, Commissioner of the St. Louis Convention Center, and as a guest lecturer at Forest Park Community College. Mr. Bommarito is a member of Confrèrie de la Chaine des Rôtisseurs, Commanderie de Bordeaux Societies, and of the National and Missouri Restaurant Halls of Fame.

Pasta con Pesce
ENTREE

Ingredients:	3 portions	6 portions	___portions
Pasta (preferably homemade)	1 lb	2 lb	
Lobster meat	5 oz	10 oz	
Crabmeat	5 oz	10 oz	
Shrimp	5 oz	10 oz	
Mushrooms, fresh, sliced	2 oz	4 oz	
Tomato, peeled and seeded	1	2	
Parsley, fresh, chopped	2 T	4 T	
Shallots, chopped	1 t	2 t	
Butter	1 lb	2 lb	
Salt and pepper	to taste	to taste	

Cook pasta very al dente. Drain off water; add butter, tomatoes, mushrooms, and shallots. Return to heat and stir until butter is creamy, then add seafood and parsley. Season. Stir until piping hot and serve on preheated plates.

Notes:

JACK L. BOWMAN F.H.C.F.A., C.P.H.M., Director of Food Services, Saint Joseph's Medical Center, Omaha, Nebraska

1975 President, American Society for Hospital Food Service Administrators

Jack Bowman is a certified professional in Health Care Material Management and a Fellow Health Care Food Service Administrator. He believes in a continuing program to improve the consumers' opinion of hospital cost containment efforts, while maintaining valid standards for quality care.

Beef Kabob

ENTREE

Ingredients:	100 portions	6 portions	____portions
Beef tips	25 lb	1½ lb	
Pineapple juice	4 c	2 oz	
Green pepper, squares	400	24	
Onion, squares	400	24	
Cherry tomatoes	400	24	

Put beef cubes in plastic bin. Pour pineapple juice over beef cubes. Marinate overnight.

Alternate 3 beef cubes, 4 green pepper squares, and 4 onion squares on skewers. Broil until well-browned on all sides. Add 2 cherry tomatoes (one at each end).

Notes:

Ingredients: 100 *portions*   ___*portions*

Ingredient	100 portions	___portions
Chili meat	30 lb	
Onions, chopped	1½ gal	
Green peppers, diced	½ gal	
Garlic powder	4 T	
Tomato puree (#10 can)	1	
Cumin, ground	12 T	
Oregano	12 T	
Paprika	12 T	
Chili powder	24 T	
Pepper	3 T	
Salt	to taste	
Beans, red	1½ gal	

Chili
ENTREE

Brown meat. Add onions, green peppers, garlic powder, and tomato puree to meat and cook. Season and cover with water. Cook until done. Add beans. Check seasoning.

Notes:

Ingredients:	40 portions	___portions
Water	3 qt	
Sugar	2 lb	
Water, cold	1 qt	
Freeze Thaw Lemon	1 lb	
Margarine	4 oz	
Lemon juice, reconstituted	1 c	
Pastry shells, prebaked	5	
Meringue	to top	

Lemon Meringue Pie
DESSERT

Place 3 qt of water in kettle and bring to a boil. Combine sugar, cold water, and Freeze Thaw Lemon and dissolve thoroughly. Add to boiling water; bring to second boil. Add margarine and lemon juice and mix well. Chill. Divide mixture into 5 prebaked pastry shells. Thoroughly chill. Top with meringue. Lightly brown meringue in 400° oven. Cut each pie into 8 pieces.

Notes:

JACK F. BRAUN C.E.C., Managing Executive Chef, The Lemon Tree, McKeesport, Pennsylvania

    1977   Chef of The Year, American Culinary Federation
    1977   Outstanding Young Man, U.S. Jaycees
    1976   President's Award, American Culinary Federation

Chef Jack Braun has been with The Lemon Tree, one of America's finest restaurants, since its opening in 1969. He has served as an officer of several chef's associations. He also played an instrumental role in federal registration of cooks' apprenticeship training and in revision of the *Manual for Culinarians*. Chef Braun was inducted into the American Academy of Chefs in 1978. He is the recipient of both the Auguste Escoffier Medal and the Thomas Jefferson Medal.

Crabmeat Imperial à la Citronier
ENTREE

Ingredients:	4 portions	6 portions	___ portions
White fish (cod, sole, etc.)	1 lb	1½ lb	
Celery, finely diced	2 stalks	3 stalks	
Oil	4 T	6 T	
Bread, small loaf	½	¾	
Alaskan crabmeat, fully cooked	1 lb	1½ lb	
Mayonnaise	3 T	4½ T	
Parsley, chopped	1 t	2 t	
Mustard, dry	1 t	2 t	
Worcestershire sauce	dash	3 drops	
Eggs	2	3	
Salt and pepper	to taste	to taste	
Butter, melted	5 T	7½ T	
Paprika	to garnish	to garnish	

Poach the white fish in boiling water and drain well. Saute the celery in oil and drain well. Trim crusts from the bread and dice it very small. Chop crabmeat and white fish slightly. Combine all ingredients except butter; mix well. Place mixture in oven-proof casserole and sprinkle with melted butter and paprika. Bake in 425° oven for about 20 minutes until slightly browned. Serve very hot with lemon wedges.

Notes:

Nottingham Bird
ENTREE

Ingredients:	6 portions	___portions
STUFFING		
Bread, large loaf	1	
Celery, diced	¼ c	
Onions, diced	½ c	
Eggs	3	
Poultry seasoning	1 t	
Salt and pepper	to taste	
Chickens, fryers, deboned, 2½ lb	3	
Ham, boiled, thin slices	12	
Sauce Espagnole	3 c	
Leeks (or onions), cooked and sliced	2	
Mushrooms, cooked and sliced	¼ lb	
Green pepper, cooked and sliced	1	

Prepare the stuffing. Trim crusts from the bread and dice it into ½-inch cubes. Saute the diced celery and onions in butter until tender. Combine bread, celery, and onions with the eggs and seasonings. Add a few drops of water if the stuffing is not moist enough.

Split chickens along the backbone into halves and debone, if not already done. Lay skin-side down and place sliced ham over entire surface. Also fill the leg cavity with a small piece of the ham. Roll a handful of stuffing into a round elongated shape and place on the ham. Also fill the leg cavity with a little stuffing. Bring edges of chicken half together, creating a rolled effect, and sew with a skewer. Place on a greased baking sheet, brush with butter, and sprinkle lightly with paprika. Bake at 350° for about 35–45 minutes.

To the Sauce Espagnole, add the cooked leeks, mushrooms, and green peppers. Heat to boiling. After the chicken is baked, remove the skewers, place in a serving casserole, and cover with the sauce. Serve very hot.

Notes:

Sauce Espagnole SAUCE

Ingredients:	6 portions	___portions
Onion, large, chopped	1	
Carrots, chopped	3	
Celery, chopped	1 stalk	
Turnip, chopped	1	
Butter, clarified	¼ c	
Bouquet garni	1	
Flour	5 T	
Brown stock	3 c	
Chicken stock, rich	1 c	
Red or white wine (depends on use of sauce)	1 c	
Tomato paste	2 T	
Veal bone, large (optional)	1	

Combine all vegetables and cook with the clarified butter and the bouquet garni until vegetables are tender. Add the flour and cook 10 minutes. Add both stocks, the wine, the tomato paste, and the veal bone (if desired), and simmer for about 45 minutes. The pot should be covered while cooking. After cooking, strain the sauce through a fine sieve and season. If sauce is not as thick as desired, a little more roux may be added. For richer taste, cook some chopped ham bone with the vegetables.

Notes:

DIETER H. BUEHLER Executive Vice-President and General Manager, Idle Wild Farm, Inc., Pomfret Center, Connecticut

1976   IFMA GOLD PLATE AWARD

Early in 1977, Dieter Buehler joined Idle Wild Farm, Inc., a company that processes food used by many divisions of the foodservice industry, as Executive Vice-President and General Manager. Before joining Idle Wild Farm, Mr. Buehler spent thirteen years with Trans World Airlines as Director of Dining and Catering Services. While with TWA, he directed a wide range of activities, including food and beverage planning, service implementation and training, scheduling, and related pricing and financial activities, including budget development and administration.

Much in demand as a speaker, Mr. Buehler has addressed a variety of food industry groups, such as the Association for Food Service Management (AFSM), IFMA symposiums, Multi Unit Food Service Operators (MUFSO), the National Security Industrial Association (NSIA), the Inflight Food Service Association (IFSA), and the Food Service Executives Association (FSEA), on a myriad of subjects ranging from menu planning and foodservice marketing to pricing and predictions for the future.

Mr. Buehler is a graduate of the Cornell School of Hotel Administration and has served as a board director, treasurer, vice-president, and conference chairman of IFSA and also as a director of the Cornell Society of Hotelmen.

Chicken Breast New England
ENTREE

Ingredients:	8 portions	___portions
Chicken breasts, halves, partially boned	8	
Butter	½ c	
Onion, chopped	¼ c	
Celery, diced	¼ c	
Green apple, peeled, cored, diced	½ c	
Stuffing mix	2 c	
Herb-seasoned croutons	2 c	
Sugar	2 t	
Chicken stock or bouillon	¾ c	
Poultry seasoning	¼ t	
Butter, melted, for basting	¼ c	
Salt and white pepper	to taste	

Have the butcher remove all bones from the chicken breasts *except* the first wing joint, which should be cut about ¾ inch from breast.

Melt the butter in a saucepan. Add the onion, celery, and apple and saute for 5 minutes over medium heat, stirring frequently. Combine this mixture with the stuffing mix, croutons, sugar, chicken stock, and poultry seasoning in a large bowl. Mix well.

Place chicken breasts flat on a sheet of wax paper with the skin down. Using a mallet, flatten breasts to about ¼ inch thickness. Place about ½ c of stuffing on each breast. Roll breast around stuffing, leaving partial wing bone sticking out at one end. Make sure that the stuffing is completely enclosed. Place the stuffed breasts, seam down, on a sheet pan. Brush each with melted butter and sprinkle with salt and white pepper. Bake in a preheated 350° oven for approximately 40 minutes, basting occasionally with melted butter. Serve with Sauce Supreme.

Notes:

Sauce Supreme SAUCE

Ingredients:	8 portions	6 portions	___portions
Chicken stock or bouillon	1 c	¾ c	
Cream, heavy	1½ c	1⅛ c	
Flour	1 T	2¼ t	
Cornstarch	1 T	2¼ t	
Salt and white pepper	to taste	to taste	
Butter	1½ T	1 T + ⅓ t	
Parsley, chopped	1 t	¾ t	

Heat the chicken stock and 1 c of cream in a saucepan. Dissolve flour and cornstarch in remaining ½ c of cream. When chicken stock is boiling, slowly add flour and cornstarch mixture, stirring continually until smooth. Reduce heat and simmer for 10 minutes. Adjust seasoning to taste. Add butter and chopped parsley; mix well. Serve Sauce Supreme over chicken or separately on the side.

Notes:

Ratatouille
VEGETABLE

Ingredients:	8 portions	6 portions	___portions
Olive oil	½ c	⅜ c	
Onions, large, sliced	2	1½	
Garlic, large cloves, minced	2	1½	
Eggplant, medium, peeled, cut into ½-inch cubes	1	¾	
Zucchini, medium, thickly sliced	6	4½	
Bell peppers, red or green, seeded, cut into chunks	2	1½	
Basil	1 t	¾ t	
Parsley, minced	½ c	⅜ c	
Tomatoes, large, peeled, seeded, cut into chunks	4	3	
Black pepper	to taste	to taste	
Salt	2 t	1½ t	
Parsley	garnish	garnish	

Heat half of the oil in a large frying pan over high heat. Add onions and garlic and cook, stirring, until onions are soft but not browned. Stir in the eggplant, zucchini, peppers, basil, and minced parsley. Add a little of the oil as needed to keep the vegetables from sticking. Cover the pan and cook over moderate heat for about 30 minutes. Stir occasionally, using a large spatula and turning the vegetables to help preserve their shape. If mixture becomes quite soupy, remove the cover to allow some of the moisture to escape.

Add the tomatoes to the vegetables in the pan and stir to blend. Again, add more oil if the vegetables are sticking. Cover and cook over moderate heat for 15 minutes, stirring occasionally. Again, if mixture becomes quite soupy during this period, remove the cover to allow some moisture to evaporate. Ratatouille should have a little free liquid, but still be of a good spoon-and-serve consistency. Season to taste with pepper and salt. Garnish with parsley and tomato. The ratatouille may be served hot. Or cover and chill it, then either serve cold or reheat to serve. The appeal of making ratatouille ahead of time is enhanced by the fact that it tastes better after standing awhile.

Notes:

BYRON L. BYRON President, American Foodservice Enterprises, Inc., Kansas City, Missouri

>1978   Ivy Award of Distinction
>1975   IFMA Silver Plate Award

Within Crown Center, Kansas City's $500-million downtown complex developed by Hallmark Cards, Inc., are nine unusual dining establishments and eleven specialty foodservice outlets. These innovative creations were developed by Byron L. Byron, a leader in the foodservice industry for thirty years. Mr. Byron was responsible for Hallmark's company-owned-and-operated foodservices, including the cafeteria and international headquarters building, four branch production plants, and one major distribution center. Over 10,000 meals are served daily in the system, which under Byron's direction became widely recognized as an outstanding example of employee feeding, modern design, and advanced technique. Foremost among the Hallmark dining facilities is the Crown Room, where company employees consume 6,000 meals a day in richly appointed surroundings, including china, silver, and stewards in gold jackets and white gloves.

As director of the restaurant operations for Crown Center, Mr. Byron supervised the planning, opening, and operation of the American Restaurant, the 3 C's Cafeteria, the Market Place, The 25 Grand, and the famous International Cafe. The latter is a composite of six cafeteria-style restaurants around a central dining arcade with seating for 600 persons at tables for two and four and with a combination seafood cocktail bar in the middle. Diners are offered a choice of authentic Italian, Oriental, and Mexican dishes; Jewish and German favorites from a New York–style deli; hamburgers and steak from the broiler; chicken and ribs in the barbeque area; and seafood from an Oyster Bar.

Currently president of American Foodservice Enterprises, Incorporated, Mr. Byron is a past president of the Society for Foodservice Management, a member of the board of trustees of the Gold and Silver Plate Society, a member of the Ivy Society, and vice-president of the Kansas City Chapter of the International Wine and Food Society of London, England.

San Francisco Cioppino
ENTREE

Ingredients:	4 portions	6 portions	___portions
Olive oil	3 T	4½ T	
Onion, coarsely chopped	1 c	1½ c	
Green pepper, coarsely chopped	1	1½	
Garlic, fresh, crushed	1 T	1½ T	
Fish stock (or canned clam juice)	2 c	3 c	
Tomatoes, fresh, coarsely chopped	1 c	1½ c	
White wine, dry	½ c	¾ c	
Parsley, fresh, finely chopped	2 T	3 T	
Bay leaf	1	1½	
Salt and pepper	to taste	to taste	
Soft-shell crab or Dungeness crab	4–8 pieces	6–12 pieces	
Mussels, in the shell	8–12	12–18	
Clams, in the shell	8–12	12–18	
Shrimp, large, shelled	4–8	6–12	
Cod, halibut, sea bass, or other firm-fleshed white fish	12 oz	18 oz	

Put olive oil into a 2- or 3-qt enameled or stainless steel pot and heat over moderate heat until a light haze forms. Add onion, green pepper, and garlic. Cook for about 5 minutes, stirring frequently, or until onions are soft and translucent, but not brown. Stir in fish stock or canned clam juice, tomatoes, wine, parsley, and bay leaf. Bring to a boil; then reduce heat and simmer partially covered for 30 minutes. Add salt and pepper.

To assemble the Cioppino, arrange the soft-shell or Dungeness crabs in the bottom of a 3- or 5-quart casserole or skillet. Lay the mussels, clams, and shrimp on top, and pour in the fish stock mixture. Bring to a boil, reduce heat to low, cover tightly, and cook for 10 minutes. Add the fish, cover again, and continue to cook for 5–10 minutes. The Cioppino is done when the mussel and clam shells have opened and the fish flakes easily when prodded gently with a fork. Discard any mussels or clams that remain closed. Serve at once, either directly from the casserole or after spooning the fish and shellfish into a large heated tureen and pouring the tomato mixture over them.

Notes:

FRANCES W. CLOYD C.F.E., Director of Food Service, Lynchburg College, Lynchburg, Virginia

Frances W. Cloyd ("Mom" Cloyd to the thousands of students attending Lynchburg College during the past twenty years) epitomizes the foodservice executive who is dedicated to the fulfillment of the highest ideals in volume feeding. Her present position as Director of Food Service at Lynchburg College in Lynchburg, Virginia, is the culmination of her extensive work, study, and travel in the interest of food excellence.

In addition to her responsibilities at Lynchburg College, Mrs. Cloyd has been president of the Piedmont Chapter of Food Service Executives Association (FSEA). In a related capacity, she serves FSEA as National Nutrition Chairman. She has served twice as president of Region II of the National Association of College and University Food Services (NACUFS), as well as being the national publication officer for the organization. Mrs. Cloyd edited a book for NACUFS entitled *Guide to Food Service Management*. In addition, she has taken an active part in many civic and food industry organizations over the years. As one might expect, her many talents include gourmet cooking and devising lovely table arrangements. She was instrumental in the formation and success of the first culinary arts exhibit ever held in central Virginia under the auspices of FSEA.

Mrs. Cloyd's most recent award (for her outstanding contribution to NACUFS) serves to illustrate the high esteem in which she is held by her colleagues in the foodservice industry.

Mushroom-Cheese Bake
ENTREE

Ingredients:	6 portions	___ portions
Celery, chopped	½ c	
Onion, chopped	¼ c	
Butter, melted	3 T	
Mushrooms, fresh, cleaned and sliced	½ lb	
Wheat bread, day-old, cubed	4 c	
Cheddar cheese, shredded	2 c	
Eggs, beaten	2	
Milk	2 c	
Mustard, dry	2 t	
Salt	1 t	
Pepper	½ t	

Saute the celery and onion in the butter until crisply tender; then stir in mushrooms and cook 5 minutes. Layer half of the bread cubes, half of the mushroom mixture, and half of the cheese in a lightly greased 2-quart casserole; repeat the layers. Combine eggs, milk, and seasonings; beat until well mixed. Pour this evenly over the bread-mushroom-cheese mixture. Bake at 325° for 45 minutes. Let the casserole stand at room temperature for 5 minutes before serving.

Notes:

Seafood Casserole
ENTREE

Ingredients:	6 portions	___portions
Butter, melted	¼ lb	
Flour	½ c	
Milk	2 c	
Half and half	1 c	
Sherry	2 T	
Shrimp, cooked	2 lb	
Crabmeat (or lobster)	1 lb	
Cracker crumbs, buttered	topping	

Make a heavy, rich cream sauce with the butter, flour, milk, and half and half. Cook on low heat until thick, stirring constantly. Add the sherry. Add the shrimp and crabmeat. Put into individual shells or a casserole and top with buttered cracker crumbs. Bake until piping hot.

Notes:

Green Bean Casserole
VEGETABLE

Ingredients:	8 portions	___portions
Green beans, French-cut, drained	2 cans	
Cream of mushroom soup, undiluted	2 cans	
Celery, diced	1 c	
Green pepper, diced	1 c	
Onion, diced	1 c	
Olives, ripe, sliced	5–6	
Potato chips, crushed	¾ c	
Almonds, slivered	¼ c	
Olives, pimiento-stuffed, sliced	5–6	

Layer half of the beans, soup, celery, green pepper, and onion in a buttered 2-quart casserole; then repeat the layers. Top with a layer of ripe olives, potato chips, almonds, and stuffed olives. Bake at 325° for 35–40 minutes.

Notes:

Black Walnut Cake
DESSERT

Ingredients:	6–10 portions	___portions
Sugar	2 c	
Butter	¾ c	
Milk	1 c	
Flour	3¼ c	
Baking powder	3½ t	
Vanilla	1 t	
Walnut meats	1 c	
Egg whites, beaten	5	

Cream sugar and butter together. Add milk and flour alternately with baking powder, vanilla, and walnuts. Fold in beaten egg whites. Bake in a tube pan at 350° for about 1 hour.

Notes:

STUART G. CROSS Managing Director, The Roof, Hotel Utah, Salt Lake City, Utah

1980   IVY AWARD OF DISTINCTION

Stuart G. Cross has been Executive Vice-President and General Manager of the Utah Hotel Company since September 1973. The Utah Hotel Company owns and operates two properties: the Hotel Utah and the Temple Square Hotel.

During his college years, Mr. Cross worked part-time for the Yosemite Park and Curry Co., the principal concessioner in Yosemite National Park. In 1950, he accepted a management position there, even though he had received a master's degree in American history from Stanford University, was teaching there, and was well on the way to getting his doctorate at that time. The Yosemite Park and Curry Co. operates hotels, restaurants, general stores, a transportation system, and a ski area; it supplies the full range of visitor services in Yosemite. Mr. Cross spent twenty-two years with the Yosemite Park and Curry Co., becoming President and later Chairman of the Board of Directors. He also met his wife, Dar, during this time.

Mr. Cross spent a year with the National Park Foundation, a nonprofit, congressionally chartered foundation supportive of the national park system, before joining the Utah Hotel Company. He takes special pride in the Hotel Utah's membership in the Preferred Hotels Association, a by-invitation-only group of forty-two independent hotels.

Among Mr. Cross's varied activities are the following: President, Preferred Hotels Association; AH&MA representative of the Utah Hotel Motel Association; honorary member (past chairman), Conference of National Park Concessioners; honorary member (past chairman), Resort Committee of the American Hotel & Motel Association; member, Advisory Committee on Food Systems Administration, Brigham Young University; and Maître de Table, Confrèrie de la Chaine des Rôtisseurs.

Gazpacho I SOUP

Ingredients:	50 portions	___ portions
Cucumbers, large, peeled and cut in half	10	
Bell peppers	3	
Onions, medium	2	
Tomatoes, diced (#10 cans), drained	2	
Garlic, finely chopped cloves	6	
Paprika	2 t	
Olive oil	½ c	
Wine vinegar	¾ c	
Consommé, strong	3 c	
Tabasco	5 drops	
Black pepper	¼ t	
Salt	to taste	

Seed the cucumbers. Chop them in buffalo chopper about 4 turns. Chop bell peppers and onions a couple of turns. Mix all ingredients. Taste for salt. More consommé mix may be needed.

Notes:

Gazpacho II SOUP

Ingredients:	6 portions	___ portions
Cucumbers, diced	1 c	
Tomatoes, diced	2 c	
Onions, red, diced	1 c	
Bell peppers, diced	1 c	
Salt	1 pinch	
Black pepper	1 pinch	
Tabasco	½ t	
Garlic, crushed	1 clove	
Beef consommé	1½ c	
Olive oil	½ c	
Wine vinegar	¼ c	

Use a 1-gallon pot. Dice all vegetables into approximately ¼-inch pieces and mix. Add salt, pepper, Tabasco, garlic, beef consommé, olive oil, and wine vinegar. Mix thoroughly. Refrigerate before serving. Flavor will improve if the soup is prepared one day in advance. More consommé may be needed. A garnish of croutons is optional.

Notes:

ANN M. CROWLEY Ph.D., Executive Director, Health Care Services Ltd., Iowa City, Iowa

1972   IFMA Silver Plate Award

Dr. Ann M. Crowley was Director of Dietetics at Abbott Hospital in Minneapolis from 1955 to 1965. She was Director of Nutrition at the University of Iowa, and concurrently Associate Professor in the College of Medicine at the University of Iowa, from 1965 to 1977. Also during that period she was Director of Graduate Nutrition Education. Dr. Crowley established Health Care Services Ltd. in 1977 and is presently Executive Director of the firm.

A column on nutrition and health written by Dr. Crowley appears in over 100 newspapers in the Midwest. She also has a series of radio programs on health that are broadcast in the Midwest. Dr. Crowley has been retained for consulting projects by General Mills, Pillsbury, Green Giant, ARA Services, the Food and Nutrition Service of the Department of Agriculture, and The Iowa Corn Promotion Board. On the international level, she conducted a survey of hospitals for the Imperial Social Services of Iran and performed a survey and proposal project for the Secretary of Health for 26 hospitals of the State of Rio de Janeiro, Brazil. Dr. Crowley developed a Dietetic Internship for Creighton University's St. Joseph Hospital in Omaha, Nebraska, and a coordinated undergraduate program in dietetics for Incarnate Word College, San Antonio, Texas.

A member of many professional societies, Dr. Crowley is a past president of The Society for the Advancement of Food Service Research. Her biography appears in the current edition of *Who's Who of American Women*.

Bran Muffins

Ingredients:	12 portions	___portions
Flour, whole wheat	1 c	
Flour, all purpose	⅔ c	
Bran flakes	2½ c	
Baking powder	3 t	
Baking soda	1 t	
Salt	½ t	
Brown sugar	⅓ c	
Molasses	¼ c	
Yogurt	1 c	
Eggs	2	
Vegetable oil	⅓ c	
Carrot, medium, shredded	1	

Combine flour, bran flakes, baking powder, baking soda, salt, and brown sugar in a large bowl. In another bowl, combine remaining ingredients except carrots. Add liquid mixture to dry mixture. Add shredded carrot. Stir until dry ingredients are moistened. Drop into greased muffin tins. Bake at 400° for 25 minutes.

Notes:

EDGAR L. DAVIS   Independent Restaurateur, Indiana

           1979   President, Society for the
                     Advancement of Food Service
                     Research

Edgar L. Davis was Director of the Food Service Division of Berkell Incorporated, a worldwide leader in food equipment with 26 plants and over 5000 employees. Formerly, Mr. Davis was with the Groen Division, Dover Corporation, and Hobart Corporation. He received his B.S. degree in business administration at Northwestern University, Evanston, Illinois.

Mr. Davis is an honorary life member of the National Association of Service Managers (NASM) and past president and chairman of the Long Range Planning Committee. He received NASM's Executive Award for distinguished service. He was also a member of IFMA's Board of Directors and Long Range Planning Committee. He received both IFMA's coveted Sparkplug Award and, in 1976, IFMA's highest honor, IFMA Key Man Award. Mr. Davis served on NAFEM's Workshop Planning Committee and as chairman of the Exhibitors' Advisory Committee of the American Dietitic Association. He is past president of the Society for the Advancement of Food Service Research. He was awarded SAFSR's Life Fellow in Food Service Research and, in 1977, an honorary doctorate in food service at the Biannual NAFEM Exposition in New Orleans.

Irish Coffee Pie
DESSERT

Ingredients:	6 portions	___portions
CRUST		
Cereal, four-grain	⅔ c	
Quaker Oats, quick-cooking	⅔ c	
Butter	⅓ c	
Brown sugar	½ c	
FILLING		
Instant coffee powder	2 T	
Sugar	¾ c	
Unflavored gelatin	1 env	
Milk	¾ c	
Eggs, separated	2	
Irish whiskey (or brandy extract, ¼ t)	¼ c	
Sugar	1 T	
Whipping cream	½ pt	
Whipped cream	½ c	
Milk chocolate curls	4 oz	

To make crust, heat cereal and oats in shallow pan for 10 minutes at 350°. Combine with butter and brown sugar until crumbly. Press firmly and evenly into a 9-inch pie pan. Chill.

Put coffee, ¾ c of sugar, and gelatin in a pan and slowly stir in milk. Cook 5–10 minutes over low heat until sugar and gelatin are completely dissolved. Beat egg yolks. Stir half of hot filling into yolks. Put back into pan and cook 3–5 minutes, stirring to keep from sticking. Chill 30–40 minutes until thick and syrupy. Add Irish whiskey or brandy extract to the filling and beat until light and frothy.

Take a separate bowl and beat egg whites until they form firm and moist peaks. Add 1 T of sugar and mix gently, then fold egg whites into chilled filling. Beat whipping cream and fold into filling. Spread into chilled pie shell and refrigerate for 2–3 hours until firm. Garnish with whipped cream and milk chocolate curls.

Notes:

PAUL B. DEIGNAN Director, Nutrition Services, United and Children's Hospitals, St. Paul, Minnesota

Paul Deignan received both his graduate and undergraduate degrees from the Cornell School of Hotel and Restaurant Administration. He is a Registered Dietitian and a "Distinguished Member" of the American Society of Hospital Food Service Administration.

Since entering the institutional foodservice management field in 1962, he has worked in both college and hospital feeding. He worked with contract management firms where he served both in the field and as a corporate technical services coordinator. Because of his interest in shared service programs among hospitals, Mr. Deignan joined United Hospitals in 1974. Here he has developed and implemented pioneering programs in hospital satellite feeding, the use of convected air tunnel microwaving, the "patient service team" approach for delivering meals and educational services to patients, and the cook-in-casing approach to cook/chill food production.

Mr. Deignan's goals include the enhancement of the foodservice industry's image through continuity of services, high level of food quality, and the building of professionalism in both the management and employee ranks. It is his hope to achieve these goals by developing and supporting opportunities to share technology among those in the industry.

Mr. Deignan is 1983 president-elect of ASHFSA.

Ingredients:	1775 portions	___portions
Navy beans	125 lb	
Water	53 gal	
Ham base	14 lb	
Onions, chopped	25 lb	
Celery, chopped	25 lb	
Tabasco	½ c	
Carrots, chopped, frozen	25 lb	
Bay leaves	18	
Ham, chopped	25 lb	
Salt	2 lb	
Pepper	3 oz	

Navy Bean Soup

SOUP

Wash beans and soak overnight.

Add water to beans, ham base, and onions. Cook until onions are tender. Add celery, Tabasco, carrots, bay leaves, and simmer 15 minutes. Add ham, salt, and pepper. Bring to 180°. Fill casings at agitator speed #5 and pump speed #7. Label, clip, and chill to 40°. Yields 1775 6-oz portions.

Notes:

Thirteen Vegetable Soup

SOUP

Ingredients:	1866 portions	___portions
Onions, chopped	23 lb	
Celery, chunk cut	23 lb	
Butter	5 lb	
Water	45 gal	
Beef Base (Minors)	11 lb	
Rutabagas, diced	10 lb	
Lima beans, large, frozen	15 lb	
Tomatoes (#10 cans)	12 cans	
Carrots, sliced, frozen	45 lb	
Kidney beans (#10 cans)	5 cans	
Corn, frozen	15 lb	
Peas, frozen	30 lb	
Green beans, cut, frozen	15 lb	
Wax beans (#10 cans)	5 cans	
Cabbage, shredded	15 lb	
Salt	8 oz	
Pepper	4 oz	

Saute onions and celery in butter until tender. Add 35 gal of water. Dissolve Beef Base in 10 gal of hot water in a separate container; add to kettle. Add rutabagas and lima beans and simmer for 10 minutes. Add the rest of the vegetables and simmer for 30 minutes. Season. Let temperature reach 180°. Fill casings with 6 qt of product at agitator speed #5 and pump speed #7. Chill to 40°. Yields 1866 6-oz portions.

Notes:

Ingredients:	1713 *portions*	___ *portions*
Tenderloin tips	180 lb
Beef stock (or water and beef base)	14 gal
Paprika	1 lb
Onion powder	3 oz
Garlic powder	3 oz
Salt	1 lb
Mushroom pieces (#10 cans)	5 cans
Mushroom soup (50-oz cans)	8 cans
Celery soup (50-oz cans)	8 cans
Sour cream	30 lb
Modified starch	5 lb
Water	1 gal

Beef Stroganoff
ENTREE

Brown the tenderloin tips. Add stock and cook until meat is tender. Add paprika, onion powder, garlic powder, salt, mushrooms, and both kinds of soup. Simmer for 10 minutes. Blend in the sour cream. Thicken with modified starch and water mixture. Heat to 180°. Fill each casing with 6 qt of product at agitator speed #5 and pump speed #10. Chill to 40°.

Notes:

STANLEY DEMOS President, The Coach House Restaurant, Lexington, Kentucky

                1973–1982   *Travel/Holiday* Award
                1978   IVY AWARD OF DISTINCTION

    Stanley Demos, the author of *Stanley Demos Cookbook,* has won a high place in the realm of gastronomy through many years of meticulous effort in many kitchens. He has consistently produced superb dishes that can be prepared easily in the average kitchen by following simple methods and using ingredients that are readily available.

    This still youthful man has the charm of his European forebears and is well known to thousands of Cincinnatians for his weekly "Stanley Suggests" recipe column in the *Cincinnati Enquirer.* Mr. Demos is a member of Confrèrie des Chevaliers du Tastevin and Confrèrie de la Chaine des Rôtisseurs.

Ingredients:	2 portions	6 portions	___portions
Mustard, prepared	4 t	3 T	
Curry powder	3 t	2 T + 2 t	
Salt	½ t	1½ t	
Lemon juice	2 t	2 T	
Mayonnaise	1 c	3 c	
Wild rice, cooked	½ c	1½ c	
Lump crabmeat	6 oz	1 lb + 2 oz	
Parmesan cheese, grated	topping	topping	

Crab Demos
APPETIZER OR ENTREE

Mix the mustard, curry powder, salt, and lemon juice with the mayonnaise. Divide the wild rice into seashells. Cover with the crabmeat. Spread the mayonnaise mixture over the crabmeat. Sprinkle grated Parmesan cheese on top, and place in a hot oven for 20 minutes. Serve as a first course or as a luncheon dish.

Notes:

Ingredients:	4 portions	6 portions	___portions
Butter	¼ c	⅜ c	
Onion, grated	3 T	4 T + 2 t	
Carrot, grated	3 T	4 T + 2 t	
Chicken broth	2 cans	3 cans	
Mustard, dry	½ t	1½ t	
Cornstarch	4 T	6 T	
Milk	¼ c	⅜ c	
Cheddar cheese, sharp, grated	1 c	1½ c	
Garlic croutons	garnish	garnish	

Cheese Soup
SOUP

Put the butter, onion, and carrot in a saucepan and saute for 3 minutes. Add the chicken broth and dry mustard; simmer for 5 minutes. Mix the cornstarch with the milk. Pour this into the boiling broth, beating with a wire whisk. Simmer the soup until it thickens. Add the grated cheese, and continue to simmer until the cheese melts. Serve in cups and garnish with garlic croutons.

Notes:

Dover Sole My Way
ENTREE

Ingredients:	4 portions	6 portions	___portions
Dover sole, fillets	12	18	
Flour	as needed	as needed	
Vegetable shortening	as needed	as needed	
Butter	⅓ stick	½ stick	
Onion, medium, diced	1	1½	
Garlic cloves, finely chopped	2	3	
Tomatoes, drained, diced	1 c	1½ c	
Parsley, chopped	2 T	3 T	
Salt and pepper	to taste	to taste	
Mornay sauce, medium	1 c	1½ c	
Romano cheese, grated	2 T	3 T	
Paprika	to garnish	to garnish	

Dust the fillets of Dover sole in some flour. Saute them in vegetable shortening until they are golden in color. When done, remove into a flat baking dish, placing fillets side by side.

To prepare the tomato sauce, melt the butter in a heavy skillet. Add the diced onion and cook until transparent. Add the garlic and saute 10 seconds longer. Add tomatoes, parsley, and salt and pepper.

To assemble this dish, first take a teaspoon and divide the tomato sauce evenly over the fillets. Over the tomato sauce, spoon on the Mornay sauce. Sprinkle with Romano cheese and dust with some paprika. Set the baking dish under the broiler; cook until the sauce is bubbly.

Notes:

Sweetbreads Sauté au Beurre Noisette

ENTREE

Ingredients:	4 portions	6 portions	___portions
Veal sweetbreads, fresh	2 lb	3 lb	
Water	3 c	4½ c	
Onion, small, sliced	1	1½	
Vinegar	2 T	3 T	
Peppercorns	12	18	
Bay leaves	2	3	
Seasoned flour	as needed	as needed	
Vegetable shortening	as needed	as needed	
Bread, toasted slices	4	6	
Butter	¾ c	1⅛ c	
Parsley, chopped	2 T	3 T	

Rinse the sweetbreads under cold running water for 10 minutes. Place them in a saucepan with water, onion, vinegar, peppercorns, and bay leaves. Bring to a boil, then lower the heat and simmer for 20 minutes. Turn off the heat and let the sweetbreads cool in the broth.

When cool, remove sweetbreads from broth. With a paring knife, remove the outer fatty membranes, being careful not to puncture the inner membrane. Slice each sweetbread into 3 pieces. Dust with seasoned flour and saute in vegetable shortening. When they are golden in color, remove them from skillet. Divide equally over toast slices on dinner plates. Discard excess fat from skillet. Into the drippings, add the butter and heat until it foams. When it takes on a brown nutty color, add the parsley; divide equally over the sweetbreads and toast.

Notes:

DON A. DIANDA Owner, Doros Restaurant, San Francisco, California

1981	IFMA SILVER PLATE AWARD
1980	Fine Dining Hall of Fame, *Nation's Restaurant News*
1977	IVY AWARD OF DISTINCTION
1961–1982	*Travel/Holiday* Award

Don A. Dianda, one of San Francisco's stellar restaurateurs, was president of the California Restaurant Association and the Golden Gate Restaurant Association and is now an honorary director of the National Restaurant Association after many years of service with that organization. Mr. Dianda has seen Doros Restaurant grow from a small establishment to its present internationally known status. This growth has been fostered by his interest in superlative cuisine. He wears the green ribbon of Balli as a member of the San Francisco chapter of Confrèrie de la Chaine des Rôtisseurs, a centuries-old organization of those interested in fine cuisine.

Award-winning Paul Bermani is the Executive Chef of Doros Restaurant working closely with Mr. Dianda to assure the quality of the food. A chef of international repute who has worked in many areas of food preparation to reach his present stature, Chef Bermani trains his staff to maintain the high level he has set as the standard in the Doros kitchen.

Doros Restaurant is located in the historic area recreating turn-of-the-century San Francisco. This area was renovated and restored after World War II. The building housing Doros Restaurant has a series of below-ground alcoves which Mr. Dianda has refurbished to provide space for food preparation, for storage of fresh and dry foods, for staff areas, and, of course, for the extensive wine cellar. The building's history goes back to preearthquake days when supposedly it was used in a way that helped create the Barbary Coast legend. After the earthquake and fire of 1906, the building was the site of a winery. Later it was a printing plant, before Mr. Dianda took it over and made it a gathering place of San Francisco gourmets.

Ingredients:	4 portions	___portions
Veal loin, thin slices, pounded flat	12	
Salt and pepper	to taste	
Flour	to coat	
Butter	1 c	
Shallots, chopped	1 T	
Dry sauterne wine	¼ c	
Brown sauce	½ c	
Mushrooms, sliced	1 lb	
Eggplant, slices	12	
Butter	2 T	
Parsley, fresh, chopped	garnish	

Veal Scaloppine alla Doros
ENTREE

Season veal with salt and pepper. Dip in flour to lightly cover both sides. Melt the butter in a large skillet; add the veal slices when it bubbles. When veal is browned on both sides, pour off excess butter. Add the shallots, pour in the wine, and simmer for 3 minutes. Add the brown sauce.

In a separate pan, saute the sliced mushrooms. In another pan, saute the eggplant slices. Arrange veal and eggplant alternately on a bed of sauteed mushrooms.

To the sauce remaining in the skillet, add the 2 T of butter. Shake the skillet to swirl and melt the butter, then pour the sauce over the veal and eggplant slices. Garnish with parsley. Serve immediately.

Notes:

Lasagna with Vegetable Protein
ENTREE

Ingredients:	336 portions	___ portions
Parsley, chopped	¾ c	
Mozzarella cheese	34 lb	
Cottage cheese	26 lb	
Beef base	15 oz	
Water, hot	15 lb	
Vegetable protein (Promate 500)	5 lb	
Ground beef	30 lb	
Onions, chopped	4 lb 11 oz	
Garlic, minced	⅔ c	
Pepper, black	2 T	
Brown sugar	5 oz	
Salt	12 oz	
Oregano, crushed	½ c + 2 T	
Sweet basil	1 T + ¼ t	
Thyme	1 T + ¼ t	
Marjoram	1 T + ¼ t	
Worcestershire sauce	¾ c + 2 T	
Tomatoes, crushed (#10 can)	2½	
Tomato paste (#10 can)	2½	
Water and beef broth	4¼ gal	
MSG	2½ T	
Beef base	10 oz	
Lasagna noodles	12½ lb	
Parmesan cheese	2 lb 8 oz	

Chop parsley. Grate mozzarella cheese (the older the cheese, the easier to grate). Drain dry cottage cheese.

Add 15 oz of beef base to hot water. Add base and water to vegetable protein. Allow to rehydrate for at least 20–30 minutes.

Brown ground beef in steam kettle. Drain well, reserving drippings. Break up meat with a wire whip. Add onions and garlic. Cook until transparent.

Chill reserved drippings. Remove fat. Reserve beef stock to use as part of liquid.

Add dry ingredients to beef and onions, blend well, and then add liquid ingredients, including beef stock. Cover and *simmer* for about 45 minutes. Add rehydrated vegetable protein and simmer another 10 minutes. Check for flavor, adding MSG and beef base as needed.

Meanwhile, cook noodles in boiling salted water to which a little oil has been added. Cook noodles until *almost* done. Rinse with cold water. *Or* cook noodles in steamer, allowing for each 2 lb of noodles, 1½ gal of boiling water, ¼ c of salt, 2 T of salad oil. Steam about 15 minutes. Rinse with cold water.

In a greased counter pan, make three layers of the following: noodles, 1 qt of *hot* meat sauce, 1 qt of mozzarella cheese, 2 c of drained cottage cheese. (Keep sauce hot while combining casserole.) Make first layer of noodles lengthwise in pan, second layer crosswise, and third layer lengthwise. Top casserole with Parmesan cheese.

Bake only until cheese melts. Overbaking will cause lasagna to be *watery*. Score 7 × 4. Send immediately to thermotainers.

Notes:

S. KENT DOHRMAN Associate Director of Housing, University of Illinois at Urbana-Champaign, Champaign, Illinois

1980 IVY AWARD OF DISTINCTION
1977 IFMA SILVER PLATE AWARD
1975 President, National Association of College and University Food Services

Currently, Kent Dohrman is the Associate Director of Housing for Food and Residential Services at the University of Illinois at Urbana. Also, for the past ten years, Mr. Dohrman has been Director of Food Services at the University of Illinois. His department oversees residence hall dining facilities feeding about 9,500 students; a central food stores operation including meat, bakery, produce, and dry stores departments; a complete test kitchen; fast food and grocery store facilities; and a self-operated vending service.

Previously, Mr. Dohrman was Director of Food Services at the University of Rochester, Assistant Director of Dining Halls at Yale University, and Director of the Student Union Food Services at North Carolina State University. He was on the faculty of the Cornell School of Hotel Administration.

Mr. Dohrman has conducted numerous educational training programs and workshops for foodservice personnel. In 1977, he joined the faculty of the annual summer Supervisory Development Workshop sponsored by Central Michigan University. He is a guest lecturer at the University of Illinois and has written many articles for national trade publications. Mr. Dohrman is a graduate of the Cornell School of Hotel Administration and of the U.S. Navy Mess Management School. He received his M.B.A. degree from the University of Illinois in 1979.

Cheese Strata
ENTREE

Ingredients:	112 portions	___portions
Broccoli, frozen	10 lb	
Bread, white, day-old 20-oz loaves	4	
Margarine, soft	1 lb	
Cheddar cheese, grated	4 lb	
Eggs, slightly beaten	7 lb	
Milk	2 gal + 1 pt	
Mustard, prepared	⅔ c	
Salt	6 oz	
Tabasco	2 T	
Paprika	sprinkle	

Thaw broccoli, drain very well, and chop coarsely. Tear bread into small pieces (approximately 1 inch by 1½ inches). Grease 2-inch counter pans with 4 oz of the soft margarine. Place ½ gal of bread pieces evenly in bottom of counter pans. Distribute 1½ qt of chopped broccoli evenly over the bread pieces. Sprinkle 1½ qt (1 lb) of grated cheese evenly over broccoli. Spread ½ gal of bread pieces evenly over cheese.

To slightly beaten eggs, add milk, mustard, salt, and Tabasco. Mix well. Pour 3 qt of this mixture over the layers in each pan. Sprinkle with paprika. Cover with wax paper. Smooth down with your hand. Refrigerate overnight.

Preheat oven to 300° on high setting. Bake uncovered for 1¼ hour, or until custard sets. Garnish with parsley. Cut each pan into 28 servings. Set pans on wire racks or inverted bun sheets.

Notes:

FRED W. DOLLAR Director of Food Services, Texas A & M University, College Station, Texas

1982	President, Society for the Advancement of Food Service Research
1978	IFMA SILVER PLATE AWARD
1978	IVY AWARD OF DISTINCTION
1977	Ted Minah Award, National Association of College and University Food Services
1976	Institutional Food Service Facility Design Award

Fred Dollar has thirty-six years experience in the food industry in the areas of purchasing, storage, distribution, development of supply systems, retail food sales, commercial food services, and institutional food services. He is a graduate of Texas A & M University and of the Food and Container Institute in Chicago. His post-graduate training was at Cornell University.

Mr. Dollar's twenty-two years in the United States military gave him the opportunity to participate in numerous facets of food programming, sales, and service, including a wide variety of innovations that have since been used successfully both within the military and in the private sector. Among the progressive concepts that he initiated or assisted in perfecting are the development of layer-packed, cut-up, frozen chicken; of eviscerated and federally inspected poultry for shipment to armed forces serving overseas; of portable kits for inspection and detection of food contamination in front line areas of combat zones; of fluid milk for armed forces serving overseas; of standards for the inspection and importation of foreign beef to augment United States supplies during periods of shortages and inflated prices; of dry packaged food mixes requiring the addition of water only; of precooked frozen bacon, which was served for the first time in 1967 at Texas A & M University; of precooked frozen sausage links and patties; of comprehensive fast food selections with conventional menus for university students who dine on the board plan; and of the "accordion" system of shopping center dining services.

Shrimp Victoria
ENTREE

Ingredients:	4 portions	6 portions	___portions
Gulf shrimp, raw, peeled and cleaned	1 lb	1½ lb	
Onion, small, finely chopped	1	1½	
Butter or margarine	¼ c	⅜ c	
Mushrooms, 6-oz can	1 can	1½ cans	
Flour	1 T	1½ T	
Salt	¼ t	⅜ t	
Cayenne pepper	dash	dash	
Sour cream	1 c	1½ c	
Rice cooked	1½ c	2¼ c	

Saute shrimp and onion in butter or margarine for 10 minutes, or until shrimp are tender. Add mushrooms and cook for 5 minutes more. Sprinkle in flour, salt, and cayenne pepper. Stir in sour cream and cook gently for 10 minutes, not allowing the mixture to boil. Serve over rice.

Notes:

CHARLES J. DOULOS President, Jimmy's Harborside Restaurant, Inc., Boston, Massachusetts

1973   IVY AWARD OF DISTINCTION

Charles J. Doulos is the second generation to operate Jimmy's Harborside Restaurant. His father, James "Jimmy" Doulos, owner and founder, was a pioneer in specialty seafood restaurants when he located his now-famous Harborside on historic Boston Harbor adjacent to the Fish Pier Exchange.

Jimmy's Harborside Restaurant has been the recipient of countless hospitality awards. The restaurant can boast of having hosted legions of dignitaries, including presidents, senators, ambassadors, movie stars, and religious leaders, as well as the equally welcome regular patrons and tourists that flock there to enjoy the warm ambiance, the famous chowder, and the abundant variety of seafood and lobsters.

Jimmy's has been recognized and honored for its many civic philanthropies, particularly its contributions to The Jimmy Fund for Children's Cancer Research. Mr. Charles J. Doulos is a member of most organizations related to the foodservice industry. He is also on the board of trustees of the Massachusetts chapter of the National Multiple Sclerosis Society and is an overseer of the Sidney Farber Cancer Institute.

Jimmy's Baked Stuffed Fillet of Sole with Lobster Newburg Sauce

ENTREE

Ingredients:	4 portions	6 portions	___portions
Bread, sliced, trimmed, diced	2 slices	3 slices	
Cracker crumbs	1 T	1½ T	
Butter	½ lb	¾ lb	
Sherry wine	2 oz	3 oz	
Parmesan cheese, grated	1 t	1½ t	
Lobster meat, cut in small pieces	½ lb	¾ lb	
Sole fillets (7–8 oz per serving)	4	6	
Milk	1 c	1½ c	
Flour	2 T	3 T	
Light cream	1 c	1½ c	
Paprika	dash	dash	

For stuffing, mix the diced bread with the cracker crumbs, 4 T of melted butter, half of the sherry, the grated parmesan cheese, and half of the lobster meat.

Roll the fillets of sole with the stuffing. Place them in a pan, brush lightly with butter, and add ½ c of milk to keep them moist. Place in a 350° oven and bake for 10 minutes.

Make a white sauce by placing 4 T of melted butter and the flour in a saucepan and whipping slowly. Warm the rest of the milk and the cream, add to saucepan, and simmer until thickened.

The Lobster Newburg Sauce is made by placing in a saucepan 1 T of butter, then adding the remainder of the lobster, sherry wine, and a dash of paprika. Saute for ½ minute. Add the white sauce and simmer for 5 minutes. Pour Newburg Sauce over fillets and bake for 5 minutes.

Notes:

PAUL R. DOYON C.F.E., F.H.C.F.A., Director, Corporate Food Service Operations, West Jersey Hospital System, Voorhees, Camden, Berlin, and Marlton, New Jersey

1979	Philadelphia's Food Executive of the Year
1977	IFSEA Grand Skillet Award
1968	Award for Excellence in Culinary Arts, Chef magazine
1966	Grand Prize of Salon Culinaire HFDA

Paul Doyon has earned a reputation as an innovator in foodservice. In the eighteen years since he made health care foodservice his career, he has influenced the way food is prepared, assembled, and served in hospitals today. Mr. Doyon believes that increased productivity, rather than cutting back in food quality, is the answer to controlling costs in the health care foodservice field. He has pioneered automation in foodservice, through the use of electronics and the mechanization of many of the menial functions in foodservice.

Mr. Doyon introduced "nouvelle cuisine" techniques of food preparation in 1972, before the term was coined by the "Trois Gros" brothers and Paul Bocuse in France. His efforts in the field of cook/freeze methods for hospital meals are known internationally. He has spoken on health care food-related matters to audiences in places as far away from his home base as England, Canada, and France. Mr. Doyon is a Certified Food Executive and a Fellow of the American Society of Hospital Food Service Administrators.

Crème Renversée
DESSERT

Ingredients:	6 portions	___portions
Milk	1 qt	
Vanilla bean	1	
Sugar	2 c	
Salt	pinch	
Egg yolks	8	
Eggs, whole	4	
Water	1 c	

Scald the milk with the vanilla bean and let seep about 15 minutes. Remove the bean (it can be washed and used over and over). In the milk, dissolve 1 c of the sugar and a pinch of salt; strain. Beat the egg yolks and the eggs together and gradually add the strained scalded milk.

Cook 1 c of the sugar with the water in a small copper-lined stainless steel saucepan until the syrup turns golden. Pour syrup into a baking dish or mold, and tip to coat the dish with the syrup (be careful not to burn yourself). Pour the custard into the dish, set the dish in a pan of hot water, and bake in moderate (400°) oven for about 45 minutes, or until a knife inserted in the center comes out clean. Cool. Invert onto a serving dish just before serving.

The purpose of the egg whites is to coagulate the milk. The purpose of the yolks is to make the cream smooth. The number of egg whites listed is the minimum that should be used for a perfect balance between thickness and smoothness. Do not let the water boil during baking; this will make bubbles in the custard. If water starts to boil, add a couple of tablespoons of cold water to the pan.

Notes:

PETER GUST ECONOMOU C.F.E., D.O.D.G., President Emeritus and Director, The Park Lane Manor House, Buffalo, New York

1970	Man of the Year, *Buffalo Courier Express*
1969	Man of the Year, Judge John D. Hillery Scholarship Foundation
1958	IFMA GOLD PLATE AWARD
1943–1945	President, International Foodservice Executives Association

From his humble immigrant origin, Peter Gust Economou has risen to become one of the most widely recognized and internationally respected restaurateurs. His superior talent as a host has won him commissions to prepare dinner events for many figures known the world over.

Mr. Economou has always sought to improve the foodservice industry and to share the vast knowledge he has acquired over many years. Incessantly active for the Statler Foundation, he has helped distribute hundreds of thousands of dollars in the form of scholarships and university trusts to eligible students in foodservice programs. He was responsible for implementing a foodservice program at Emerson Vocational High School, a program used as a model for secondary school foodservice training throughout the country. He was called on to counsel the United States Army, Navy, Air Force, and Civil Defense in matters of food preparation and service, a duty he performed with great fervor.

At an early age, Peter Gust Economou adopted this creed to live by, to work by, and, as he always taught his employees, to maintain in every endeavor in life: "Good will is like a good name, won by many acts but lost by only one."

Biography from *Your Host Peter Gust,* by Ellen Taussig (1979).

Moussaka
ENTREE

Ingredients:	10 portions	6 portions	___portions
Eggplant, medium	1	⅔	
Vegetable shortening or oil	½ c	⅓ c	
Butter	¼ c	2 T	
Ground beef or lamb	2 lb	20 oz	
Onion, large, finely chopped	1	⅔	
Salt and pepper	to taste	to taste	
Catsup	½ c	⅓ c	
Oregano	½ t	⅓ t	
WHITE SAUCE			
Butter	1½ T	2¾ t	
Cornstarch	2 T	3½ t	
Salt	½ t	⅓ t	
Milk	3 c	14½ oz	
Eggs	4	2½	
Catsup, diluted in a little water	1 T	1¾ t	
Cinnamon	½ t	⅓ t	

Wash the eggplant and cut in ½-inch slices. Sprinkle with salt and let stand in a bowl for ½ hour. Rinse in cold water and place on towel to dry. Melt oil and butter together. Place eggplant slices close together on an oiled cookie sheet. Brush tops of eggplant slices with oil and butter mixture. Bake them in a 350° oven for about 15 minutes, or until slightly browned.

Place a tablespoon of the oil and butter mixture in a frying pan and cook the ground meat, chopped onion, salt and pepper, catsup, and oregano for about 10 minutes, or until slightly browned.

Make the white sauce. Heat butter. Stir in the cornstarch and salt until it bubbles, then add the milk gradually and heat until thickened. Beat the eggs and add them to a small quantity of the white sauce; mix well. Add this to the rest of the sauce with the catsup.

Oil the bottom and sides of baking pan (9 × 12 inch) with the oil and butter mixture. Divide the eggplant into three portions and the meat into two portions. Spread one layer of eggplant on the bottom of the pan, then one layer of meat, another layer of eggplant, a layer of meat, and finally a last layer of eggplant. Pour the white sauce and egg mixture over the layers and sprinkle with the cinnamon. If there is any oil and butter mixture left, it may be added before baking if desired. Bake at 325° for ¾–1 hour, or until nicely browned.

Notes:

RICHARD N. FRANK   President and Chief Executive Officer, Lawry's Foods, Inc., Lawry's Restaurants, Inc., Los Angeles, California

According to his father, Richard N. Frank was a man who "doesn't know a peanut from a watermelon." Lawrence Frank delivered that unflattering judgment when Richard informed him that he believed he could make a success out of Lawry's Seasoned Salt, which Lawrence had created, and would prefer trying his hand at that, rather than join Lawrence's multimillion-dollar bakery business. In spite of the perceived handicap, Richard Frank oversaw the development of Lawry's Foods, Inc., from annual net sales of about $350,000 in the early 1950s to a present sales volume of over $70 million.

Lawry's Foods, Inc., is today a leader in marketing specialty food items, including seasoning blends, foil-packaged seasoning mixes, and Mexican food products, to general consumers and to the foodservice industry around the world. Richard Frank has developed the company's headquarters in Los Angeles into a major Southern California visitor attraction. Lawry's California Center combines outdoor dining, shopping, and plant touring in an attractive thirteen-acre oasis setting.

Richard Frank is also the president of a separate company, Lawry's Restaurants, Inc. This company owns and operates the world-famous Lawry's The Prime Rib in Beverly Hills and Chicago, Lawry's Westside Broiler in Beverly Hills, The Great Scot in Los Angeles, and The Five Crowns in Corona del Mar. The success of these award-winning restaurants and the high esteem in which Lawry's Foods, Inc., is held by the food industry have established Mr. Frank as a restaurateur entrepreneur quite capable of distinguishing a peanut from a watermelon.

Richard Frank's Famous Leftover Hash
ENTREE

Ingredients:	4 portions	6 portions	___portions
Onions, thinly sliced in rings, then quartered	2	3	
Olive oil	as needed	as needed	
Potatoes, cooked, peeled, diced in ¼-inch cubes	1 lb	1½ lb	
Lawry's Seasoned Salt	1 t	1½ t	
Lawry's Pinch of Herbs	1 t	1½ t	
Roasted meat, diced in ¼" cubes	1 lb	1½ lb	
Mexican red peppers, dried, finely chopped (or cayenne pepper to taste)	2	3	
Green pepper, thinly sliced in rings, then quartered	1	1	
Eggs, poached	4–6	6–9	

Saute onions in oil until golden brown; drain and set aside. Cook potatoes with Seasoned Salt and Pinch of Herbs in a small amount of oil over high heat until they are brown; set aside. Saute meat and red peppers, also over high heat, until meat is crisp and brown. Add onions, potatoes, and green pepper to meat mixture, and continue cooking 5–10 minutes. Mix constantly to keep mixture from overbrowning at the bottom of the pan. Top each serving with a poached egg.

Salad oil, butter, or margarine may be substituted; however, olive oil is recommended. Oregano or Italian seasonings may be substituted. Any leftover meat may be used, such as roast beef, prime ribs of beef, pot roast, steak, roast leg of lamb, lamb chops, lamb shanks, etc. Small portions of corned beef and pork may be used, mixed in with other meat. Beef and lamb may be used separately or combined. Boiled potatoes work best; however, fried, baked, or even frozen hash browns may be used.

Notes:

CHARLES F. FREDERIKSEN Director of Housing and Food Service, Iowa State University, Ames, Iowa

1978	IVY AWARD OF DISTINCTION
1972–1973	President, Association of College and University Housing Officers

Charles Frederiksen has published articles in the *Journal of College and University Housing,* a monograph of residence hall programming, and articles in the *ACUHO News.* He has served in many capacities in the Association of College and University Housing Officers (ACUHO) during the past fifteen years, including secretary, editor of the magazine, and president.

Mr. Fredericksen is a strong supporter of the principle of "oneness of purpose" in university housing and food service. He works hard to realize that goal in the Iowa State housing and food service program, which accommodates nearly 12,000 students.

Iowa State Bean Soup
SOUP

Ingredients:	100 portions	6 portions	___portions
Beans, navy or white	6 lb	6 oz	
Onion, chopped	1 lb 4 oz	1¼ oz	
Bacon, finely diced cubes	1 lb 4 oz	1¼ oz	
Flour	8 oz	½ oz	
Beef base	8 oz	½ oz	
Chicken base	8 oz	½ oz	
Water	4 gal	1 qt	
Tomatoes, diced	1 #10 can	7 oz	
Celery, tops and leaves, minced	12 oz	1 oz	
Parsley, fresh, minced	⅓ c	1 T	
Ham, scraps and ends, minced	1 lb 8 oz	1½ oz	
Black pepper	1½ t	⅛ t	
Liquid Smoke	½–1 t	6–10 drops	

Check dry beans for foreign matter; soak in cold water overnight.

Steam beans and onions in low-pressure steamer until beans are tender. Saute bacon in steam-jacketed kettle until crisp. Add flour and make a roux. Cook roux 5 minutes.

Mix beef and chicken bases with part of the water to make a stock. Add beans, onions, stock, rest of the water, tomatoes, celery, parsley, ham, black pepper, and Liquid Smoke to kettle. Heat to boiling; simmer until celery is tender and beans are cooked.

Notes:

Pizza Meatloaf Pie
ENTREE

Ingredients:	196 portions	6 portions	___portions
Ground beef	50 lb	1½ lb	
Milk, evaporated	2 gal	8 oz	
Bread crumbs, fine	5 qt	5 oz	
Garlic salt	½ c	1 t	
Salt	¼ c	dash	
Tomato paste	1 gal	4 oz	
Mushrooms, drained	7 lb	3½ oz	
Cheddar cheese, shredded	7 lb	3½ oz	
Oregano	¼ c	1 t	
Parmesan cheese	1½ lb	¾ oz	

Mix ground beef, milk, bread crumbs, garlic salt, and salt. Scale 10¾ lb of meat mixture per pan (7 pans, 12″ × 20″ × 2″). Pat down evenly. Spread 2 c of tomato paste over each pan. Top each pan with 1 lb of mushrooms and shredded cheese. Sprinkle on oregano and parmesan cheese. Bake 250° (convection oven) for 1 hour. To serve, cut 2 by 7 pieces, then cut each piece diagonally in half. (For 6 portions, use 9-inch square pan.)

Notes:

Carrot Cake with Cream Cheese Frosting

DESSERT

Ingredients:	120 portions	___portions
Eggs, whole	2 lb 11 oz	
Sugar	5 lb	
Oil	½ gal + 1 c	
Flour	3 lb 10 oz	
Soda	¼ c	
Salt	1 T	
Cinnamon	2 T	
Carrots, finely grated	6 lb	
Vanilla	2 T	
Nuts	1 lb 5 oz	
FROSTING		
Cream cheese, softened	8 oz	
Margarine, softened	5 oz	
Vanilla emulsion	2½ t	
Sugar, powdered	2 lb	
Milk, whole	as needed	

Cream together eggs, sugar, and oil. Sift in dry ingredients and blend. Add grated carrots; mix. Add vanilla and nuts; mix well. Scale 12 lb into each of two greased sheet pans (18" × 26"). Bake at 350° for 25–30 minutes. Cool and ice with Cream Cheese Frosting. To make frosting, beat together all of the ingredients except the milk. Add milk only if necessary, being careful not to add too much. This frosting has a tendency to be soft when warm.

Notes:

JOHN C. FRIESE　　Food Service Systems Specialist, USDA Food and Nutrition Service, Atlanta, Georgia

      1978 USDA Distinguished Service Award
      1971 IFMA SILVER PLATE AWARD
      1970 President, NACUFS

 John Friese is a 1950 graduate of Pennsylvania State University. He worked in the restaurant business for several years before devoting twenty-two years to college foodservice. After that, for three years he was an independent consultant. He is now a USDA school food service and Title VII consultant.

Depression Dessert

DESSERT

Ingredients:	8 portions	___portions
Jello Vanilla Pudding, not instant, large size (or 2 small size)	1 pkg	
Eggs, separated	2	
Sugar	¼ c	

CRUST AND TOPPING

Zwieback	1 pkg	
Margarine, melted	½ c	
Brown sugar	½ c	

Cook pudding according to directions on package. When just about thick, add 2 egg yolks. Make meringue with egg whites and sugar; beat until stiff. Make crust with zwieback, margarine, and brown sugar. Press half into square 12-inch baking dish. Put pudding on top and pile on meringue. Sprinkle half of the crust crumbs on top. Bake in a 375° oven for 10 minutes. Watch carefully.

During the "dust bowl" depression years of the early 1930s, the combination of low cost with high nutritive value made this dessert the perfect end to simple meals.

Notes:

ANGELO GAGLIANO   Director of Food Service, Memorial Sloan-Kettering Cancer Center, New York, New York

> 1977   IFMA SILVER PLATE AWARD
> 1976   IVY AWARD OF DISTINCTION
> 1968   President, American Society for Hospital Food Service Administrators

Mr. Gagliano, a graduate of the University of Miami, held positions with IBM, the Army and Air Force Exchange, and Grumman Aircraft before coming to Sloan-Kettering in 1963. While with the Exchange, he was responsible for the foodservice operations on twelve bases spread from Panama to Greenland.

Mr. Gagliano supervised the transformation of the Memorial Sloan-Kettering Cancer Center hospital kitchen from an antiquated, decentralized 265-bed operation to an ultra-modern facility in a new 600-bed tower. His design innovations of a 43-foot computerized tray assembly line and an automated delivery system set a standard back in 1970 that is rarely matched in hospitals being built today. Mr. Gagliano's operation is able to deliver to patients high-quality food at optimum temperatures within ten minutes of tray assembly.

Mr. Gagliano is the second ASHFSA president, is active in many organizations, and is much sought-after as a speaker and consultant.

Poulet Farci Bon Vivant
ENTREE

Ingredients:	4 portions	6 portions	___ portions
Almonds, blanched, sliced, crushed	4 oz	6 oz	
Onion, small, very finely chopped	1	1½	
Chicken livers, very finely chopped	3	4–5	
Mushrooms, very finely chopped	4	5	
Parsley, very finely chopped	1 T	1½ T	
Chives, very finely chopped	1 T	1½ T	
Egg	1	1½	
Cream	3 T	4½ T	
Raisins, marinated in 1 oz cognac and 1 oz white wine	2 oz	3 oz	
Apple, diced	½	¾	
Salt and pepper	to taste	to taste	
Chicken breasts, double, boned (8 oz each after boning)	4	6	
Butter	¼ lb	⅜ lb	
Supreme Sauce	1½ c	2¼ c	
Almonds, sliced blanched, lightly roasted	2 oz	3 oz	

Saute crushed almonds until lightly roasted. In another pan, saute onion until lightly browned or transparent. Add chicken livers, mushrooms, parsley, and chives. Stir over high heat for a few minutes. Turn off heat.

Mix egg with cream. Stir into chicken liver mixture. Mix in crushed almonds, drained marinated raisins (save the marinade), and diced apple. Season to taste with salt and pepper. Cool partially, then chill. (Stuffing is easier to handle when cool.)

Lay chicken breasts out flat. Place some stuffing on each breast. Roll breast around stuffing. Place seam-side down in melted butter in roasting pan. Bake at 450° for 5 minutes. Reduce heat to 325° and bake 25 minutes longer, basting occasionally.

Flavor the Supreme Sauce with cognac and wine marinade. Spoon over chicken. Sprinkle with sliced almonds. Sprinkle with additional minced parsley, if desired.

Notes:

PETER GOLDMAN General Manager, Hyatt Regency, San Francisco, California

1972 Ivy Award of Distinction

Peter Goldman joined the Hyatt Regency in San Francisco in September of 1979 as General Manager and Regional Vice-President. Mr. Goldman was formerly the Managing Director of Fairmont Hotel Company.

Born in Vreslau, Germany, Mr. Goldman began his hotel career in San Francisco in 1949. In addition to managing the Hyatt Regency in San Francisco, he also supervises the operation of seven other Hyatt hotels in northern California and in Seattle. His civic activities include service as Director of the Hotel Employers Association of San Francisco, Chairman of the Board of the California Tourism Council, and President-Elect of the San Francisco Convention and Visitors Bureau. Mr. Goldman is a definite asset to Hyatt Hotels.

At the Fairmont, Mr. Goldman created a mix of restaurants offering everything from Creole cuisine to a Polynesian room with a pool and hourly rainstorms. In his thirty-two years with that hotel, he built up a strong catering department, in part by making sure to rebook meetings before they adjourned and by personally meeting the attending executives.

Mousseline of Salmon
ENTREE

Ingredients:	2 portions	6 portions	___portions
Salmon, fresh	1 lb	3 lb	
Egg whites	2 doz	3 doz	
Whipping cream	½ pt	3 c	
Salt and white pepper	to taste	to taste	
Worcestershire sauce	to taste	to taste	
Lemon juice	to taste	to taste	

Blend ingredients into fine creamy substance and fill individual forms of your choice. Poach in bain marie (water bath) for 30 minutes over low heat. Serve with sauce vin blanc or champagne and oyster sauce.

Notes:

Ingredients: *___portions*

PANCAKES

Eggs	1 gal
Milk	3 gal
Cake flour	19 lb
Shortening	2 qt
Baking powder	1 lb
Sugar	2 lb 8 oz
Salt	3 oz

MARSHMALLOW SAUCE

Sugar	16 lb
Egg whites	1 gal
Corn syrup	3 lb

FRESH STRAWBERRY SAUCE

Strawberries, fresh or frozen
Brandy
Cointreau

Pancakes Oscar

ENTREE

 Prepare pancakes as by usual method. Pancakes can be individual stacks or can be large cake size, stacked five high and cut like a cake.
 To prepare Marshmallow Sauce, mix ingredients in a double boiler until sugar dissolves. Whip until creamy stiff.
 Cut up fresh or frozen strawberries and marinate them with brandy and Cointreau. Then crush into a saucy substance.
 Cover each pancake with a layer of Fresh Strawberry Sauce then Marshmallow Sauce, and brown under broiler.

Notes:

ROLAND AND VICTOR GOTTI Owners, Ernie's, San Francisco, California

1981	Fine Dining Hall of Fame, *Nation's Restaurant News*
1963–1982	Mobil 5-Star Award
1953–1982	*Holiday* Award for Distinctive Dining
1971	IVY AWARD OF DISTINCTION

Located in San Francisco on a historic site, Ernie's stands where a building known as the Frisco Dance Hall was located prior to its destruction in the earthquake and fire in 1906. Later, when it was rebuilt, the name of the structure was changed to Il Trovatore. The birth of the current restaurant took place in the early 1930s, when Ernie Carlesso and Ambrogio Gotti purchased Il Trovatore and, a few years later, rechristened it Ernie's. The two men operated the restaurant jointly until Mr. Carlesso's death in 1946, when Mr. Gotti assumed sole ownership. During the following year, Mr. Gotti retired from the business, turning over ownership and control of the restaurant to his two sons, Roland and Victor, who have operated it ever since.

Ernie's has gained international recognition for its superlative French cuisine and its impeccable service. The late Lucius Beebe, one of the nation's foremost gourmets and bon vivants, dined regularly at Ernie's and also was the Gotti brothers' "unofficial" counsel in building their extensive wine list, which now offers a selection of more than 200 fine imported and domestic wines. A popular location choice with studios, Ernie's has been featured in many movies and TV shows. Notable among these are *The High and the Mighty* and the Hitchcock thriller *Vertigo*. More recently, it has been featured in several episodes of *The Streets of San Francisco*.

Perhaps some of the greatest tributes to Ernie's have come from noted restaurant critics who have saluted its beauty. Roy Andries de Groot, contributing editor of *Esquire,* has commented: "Ernie's is more than the most famous and handsome restaurant in the country—it is a national institution." Elegant decor, an outstanding wine cellar, and excellent cuisine are important factors in Ernie's success, but there are other aspects on which the management concentrates. According to the Gotti brothers, these include constant attention to every detail, no matter how minute, that will ensure customer satisfaction and unceasing care in maintaining the highest standards of quality.

Chicken Cynthia à la Champagne
ENTREE

Ingredients:	4 portions	6 portions	___portions
Chickens, 2¼ lb each	2	3	
Salt	to taste	to taste	
Flour	to coat	to coat	
Butter	1 T	1½ T	
Oil	1 T	1½ T	
Curaçao	1 oz	1½ oz	
Champagne, dry	6 oz	9 oz	
Bouillon	1 c	1½ c	
Mushrooms, sliced	1 c	1½ c	
Butter	1 T	1½ T	
Whipping cream	½ c	¾ c	
Orange wedges	garnish	garnish	
Seedless grapes	garnish	garnish	

Disjoint chickens. Set wings and legs aside. Bone remaining parts. Salt and flour chicken. Saute in butter and oil for ten minutes on each side. Remove from stove and continue browning in 350° oven for 20 minutes.

Remove fat, add Curaçao and champagne. Cover with bouillon, let simmer on top of stove until tender, approximately 20 minutes. Add mushrooms, which have been sauteed in butter and whipping cream. Serve in chafing dish. Decorate with orange wedges and seedless grapes.

Notes:

MICHAEL GRISANTI and VINCENZO GABRIELE Owners, Casa Grisanti, Louisville, Kentucky

> 1982 Fine Dining Hall of Fame, *Nation's Restaurant News*
> 1981 IVY AWARD OF DISTINCTION

Michael Grisanti and Vincenzo Gabriele, the imaginative young owners of Casa Grisanti, know how to fulfill their civic duties. It helps that Grisanti, who is twenty-nine, chairs the executive board of Louisville's School of Fine Art, the only accredited art school in Kentucky. But the Grisanti-Gabriele team best meets the city's hunger for taste and style through excellent service and food at Casa Grisanti.

"Confidence, that's the word we use all the time," says Mr. Gabriele. When people walk into the copper-walled Casa Grisanti, they place themselves in the care of its management. It's a matter of trust, the end result of years of service, beginning with Michael Grisanti's father Albert, who opened the restaurant on its offbeat site back in 1959. "Our regular customers, they don't order off the menu," continues Mr. Gabriele. "They know we'll do something special for them. They know we'll give them something they'll like."

The Grisanti touch with people and with the community's needs has been passed on, father to son. In the early 1970s, when Michael Grisanti joined his father in the family business, he took a hard look at Louisville. At that time, the neighborhood around the restaurant was deteriorating into what is today a vacant-looking area with a smattering of light industry. "At that time, I kept hearing people say they wished Louisville had a nice French restaurant," says Grisanti, who offers Italian cuisine in Mama Grisanti and Casa Grisanti, and American cuisine in the newly opened Sixth Avenue. "What they were really saying was that they wanted a first-class restaurant. We had to do something special to compete with the suburbs and keep people coming here. Now, if we mentioned moving, our customers would be up in arms. We've got a terrific reputation."

Biography courtesy of *Restaurants and Institutions*, May 1, 1981, p. 54.

Ingredients:	1 portion	___portions
Fettucine		
Basil leaves (no stems), finely chopped	2 c	
Salt	1 t	
White pepper	½ t	
Garlic, finely chopped	2 t	
Pine nuts, finely chopped	2 T	
Olive oil	½ c	
Parmesan cheese	½ c	

Fettucine con Pesto

ENTREE

Cook desired amount of fettucine (al dente). Mix the rest of the ingredients to make pesto sauce. Then, in a pan over medium heat, add pesto sauce and 6 oz of pasta water to cooked fettucine; mix and serve.

Notes:

Ingredients:	1 portion	6 portions	___portions
Veal, 3-oz pieces	2	12	
Prosciutto, slices	2 oz	24 oz	
Cheese, Jarlsberg or Swiss	2 oz	24 oz	
Flour	to coat	to coat	
Butter	to saute	to saute	
Madeira wine	1 oz	6 oz	
Veal stock	2 oz	24 oz	

Veal Michelangelo

ENTREE

Stuff thin slices of veal with prosciutto and Jarlsberg (or Swiss) cheese; lightly flour and saute in butter. Then cook with Madeira wine and veal stock.

Notes:

KENNETH F. HANSEN Owner, Scandia, Los Angeles, California

1975   IVY AWARD OF DISTINCTION

Kenneth Hansen, Danish-born founder of the renowned Scandia restaurant in West Hollywood, was a master chef considered by many to be the "dean" of Southern California restaurateurs. Mr. Hansen began his Sunset Boulevard restaurant career in 1936 when he became associated with the Bit of Sweden, located at Sunset and Doheny. He acquired that restaurant in 1940, and in 1946 he opened his original Scandia just a block away. As his business and reputation grew, a larger restaurant was dictated, and in 1958 the current Scandia was opened at 9400 Sunset Boulevard.

In 1961, Kenneth Hansen was knighted by King Frederick IX of Denmark, as a tribute from the King to a fellow countryman who had left his homeland as a cabin boy on a Danish vessel and had become the foremost exponent of Scandinavian cuisine in America. While knighthood was probably Mr. Hansen's most gratifying award, he also received many other salutes in the restaurant field. Scandia has won the coveted Holiday Magazine Award for distinctive dining consistently for more than twenty years. Mr. Hansen's exacting attention to quality and detail was his trademark, and it helped to spark the careers of numerous other successful restaurateurs. Mr. Hansen was the founder of the Vikings of Scandia, a philanthropic group of 500 men who have given away more than $3 million to various children's charities in the past 30 years.

Deceased, December 1980.

Béarnaise Sauce

SAUCE

Ingredients:	6 portions	___portions
Peppercorns, crushed	8	
Shallots, chopped	2	
Bay leaf	1	
Parsley, branches	4–5	
Tarragon vinegar	½ c	
Egg yolks	5	
Lemon juice	½ lemon	
Water	1 T	
Butter, melted clear	½ lb	
Salt	to taste	
Cayenne	to taste	
Parsley, chopped	1 t	
Tarragon leaves, chopped	1 t	

Place in a small heavy bottom casserole the peppercorns, shallots, bay leaf, parsley branches, and vinegar. Heat until volume is reduced to ¼ of initial size. Strain.

Beat egg yolks with lemon juice and water in the top of a double boiler until thick. Then add melted butter very slowly, stir in the reduction of vinegar and spices, season with salt and cayenne, and add chopped parsley and chopped tarragon leaves.

Notes:

Kalvfilet Oscar
ENTREE

Ingredients:	6 portions	___portions
Veal cutlets, ¼-inch slices, flattened	6	
Salt and pepper	to taste	
Flour	to coat	
Butter	to saute	
Asparagus tips	30	
Crab legs	5–6	
Water	2–3 T	

Season veal cutlets with salt and pepper, dip in flour, and saute in butter in a skillet over a brisk fire, turning cutlets several times until done to a golden brown. Place cutlets on a platter. On each cutlet, place 4 or 5 warmed asparagus tips. On top of the asparagus, place the crab legs that have been slightly warmed in butter. Pour 2–3 T of water into the skillet where the cutlets were fried and reduce. Pour over cutlets. Place platter in oven to keep warm until ready to serve, at which time Béarnaise Sauce should be poured over each cutlet.

Notes:

SISTER MARY KATERI HARKINS R.D., Director of Dietetics, Mercy Hospital, Rockville Centre, New York

1971	President, American Society for Hospital Food Service Administrators (ASHFSA)
1970	IFMA SILVER PLATE AWARD, HOSPITAL AND HEALTH CARE
1970	Woman of the Year, Business and Professional Women's Club of Nassau County
1961–1965	Secretary, Treasurer, and President of the Long Island Dietetic Association

Sister Mary Kateri Harkins instituted the five-meal plan for patients' services at Mercy Hospital in 1969. The program is still in effect and is as successful as ever. Along with the five-meal plan, a program of medical dietetics was introduced. The patient's menu is used as a teaching tool. When special diet patients are discharged, they have been well instructed in the food selection process they must follow if they are to adhere to the doctor's diet prescription.

Chocolate Chip Cookies
DESSERT

Ingredients:	72 portions	___portions
Flour, all-purpose	1 qt	
Baking soda	1 T	
Salt	½ t	
Margarine	1 lb	
Sugar, dark brown	⅔ c	
Sugar, white	1 c + 3 T	
Eggs	4	
Vanilla flavoring	1 T	
Chocolate chips	1 qt	

Sift flour, soda, and salt together. Cream margarine, brown sugar, and white sugar thoroughly; add eggs and vanilla, beating until light. Gradually add flour mixture, beating until blended. Add chocolate chips. Drop with No. 40 scoop onto greased baking sheets. Bake for 10–12 minutes at 375°. Yields 6 dozen cookies.

Notes:

G. "JIM" HASSLOCHER President and Chairman of the Board, Frontier Enterprises, Inc., San Antonio, Texas

1974 IFMA GOLD PLATE AWARD

A graduate of St. Mary's University, Mr. Hasslocher started his chain of eating establishments in 1947. He was named "Outstanding Restaurateur of Texas" in 1961 by the Texas Restaurant Association. His civic activities have been extensive, including involvement with San Antonio's Chamber of Commerce, Research and Planning Council, and Associated Employers. Mr. Hasslocher is a director of the San Antonio Livestock Exposition and a past president of the Texas Restaurant Association.

Enchilada Verde Casserole
ENTREE

Ingredients:	8 portions	___portions
Chicken breasts, whole	2	
Spikes	1 t	
Cumin	½ t	
Salt and pepper	to taste	
SALSA VERDE		
Garlic minced	1	
Green pear tomatoes	2½ lb	
Onion, large	1	
Cilantro, chopped	⅛ c	
Salt	1 t	
Butter	2 T	
Onion, chopped	⅛ c	
Sour cream	1 c	
Tabasco	6 drops	
Tortillas	8	
Broccoli, steamed and seasoned	1 lb	
Monterey Jack cheese, grated (or Jalapeno Jack)	1 lb	

Bake chicken with spikes, cumin, and salt and pepper at 325° for 1 hour. Cool and remove from bone. Chop coarsely.

To make Salsa Verde, mince garlic in processor or blender. Add tomatoes, onion, and cilantro, chop medium fine, and pour sauce into pan to simmer for 30–40 minutes.

Melt the butter in a skillet. Saute chopped onion until transparent. Add coarsely chopped chicken. Add sour cream and mix well; saute until sour cream is completely mixed in chicken. Add Tabasco.

Grease a casserole dish and cover bottom with 2 oz of Salsa Verde. Dip tortillas in Salsa Verde to soften them. Line the bottom of the casserole dish with tortillas. Add some of the chicken mixture. Top with some broccoli and grated cheese. Add Salsa Verde to cover. Repeat until all ingredients are used (two or more layers). Bake uncovered at 350° for 30 minutes.

Notes:

KEITH HAZELTINE   Director of Dining Services, Sam Houston State University, Huntsville, Texas

1981 Ivy Award of Distinction

Keith Hazeltine is a prolific writer who has published dozens of articles. Ranging in subject matter from chemistry of foods to management principles, these have appeared in various journals in the fields of food service and university administration. Mr. Hazeltine has been an active speaker on programs across the continent. His professional affiliations include the National Association of College and University Food Services and the Society for the Advancement of Food Service Research.

Mr. Hazeltine is a firm believer that the dining staff performs the most important function on the college campus: "After all, we are in the business of feeding other people's children." At Sam Houston State, he tries to foster good eating habits that can have a healthy, lifelong influence. Purchasing specifications for the dining service seek to minimize additives in the food supply. The dining service is a nearly pure example of participative management, because Mr. Hazeltine knows that student input is vital to success; employee committees assist management in every area. Innovative systems and designs have produced unique and efficient dining services for the students. Happy diners in a galleria of foodservice boutiques help themselves to flavorful, colorful, crunchy vegetables cooked in the serving area.

Mr. Hazeltine, a 1955 graduate of Cornell University, has benefited from his experience in hotels and restaurants and at Rutgers University, Penn State, and SUNY. He also gives credit to the influences of Ray Cantwell, Bill Muser, E. H. Schmidt, and Fred Dollar.

Pork Chops Supreme
ENTREE

Ingredients:	25 portions	6 portions	___portions
Pork chops, loin, 4 oz each	50	12	
Salt	3⅔ T	2⅔ t	
Lemon, thin slices	50	12	
Brown sugar	1½ lb	5¾ oz	
Catsup	1½ lb	5¾ oz	
Water	1½ pt	5¾ oz	

Place pork chops on baking sheets. Season with salt. Top each pork chop with lemon slice. Mix brown sugar, catsup, and water. Pour this mixture over the pork chops. Cover and bake at 325° for 1 hour. Uncover and bake 30 minutes longer.

Notes:

Ingredients:	6 portions	___portions
Bulgur wheat	2 c	
Water, cold	2 c	
Parsley, finely chopped	1 c	
Green pepper, finely chopped	½ c	
Green onion, minced	1 c	
Mint, fresh, minced (or 2 T dry mint)	½ c	
Olive oil	½ c	
Lemon juice	½ c	
Salt	2 t	
Tomato, chopped or sliced	1	
Green pepper, chunks	garnish	

Tabbuli

VEGETABLE

Combine the wheat and water; allow to stand 1 hour. Add the remaining ingredients and stir together. Chill well. Garnish with chopped or sliced tomato and chunks of green pepper. May be eaten by hand, by scooping with pepper chunks.

Notes:

Ingredients:	12 10" pies	___pies
Butter	4 lb	
Sugar, confectioners'	1½ qt	
Bitter chocolate, melted	1 lb	
Vanilla	5 T	
Eggs, chilled	32	
Pie shell, baked	12	
Whipped cream	to top	
Almond slivers, toasted	garnish	

Chocolate Silk Pie

DESSERT

Using an electric beater, cream butter with sugar, then add chocolate and vanilla. Add eggs *one at a time*, beating 2 minutes after adding *each* egg. Pour into baked pie shell. Chill for 1 hour. Top with whipped cream and sprinkle with toasted almond slivers before serving. Delicious and very rich.

This should be made only in the above quantity or a smaller quantity. Larger quantities may separate. Be sure that eggs are chilled.

Notes:

SAMUEL L. HUFF Foodservice Director (retired), Washington State University, Pullman, Washington

> 1978 Certificate of Recognition, NACUFS
> 1972 IVY AWARD OF DISTINCTION

After retiring from a career in the Navy Medical Service Corps, which included eight years as a hospital foodservice officer, Sam Huff took the position of Foodservice Director at Washington State University because "I believed it to be an exceptionally good operation at the time." Mr. Huff believes that if there is a secret to success in foodservice endeavors, it must include WORK—Willingness, Organization, Responsibility, and Knowledge. An observer of his operating methods would be inspired to add that he also exhibits a creative approach to students and staff.

To better serve the students, Mr. Huff worked with them to find out their needs. One way he did this was in food committees, which served both dining hall members and management in an advisory capacity and as an important communications link. Based on input from the various food committees, along with his own and his staff's ideas, menus were adjusted to meet changing student preferences, special diet items were made available, guest meals were provided, and, in general, as much variety as possible was offered.

Mr. Huff ran an efficient and successful operation, which was in no small part the result of his concern for staff as well as students. He put a high priority on obtaining recognition and compensation for his staff, a difficult task in a state institution where working hours and salaries are largely established by others. He found compliments for work well done and promotions from within to be helpful. To facilitate the latter, he kept his employees informed of ways in which they could improve themselves and encouraged them in efforts that would make them eligible for advancement.

Swedish Meatballs
HORS D'OEUVRES

Ingredients:	80 portions	___portions
Ground beef	35 lb	
Pork sausage	15 lb	
Onion, finely ground	2 qt	
Celery, finely ground	2 qt	
Allspice	¾ c	
Bread crumbs	2½ gal	
Pepper	½ c	
Salt	1 c	
Sugar	1 c	
Eggs, whole	1 gal	
Tomato sauce	to cover	

Combine all ingredients. Shape into 1-inch balls. Saute slowly until done. Pour off excess fat during cooking. Place meatballs in chafing dish pans. Cover lightly with tomato sauce just before serving. Keep hot. Yields 400 meatballs.

Notes:

Shrimp Cocktail Sauce

SAUCE

Ingredients:	100 portions	___portions
Chili sauce (#10 can)	1	
Horseradish	1 c	
Salt	to taste	
Tabasco	½ t	
Worcestershire sauce	1 T	

Combine all ingredients. Serve chilled. Allow about 1 oz per person.

Notes:

Sweet and Sour Pork Cubes
ENTREE

Ingredients:	48 portions	6 portions	___portions
Pork loin, boneless	30 lb	3¾ lb	
Vinegar	1 gal	1 pt	
Water	2¼ gal	2¼ qt	
Salt	1 c	⅛ c	
Pepper	6 T	2¼ t	
Garlic powder	3 T	1⅛ t	
SWEET AND SOUR SAUCE			
Pineapple juice	1 qt	2 oz	
Vinegar	½ c	½ oz	
Brown sugar	¾ c	¾ oz	
Paprika	1 T	¾ t	
Ginger, powdered	1 T	¾ t	
Salt	1 T	¾ t	
Pepper	2 t	¼ t	
Cornstarch	½ c	½ oz	

Trim and cut pork into 1-inch or bite-size cubes. Place cubes in steam-jacketed kettle. Add vinegar, water, salt, pepper, and garlic powder. Bring to a boil, then lower heat and simmer until a small amount of liquid is left. Drain and save stock for possible later use. (Add to any remaining pork cubes and sauce, reheat and serve over steamed rice.) Saute cooked pork in hot, melted shortening until brown. Place in chafing dishes and cover lightly with Sweet and Sour Sauce.

To make sauce, combine all ingredients except cornstarch; heat. Add cornstarch to thicken. Test for taste. Adjust ingredients for typical sweet-sour flavor.

Plan on 8–10 oz of meat per person.

Notes:

BARRY B. HUTCHINGS F.H.C.F.A., Director of Food Service, Swedish Medical Center, Craig Hospital, Englewood, Colorado

1980	President, American Society of Hospital Food Service Administrators (ASHFSA)
1980	General Foods Grand Champion Salad Award
1974–1976	Kraft Foods Finalist Salad Award

Barry Hutchings started his college education intending to become a doctor. However, after four years of premed, he changed his career objective to business administrator. Mr. Hutchings is a strong believer in people. In fact, he states, "We are not in the food business—but the people business. It is people we serve and people we motivate to give service." His constant monitoring of his food service demonstrates his commitment to his concept. He constantly receives a 92 percent to 96 percent satisfaction rating in patient care audits.

Mr. Hutchings is currently involved in consulting with rural hospitals in Colorado. Mr. Hutchings has written numerous articles. As if this active career in food service were not enough, he devotes any "spare" time to the stage, appearing in numerous musical and dramatic productions.

Hot and Cold Salad
APPETIZER

Ingredients:	50 portions	6 portions	___portions
Lime Jello	1½ lb	1 pkg, large	
Water, hot	3½ qt	1½ c	
Mayonnaise	3 c	¼ c	
Avocados, diced	2 lb	¼ c	
Lemon juice	1½ c	½ c	
Pineapple, chunks, drained	2 lb	½ c	
Bean sprouts, drained	2 lb	½ c	
Pimiento, chopped	2 c	4 T	
Onion, finely grated	2 t	½ t	
French dressing	3 c	½ c	
Sour cream	3 c	½ c	
Tabasco	15 drops	4 drops	

Dissolve Jello in hot water; let cool. Blend in mayonnaise. Add avocados that have been covered with lemon juice, pineapple chunks, bean sprouts, pimiento, and onion. Chill until set. Mix French dressing, sour cream, and Tabasco. Cut Jello into squares, place on lettuce, garnish with French dressing mixture.

Notes:

PAUL HYSEN   President, Hysen & Associates, Inc., Novi, Michigan

1980   President, Food Consultants Society International
1979   Design Award for St. Lawrence Hospital, Lansing, Michigan, *Institutions/Volume Feeding* magazine's design competition
1977   Design Award for St. Mary's Hospital, Grand Rapids, Michigan, *Institutions/Volume Feeding* magazine's design competition

Paul Hysen has over twenty-three years experience in planning, designing, and implementing foodservice facilities. His firm provides professional consulting services to all facets of the foodservice industry. The firm's services include preliminary evaluation and analysis, feasibility studies, program development, facility engineering, and implementation assistance. At any given time, the firm has from sixty to eighty active projects located in over twenty states. Mr. Hysen is responsible for marketing activities and the Management Advisory Services Group, as well as for overall corporate direction.

Mr. Hysen is a past president of the Foodservice Consultants Society International. He is a member of the Society for Food Service Management, the American Society for Hospital Food Service Administrators, and the Society for the Advancement of Food Service Research. He is also a Professional Affiliate Member of the Michigan Society of Architects.

Cheese and Leek Soup

SOUP

Ingredients:	4 portions	6 portions	___portions
Leeks, finely chopped	2	3	
Celery stalks, finely chopped	2	3	
Onion, small, finely chopped	1	1½	
White pepper	¼ t	⅜ t	
Nutmeg	⅛ t	3/16 t	
Chicken stock (or canned clear broth)	4 c	6 c	
Cheddar cheese, sharp, grated	2 c	3 c	
Cornstarch	1 T	1½ T	
Egg yolk	1	1½	
Cream	½ c	¾ c	
Sherry	2–3 T	1 T	

Simmer first six ingredients for 30 minutes. Whisk in ¼ c of cheese at a time; mix well. Whisk cornstarch mixed with a small amount of water into soup mixture.

Whisk together egg yolk and cream, then slowly mix in 1 c of soup mixture to temper. Whisk back into remainder of soup. Do not boil or overheat because soup will separate. Add sherry before serving.

Notes:

Ratatouille
VEGETABLE

Ingredients:	6 portions	___ portions
Eggplant, diced ½" thick	1	
Tomatoes, quartered	8	
Zucchini, sliced ½" thick	4	
Green peppers, sliced into strips	4	
Olive oil	½ c	
Garlic cloves, finely chopped or crushed	2	
Shallots, finely chopped (or 1 medium onion)	2	
Salt and pepper	to taste	

Heat first five ingredients in 4-qt stock pot. Saute garlic and shallots. Stir into vegetables to coat with oil. Cover and simmer 1 hour; stir only occasionally so as not to mash vegetables. Season to taste.

Notes:

Chocolate Mousse
DESSERT

Ingredients:	6 portions	___portions
Chocolate, extra bittersweet	4 oz	
Egg yolks	4	
Butter, unsalted	4 T	
Egg whites, beaten until very stiff	4	

Melt chocolate in double boiler. Whisk egg yolks into chocolate. Whisk butter into chocolate mixture. Fold chocolate mixture gently into egg whites, and refrigerate to set.

Be careful not to overheat the chocolate in the double boiler. The mixture should not boil or even bubble.

Notes:

TONY JAEGER   Executive Vice-President, Restaurant Operations, Movenpick Enterprises, Geneva, Switzerland

Tony Jaeger is Executive Vice-President in charge of Restaurant Operations for Movenpick Enterprises. For the last twenty-two years, he has been responsible for the development of Movenpick Restaurants' concepts and products. His career in catering has covered cooking, patisserie, and service to the wine trade. He is a member of the American Management Association, Confrèrie de la Chaine des Rôtisseurs, and Confrèrie du Guillon.

Mr. Jaeger strives for innovations in the almost seventy Movenpick Restaurants by means of various creative conceptions tempered by common sense. He is utterly convinced that dynamic, flexible, high-class "à la carte catering" can succeed if a company's senior management allows the management to add a personal touch in its daily interpretation of the clearly defined concept and policies.

Among Mr. Jaeger's outstanding projects were the development and launching of the unique Movenpick Ice Cream in Switzerland and Germany in 1972, which made Movenpick the trendsetter in this particular product area and inspired many imitators in the field; and the streamlining and upgrading of "Baron de la Mouette," Movenpick's table gourmande, and the "Backstube," Movenpick's place for ovenfresh fruit tarts, quiches, gratins, and so on.

Ingredients:	6 portions	___portions
Butter, cooking	3 oz	
Onions, finely chopped	1 oz	
Shrimp, peeled	1 lb 10 oz	
Salt	to taste	
Pepper	to taste	
Cognac (brandy)	2 fl oz	
Tomatoes, peeled, cut into small cubes	10 oz	
Garlic, crushed	1 T	
Oregano	to taste	
Rosemary	to taste	
Thyme	to taste	
Cream	1 pt	
Pernod	2 fl oz	

Scampi Miracle

ENTREE

Heat the butter in a large frying pan. Add chopped onions and fry gently for 5 minutes until transparent. Add shrimp, continue frying for 3 minutes, and season with salt and pepper. Add brandy and set alight. Remove shrimp from pan, put them into a serving dish, and keep them warm.

In the same pan, put the tomato cubes, garlic, oregano, rosemary, thyme, salt, and pepper, as well as the cream. Bring to a boil and then keep simmering until the sauce is reduced by one third. Return the shrimp to the sauce, add the Pernod, bring to a boil again, and then pour into the serving dish.

Notes:

FAISAL A. KAUD Assistant Administrator, Dietary, Environmental Services, and Materials Management, University of Wisconsin Hospital and Clinic, Madison, Wisconsin.

> 1982 The Distinguished ASHFSA Award
> 1981 IFMA SILVER PLATE AWARD
> 1979 President, American Society of Hospital Food Service Administrators

In 1970, at the University of Wisconsin Medical Center, Faisal A. Kaud implemented an innovative chilled food system with mobile refrigerated carts equipped with microwave ovens and beverage facilities. After thorough and comprehensive planning, the functions of the ingredient room were organized and the activities of the hot and cold food production were centralized in order to deliver efficient patient and nonpatient food services. Mr. Kaud's extensive background in the management of commercial food services, including airline catering, has greatly contributed to his enhancing of effective management practices, the menu, food quality, service, and marketing techniques. The nonpatient cafeteria, which serves 5000 customers each weekday, has become significant competition for a nationally franchised fast food facility located one block from the hospital and for the campus-wide dining service.

In 1979, Mr. Kaud planned the foodservice activity for a new 555-bed teaching hospital in a modern clinical science center, housing the University of Wisconsin Medical School, School of Nursing, the Wisconsin Clinical Cancer Center, and other university research facilities. Mr. Kaud, with his competent staff of managers, dietitians, office clerks, and foodservice workers, met a formidable challenge by serving breakfast to 312 patients in the old facility and then, immediately after the physical move, resuming patient nourishment service at 10:00 a.m. at the new hospital. In addition, every patient was visited by the clinical dietetic staff that morning.

Mr. Kaud received a B.S. degree from the Cornell School of Hotel and Restaurant Administration. He earned his master's degree in health services administration and an advanced program certificate in health care financial planning and control from the University of Wisconsin at Madison.

Cheese Soufflé
ENTREE

Ingredients:	48 portions	6 portions	___portions
Butter (or margarine)	1½ c	1½ oz	
Flour	2½ c	1¼ oz	
Milk, hot	7 c	7 oz	
Salt	1 T	⅓ t	
American cheese, grated	3 qt	6 oz	
Egg yolks, slightly beaten	50	6	
Egg whites	50	6	
Cream of tartar	3½ t	⅓ oz	

Melt the butter, add flour, and blend. Add hot milk and whip until smooth. Season with salt. Add grated cheese and stir until melted. Add slightly beaten egg yolks, first adding a portion of the hot mixture to the yolks. Cool.

Whip egg whites with cream of tartar until they are stiff but not dry. Fold into cool mixture. Grease *only* the bottoms of two 2-inch full-size pans (or regular soufflé pan for 6-portion size). Divide soufflé mixture into the pans. Place the pans in a tray containing a small amount of water. Bake in convection oven at 300° until set. Keep fan on *low*. For doneness, test with a silver knife; knife must come out clean.

Notes:

JOHN H. KONIARES Owner/Operator, Kernwood at Lynnfield, Lynnfield, Massachusetts

1976 IFMA Silver Plate Award

John Koniares, the son of a well-known restaurateur, has carried on the family tradition for more than forty years. A noted authority in restaurant sanitation, Mr. Konaires also employs the most modern energy-saving equipment in his restaurant.

Mr. Koniares has been active as a director of the Massachusetts Restaurant Association and the National Restaurant Association, as well as an advisor to the culinary arts departments at Northeastern Metropolitan Regional Vocational School and at Johnson and Wales College. He was a member of the prestigious survey team for the 1974 U.S. Air Force Hennessy Award and was the Massachusetts Restaurant Association's "Restaurateur of the Year" in 1977. An avid yachtsman and deep-sea fisherman, Mr. Koniares belongs to sporting clubs in both the Northeast and Florida. He also serves as a bank director and a hospital trustee in Malden, Massachusetts.

Spaghetti Carbonara
ENTREE

Ingredients:	6 portions	___portions
Bacon, sliced	½ lb	
Spaghetti, imported (Spigadora)	1 lb	
Eggs, large	6	
Parmesan cheese, imported, grated	1 c	

Chop the bacon and fry it. Hold it in the hot bacon fat. Boil the spaghetti until al dente; drain. Pour hot bacon and bacon fat over spaghetti. Toss. Add raw eggs. Toss again. Add Parmesan cheese. Toss again and serve.

Notes:

GEORGE LANG   President, The George Lang Corporation, New York, New York

George Lang is a man of many parts—chef, food consultant, concert violinist, and author. He is perhaps best summed up by Lin Yutang's description of him as "the poet of the possible." Mr. Lang was born in Hungary and came to the United States after completing his studies in Hungary, Austria, and Italy. Since that time he has worked as a chef-saucier and chef-decorateur in many hotels and restaurants, including the Plaza under the direction of Chef Gatti; operated a "wedding factory" in the Bowery; arranged a state dinner for Queen Elizabeth at the Waldorf-Astoria and a Jeffersonian dinner at the Savoy in London; run the famous Four Seasons Restaurant in New York City; participated in the development of many of the Restaurant Associates restaurants and projects; reformulated airline cuisine for several international carriers; and lectured on international project development at Cornell University. The phrase most often heard in connection with George Lang is "the expert's expert," and it is this expertise that won him the Hotelman Award in 1975.

George Lang heads The George Lang Corporation, which, according to a recent issue of *Hospitality Magazine*, is "the only think-tank in the food and beverage industry." The corporation's services include a total analysis of clients' needs, followed by a totally integrated merchandising plan through realistic interpretation of the analysis. The clients range from international hotel chains to restaurants, resorts, cruise ships, airlines, convention centers, and governments with highly specialized problems, often not in the food and beverage area.

In a switch from creative business to creative writing, Mr. Lang parlayed his gastronomic lore into the book *The Cuisine of Hungary* (Atheneum, 1971), a cultural-culinary history regarded as the definitive book on the subject. He was consultant for several of the Time-Life *Foods of the World* cookbooks, a contributor to *The Great Cooks' Cookbook* (Doubleday, 1974), and an advisor on *The Four Seasons Cookbook* and the delightful *Chinese Gastronomy* by the Lin family. His articles on food and wine, architecture, design, calligraphy, Renaissance history, and other subjects have appeared in various national magazines. The fifteenth edition (1974) of the *Encyclopedia Britannica* has two major pieces by him on "Restaurants" and "Gastronomy," the latter being, according to his lead sentence, "the art of selecting, preparing, serving, and enjoying fine food." It is his mastery of this art, among others, that has enabled George Lang to achieve a unique position in the hospitality industry as an international tastemaker of considerable reputation and renown.

The New Yorker has described George Lang as combining "the head of a scientist with the heart of an artist, the ingenuity of a used car salesman with the energy of a marathon runner."

Source: Biography and recipe reprinted with the author's permission from *The Great Cooks' Cookbook* (Chicago: Ferguson/Doubleday, 1974).

Potée Paysanne SOUP

Ingredients:	6 portions	___portions
Pork knuckles, split in half	2	
Salt pork, lean	½ lb	
Beef flank	3–4 lb	
Savoy cabbage, small head, cored and sliced	1	
Carrots, whole, peeled	3	
Turnips, small, peeled and halved	2	
Leeks, large, trimmed, washed, and split lengthwise	2	
Garlic sausage, fresh,	1 ft	
Potatoes, whole, peeled	3–4	
Bouquet garni (parsley, thyme, bay leaf)	1	

Bring pork knuckles, salt pork, and beef almost to the simmering point in 2½ qt of water. Delay simmering by adding ½ c of cold water two or three times to bring most of the impurities to the top so they can be skimmed. Then cook about 1½ hours, or until meat is almost tender. Remove meat and set aside. Add all the vegetables to the broth, except the potatoes, and cook 20 minutes longer. Add the sausage, potatoes, and bouquet garni. Add 2 c of water if the soup seems too thick. Cook 20 minutes more over medium heat. If all vegetables are properly done, that is, not overdone, turn the heat down to very low and simmer gently for a few minutes more. Skim off the fat.

There are many ways to make a fine presentation of Potée Paysanne. For example, arrange the salt pork, pigs' knuckles, sausage, and beef in a pile on a serving platter—possibly one that is lined with a wooden board—and surround them with the large vegetables: potatoes, carrots, and leeks. The soup, including the Savoy cabbage, is served in a soup tureen and accompanied by toasted French bread or any good crusty one.

If you happen to be a native of any one of certain European countries, you may want to add a much larger piece of salt pork to the potée. If it's not completely fresh, boil it separately first for a couple of minutes and discard the water; it's then ready to use. In any case, be sure to skim the fat from the soup before serving it. The sausage can be Italian, German, Hungarian, or Polish, as long as it's not smoked. Depending on the type you choose, it will need a little more or a little less cooking time. You may also use other vegetables, such as whole string beans. Other ingredients can be added too, such as smoked pork shoulder or even preserved goose. You may add garlic if you are fond of it.

The most important thing to remember about potées is that they must be cooked as slowly as possible; the water should always be kept at a simmer.

In France, the family of potées is a large one, and, in fact, no single source agrees with another on the precise definition. A potée can be loosely described as a soup, meat, and vegetable dish, the ingredients of which have been cooked together in a special pot and which is never pureed, creamed, or thickened with anything. Every nation has a dish like it—from the Chinese hot pot to the New England boiled dinner. Actually, a pot au feu is a sort of potée, although some Gallic purists might argue the point. Probably the most famous potée comes from Auvergne and contains almost anything that is found in the local kitchens, including pickled pork and many kinds of sausages.

Notes:

STUART LEVIN   Owner/Operator, Top of the Park Restaurant, New York, New York

1972 IFMA Silver Plate Award

"The sheer pleasure of dining out," in the opinion of Mr. Levin, author, lecturer, world traveler, and former owner of America's most famous restaurant, Le Pavillon, "will linger with the American public for as long as time immemorial, whether it be at moderately priced restaurants or inexpensive restaurants, or dining luxuriously on an aircraft." Mr. Levin has catered for five United States presidents, five other heads of state, and members of the royal family of England. He has lectured extensively on the subject of fine dining at Cornell University, Harvard University, and Boston University, as well as at the National Hotel and Restaurant Show in New York City.

Mr. Levin became a restaurateur in 1951, following service in the Quartermaster Corps in Japan on the island of Eta Jima, where he ran an Officers' Club. Later, he joined Restaurant Associates, which was just beginning to grow at the time. He was part of the team that built the well-known Forum of the Twelve Caesars and the posh Four Seasons.

The parties and dinners he has catered include a gastronomical delight for newlyweds aboard a helicopter flying from atop the Pan Am Building to Kennedy Airport and a kitchen party for Princess Margaret, where 250 guests selected and sauteed their own live trout under his supervision. In the last ten years, Mr. Levin has journeyed to Uganda, Kenya, Morocco, France, England, Spain, Italy, Austria, Denmark, Sweden, Germany, as the Caribbean, and Venezuela, as well as throughout the United States, to study international cuisine. Mr. Levin is an officer or board member of the New York State Restaurant Association, Continental Restaurants of America, the Culinary Institute of America, New York City's Mayor's Midtown Citizens Committee, and the New York Convention and Visitors Bureau.

Ingredients:	50 portions	___portions
Black Russian pumpernickel, approx. 15 × 8 × 6 inches	1 loaf	
Butter, unsalted	⅛ lb	
Onions, large white, very thinly sliced	2	
Capers, chopped	½ c	
Smoked salmon, thinly sliced	1 lb	
Parsley, fresh	garnish	

Tiny Smoked Salmon Sandwiches in Black Bread

APPETIZER

Preparing the Bread. Cut off top part of pumpernickel loaf, keeping it in one piece. With a very sharp thin knife, make an incision in the bread about ½ inch from the crust. Then cut completely around the loaf so that the inside of the bread has been cut away from the crust. Cut deep, but not all the way through to the bottom of the loaf. When that is done, make a series of five cuts in the side of the loaf (through the crust) so that the bread is loosened from the loaf. Remove the bread from the loaf. Make four complete slices of bread from the bread that you have just taken out of the loaf.

Making Sandwiches. Spread the butter on the four slices of bread. On *two* of the slices of bread, place the sliced onion, covering the entire surface. Then sprinkle the chopped capers over the onions. Next, place the smoked salmon over the capers. Cover the smoked salmon with the other slices of bread, buttered side down. With a sharp knife, cut small triangular sandwiches.

Assembling the Loaf. Place the first layer of sandwiches in the hollow loaf, alternating the triangles so that they fit neatly on the bottom. Place the second layer on top of the first in the same manner. Put a toothpick in each sandwich, with a little of the toothpick sticking out of the sandwich so that people can pick it up easily. Place the assembled loaf on a tray and garnish with large pieces of parsley around the bottom of the loaf. Put the top of the loaf against the back of the bread so that people see it as a whole loaf.

Notes:

LEON LIANIDES Owner/Operator, The Coach House, New York City, New York

1980 Fine Dining Hall of Fame, *Nation's Restaurant News*

For thirty-two years, Mr. Lianides has operated a restaurant that cannot be directly compared with any other in the country. The Coach House serves a unique blend of the marvelous dishes of the past and the best of contemporary "crossroads of the world" dishes. The food quality at the Coach House is rarely equaled even in New York City. The food served is no less extraordinary than are the floral arrangements and the rich collection of nineteenth century paintings that grace this intown country inn.

A native of Corfu, Greece, Leon Lianides came to New York to become an industrial engineer. After a short term as an engineer, the young man bought a charming tearoom that once was the coachhouse and stable of the John Wanamaker estate in Greenwich Village. The tearoom was converted into a fine restaurant, and the young Lianides spent summers studying cuisine in France.

The Coach House Seafood à la Méditerranée

ENTREE

Ingredients:	4 portions	___portions
Shrimp, large	12	
Clams, cherrystone	12	
Lobster tails, ½ pound	4	
Olive oil	½ c	
Garlic cloves, finely minced	4	
White wine, dry (preferably chablis)	¾ c	
Plum tomatoes, canned, drained	2 c	
Bay leaves	2	
Oregano	½ t	
Salt and pepper	to taste	
Parsley, finely chopped	2 T	

Using a sharp pointed scissors, slit the shells of the shrimp, but do not remove them. Devein the shrimp, wash them, and dry them. Scrub the clams and dry them. Do not open the shells. Wash and dry the lobster tails. Cut them, unshelled, into 1-inch pieces.

In a large deep skillet, heat the olive oil. Add the minced garlic and cook over low heat for 1 minute, taking care that it does not brown. Add the prepared shrimp, clams, and lobster tails; cook them for 3 minutes. Pour in heated dry white wine, increase the heat, and cook the ingredients briskly for 3 minutes more. Then stir in plum tomatoes, and add bay leaves, oregano, and salt and freshly ground black pepper to taste. Reduce the heat to moderate, cover the pan, and continue cooking for 10–12 minutes, or until the clam shells open. Remove the bay leaves. Transfer the seafood with its sauce to a heated serving dish, and sprinkle chopped parsley over it. Serve the Seafood à la Méditerranée with steamed rice.

Notes:

The Coach House Bread and Butter Pudding
DESSERT

Ingredients:	10 portions	___portions
French bread, thin slices	12	
Butter	as needed	
Eggs, whole	5	
Egg yolks	4	
Sugar	1 c	
Salt	⅛ t	
Milk	4 c	
Heavy cream	1 c	
Vanilla extract	1 t	
Sugar, confectioners'	to top	

Trim the crusts from the bread, and butter the slices on one side. Beat together the eggs, egg yolks, sugar, and salt until the dry ingredients are thoroughly incorporated. In a saucepan, combine the milk and cream. Scald them and then blend the heated liquids very gradually into the egg mixture. Stir in the vanilla extract. Arrange the slices of bread, buttered sides up, in a 2-quart baking dish and strain the custard mixture over them. Set the dish in a roasting pan filled with hot water to a depth of about 1 inch. Bake the pudding in a 350° preheated oven for 45 minutes, or until a knife inserted in the center of the pudding is withdrawn clean. Sprinkle the pudding generously with confectioners' sugar and glaze it under a hot broiler. At the Coach House, this elegant pudding is served with a puree of fresh raspberries.

Notes:

G. E. LIVINGSTON Ph.D., President, Food Science Associates, Inc., Dobbs Ferry, New York

    1980–Present   President, The Society for Foodservice Systems

Dr. Livingston holds a B.A. degree in chemistry from New York University and M.S. and Ph.D. degrees in food technology from the University of Massachusetts. Dr. Livingston's career has combined teaching and research in food science and food service with industrial, consulting, and government service.

From 1951 to 1953, Dr. Livingston was assistant professor and, from 1953 to 1959, associate professor of food technology at the University of Massachusetts. In 1954, he served as visiting professor at Laval University. From 1966 through 1972, he was adjunct professor of public health nutrition at Columbia University, where he directed the food science program and a special training program in public health nutrition. Since 1973, Dr. Livingston has been adjunct professor in the Department of Nutrition and Dietetics of the Pratt Institute in Brooklyn, New York, and also, since 1978, adjunct professor in the Department of Home Economics and Nutrition of New York University. From 1959 to 1962, Dr. Livingston served as a research supervisor for the Continental Baking Company. From 1962 to 1965, he was the manager of the institutional products department of Morton Frozen Foods.

Dr. Livingston founded Food Science Associates in 1956 in Amherst, Massachusetts. In 1959, the firm was moved to Rye, New York, and, in 1972, to its present location in Dobbs Ferry. Dr. Livingston is the author of about 100 research and technical publications, including several book chapters. He holds two federal patents. He is the coauthor and coeditor of *Food Service Systems: Analysis, Design and Implementation* published by Academic Press. Dr. Livingston is a consultant to the U.S. Army Natick Research and Development Command, chairman of the Food and Nutrition Committee of the American Health Foundation, and coeditor of the *Journal of Food Service Systems.*

Poached Salmon with Sauce Mousseline "Belle Polonaise"
ENTREE

Ingredients:	8 portions	6 portions	___ portions
Salmon, pieces or steaks	8	6	
Heavy cream	8 oz	6 oz	
Mayonnaise	8 oz	6 oz	
Horseradish, white, grated	2 T	4½ t	
Capers	½ oz	½ oz	

Poach salmon in court bouillon. Whip heavy cream until stiff (approximately half a minute). Add mayonnaise to whipped cream, fold and whip. Add horseradish, whip for a few seconds. Add capers.

The sauce can be chilled and served cold on cold salmon or heated gently in a double boiler and served with the fresh poached salmon. The recipe yields approximately 16 oz of sauce; serve about 2 oz per person.

Notes:

GARRETT DAWSON "SONNY" LOOK President, Look's Sir-Loin House, Inc., Houston, Texas

1977	Diplomat Award, National Institute of the Food Service Industry
1968	IFMA SILVER PLATE AWARD
1955	Outstanding Restaurateur of Texas
1954	Outstanding Restaurateur of Houston

"Sonny" Look, a restaurateur since his first opening in 1946, operates his fine restaurants and several Ramada Inns. His first establishment with only forty-six seats became so famous for serving families, athletes, and newspaper people that Mr. Look was forced to expand. His company became a premier catering firm for Texas, Louisiana, and Mississippi. The Sir-Loin Inn in Houston is one of American's largest restaurants, seating 1,600 in a one-level operation.

A native of Brenham, Texas, and a graduate of the University of Houston, Mr. Look served for fourteen years as a director of the National Restaurant Association. He helped to create the Houston Convention and Visitors Bureau and the Texas Tourist Bureau. His personal interests have led him to close involvement with the Houston Livestock Show and Rodeo and the Houston Farm and Ranch Club.

Barbecued Shrimp
ENTREE

Ingredients:	4 portions	___portions
Shrimp, jumbo size	12	
Flour	½ c	
Egg	1	
Sweet milk	1 c	
Salt and pepper	to taste	
Cracker crumbs, fine	1 c	
Cooking oil	1 qt	
Hickory House Smoke Sauce	1 pt	

Peel and devein the shrimp, leaving shell on tails. Wash and clean them thoroughly. Dust shrimp with flour. Break egg in bowl; beat well. Add milk, and salt and pepper to taste. Dip shrimp in egg and milk then roll in fine cracker crumbs.

Pour oil in deep saucepan and heat to 350°. Drop in shrimp and fry for 4 minutes to seal moisture in shrimp. Remove shrimp from deep fat and saturate in Hickory House Smoke Sauce. Put shrimp in shallow pan and place under broiler or in oven for 5 minutes, or until the shell or the tails becomes brown and crisp. Serve a mild barbecue sauce with shrimp.

Notes:

Golden Mushroom "Sir-Loin" Beef Tips
ENTREE

Ingredients:	8 portions	___portions
Beef, cut in 1-inch cubes	2 lb	
Butter (or margarine)	¼ c	
Sherry	¾ c	
Garlic clove, minced	1	
Campbell's Golden Mushroom Soup	2 cans	
Onions or shallots, finely chopped	1 T	
Water	½ c	

In a skillet, brown the beef in butter. Add the remaining ingredients. Cover and cook over low heat for 2 hours, or until tender. Stir occasionally. Serve over noodles.

Notes:

"Texas" Chili
ENTREE

Ingredients:	32 portions	___portions
Ground beef, 10% fat	20 lb	
Onions, yellow, finely diced	2	
Chili powder	½ lb	
Chili pods	2 lb	
Cayenne pepper	1 T	
Garlic powder	3 T	
Tomato puree	2 gal	
Salt and pepper	to taste	

Use a large stew pot to saute the ground beef. When meat is ⅓ done, add onions, chili powder, chili pods, cayenne pepper, and garlic powder. Simmer until ¾ done; then add tomato puree, plus salt and pepper. Cook until meat is tender.

Notes:

Tudie's Chicken Dinner
ENTREE

Ingredients:	4 portions	___portions
Chicken, 2 to 2½ lb, cut up	1	
Salt and pepper	to taste	
Butter, melted	⅓ c	
Cream of celery soup	1 can	
Cream of mushroom soup	1 can	
Dry white wine	½ c	
Rice, cooked	3 c	
Parsley, finely chopped	¼ c	

Wash chicken and pat dry. Sprinkle pieces with salt and pepper. Brown chicken on all sides in butter. Pour off excess fat. Add canned soups and wine. Stir to blend. Cover and simmer for 40–45 minutes, or until the chicken is tender.

Place hot rice on a large platter; pour the chicken and gravy over rice. Garnish with chopped parsley. Serve the chicken with fruit salad or cranberry sauce, a green vegetable, and dessert to complete the dinner.

Notes:

BEVERLY M. LOWE R.D., C.F.E., Director of Food Services, Hampton City Schools, Hampton, Virginia

1982	IVY AWARD OF DISTINCTION
1980–1982	Vice President, IFSEA
1974–1980	Secretary, IFSEA
1979	Distinguished Service Citation, IFSEA
1978	IFMA SILVER PLATE AWARD
1965	Outstanding Young Woman of America

Beverly Lowe has distinguished herself by garnering two dozen industry, civic, and academic awards. These are in recognition of her vast contributions to school food service and community affairs and of her unstinting service on the IFSEA board and the advisory boards of three college hotel, restaurant, and institutional education programs.

Pecan Pie
DESSERT

Ingredients:	6–9 portions	___portions
Eggs	3	
Sugar	¼ c	
Karo corn syrup (Blue Label)	1 c	
Vanilla	1 T	
Butter, melted	4 T	
Salt	¼ t	
Pecan meats, broken into large pieces	1 c	
Pie shell, unbaked	1	

Beat eggs slightly; add sugar, corn syrup, vanilla, melted butter, and salt. Blend well. Add pecans. Pour mixture into unbaked pie shell. Bake at 325° for 1 hour, or until inserted knife blade comes out clean.

Notes:

Spoon Bread

Ingredients:	6 portions	___portions
Water, boiling	1 c	
Corn meal, white	½ c	
Milk	½ c	
Salt	½ t	
Baking powder	1½ t	
Butter, soft	1 T	
Sugar	2 T	
Eggs, well beaten	2	

Pour boiling water over corn meal. Beat in remaining ingredients. Pour into buttered 1-quart casserole or baking dish. Bake at 400° for 20–25 minutes until just set. Serve piping hot with butter.

Notes:

KENNETH T. G. LUM   President and General Manager, Princess Pauahi Coffee Shop Restaurant, Royal Hawaiian Center, Honolulu, Hawaii

1975–1978   IFSEA Board of Directors

Kenneth Lum's Princess Pauahi Coffee Shop Restaurant interfaces the concepts and practices of fine dining with many practical and economical applications of menu planning and pricing. He seeks to provide the patrons of his restaurant with a high-quality environment at the lowest possible prices.

Pineapple Flambé
DESSERT

Ingredients:	10–12 portions	___portions
Pineapples, large (4–5 lb each), ripe	2	
Powdered sugar	sprinkle	
Kirsch liqueur	2 oz	
Cornstarch	dash	
Rum, 151 proof	2 oz	
Brandy, domestic	2 oz	
Ice cream	for 10	
Whipped cream	to garnish	

Clean and cut one of the pineapples into 1-inch cubes. Cut off the crown of the other pineapple about 2 inches from the top of the fruit. Using a grapefruit knife, carefully core out all the fruit from the pineapple. Be sure to avoid piercing the shell. Core out as close to the bottom of the shell as possible. The shell is ready to hold the cubes from the first pineapple, plus any extra from the second pineapple.

Place the pineapple cubes in a saucepan with a slight sprinkle of powdered sugar over the top. Add Kirsch liqueur. Saute over medium heat for no more than 3–5 minutes; add a pinch of cornstarch, just enough to form a very thin gravy. Remove from the stove and pour into the pineapple shell. Place the shell without the crown into a preheated oven and bake for 20 minutes at 375°.

Take the shell out of the oven and place it on a nice-sized platter. Pour 151-proof rum and domestic brandy over the top. Work a long-handled spoon into the fruit to allow some of the rum and brandy to seep down. Put a dash of brandy on the long-handled spoon, light it, and touch the shell for the fruit to flame. Toss lightly until flaming subsides. Some spillage of rum and brandy onto the platter will allow a little flaming on the side. Spoon over ice cream with a whipped cream border.

Notes:

TOM G. MARGITTAI   The Four Seasons Restaurant, New York, New York

>   1981 Fine Dining Hall of Fame, *Nation's Restaurant News*
>   1974 IVY AWARD OF DISTINCTION

Mr. Margittai, the son of a Hungarian industrialist, was born in Transylvania, Rumania. Educated in Western Europe, primarily in Switzerland, he came to the United States in 1950 and trained at the Waldorf-Astoria in New York City. He was the catering manager of the original Park Lane Hotel in New York City, and later Director of Sales and Catering of the Mark Hopkins Hotel in San Francisco when it was designated a "State Department Hotel" for state visits. Mr. Margittai received and catered to such dignitaries as the Shah of Iran, the King of Belgium, Khruschev, De Gaulle, and Chancellor Adenauer.

In 1962, he was singled out to join Restaurant Associates, then the most dynamic and innovative restaurant company operation in the United States. After handling a variety of assignments during the company's growth period, he was named Director of Operations for its Service Restaurant Division in 1969 and a Group Vice-President in 1970. In 1973, with Paul C. Kovi as partner, Mr. Margittai acquired the famed Four Seasons Restaurant from Restaurant Associates; it since has become an internationally known institution and a hallmark for quality.

Baked Red Snapper and Scallop Tartare

ENTREE

Ingredients:	6 portions	___portions
Scallops	1 lb	
Red snapper fillets, trimmed	2 lb	
Peppercorns, green, crushed	1 T	
Brandy	3 T	
Lemon juice	½ lemon	
Butter, softened to room temperature	½ c	
Salt	½ t	
Bread crumbs, white, fine	2–3 c	
Heavy cream	1½ c	
Peppercorns, green	¼ c	

Push the scallops, red snapper fillets, and crushed green peppercorns through the coarse blade of a food chopper. Add brandy, lemon juice, butter, and salt and mix lightly but thoroughly with fingers. Shape into rounds, each about ¾ inch thick. Roll in fine white bread crumbs.

Butter a large shallow ovenproof dish. Cover the bottom with heavy cream. Arrange the rounds in one layer and dot each with 8–10 green peppercorns. Bake in a preheated 300° oven for 20 minutes. Serve hot.

Notes:

Baked Fennel Parmesan
VEGETABLE

Ingredients:	6 portions	___portions
Fennel, large heads	3	
Milk	2 c	
Onion, yellow, sliced	1	
Salt	2 T	
Pepper, freshly ground	to taste	
Butter, salted	1 t	
Parmesan cheese, grated	¾ c	
Bread crumbs	2 T	
Olive oil	1 T	
Sour dough bread, large piece	1	

Trim the fennels, but leave them whole. Make a white stock in a deep kettle with the milk, onion, and 2 qt of water. Bring to boil. Add the fennel, and if necessary, cover with more water. Simmer 55 minutes, or until tender. Drain well; reserve ¼ c of the cooking liquid.

Trim, halve, and core the fennels. Arrange them overlapping in a buttered baking dish. Sprinkle with salt and pepper and dot with butter. Scatter cheese and bread crumbs on top and moisten around the sides with the reserved cooking liquid. Brown in a hot oven. Finish with a drizzle of olive oil. Serve with sour dough bread and fish baked in thin pastry leaves.

Notes:

ELLA BRENNAN MARTIN   Owner, Commander's Palace, New Orleans, Louisiana

    1982   Fine Dining Hall of Fame,
                Nation's Restaurant News
    1977   IVY AWARD OF DISTINCTION
    1973   IFMA SILVER PLATE AWARD
    1971   IVY AWARD OF DISTINCTION

    Ella Brennan Martin is the owner of Commander's Palace. Housed in a Victorian mansion that is a New Orleans landmark, the restaurant is located in the city's Garden District. This lovely area, filled with large beautiful homes (many antebellum) is the city's most prestigious residential area. The excellent food draws many patrons to Commander's Palace, but the warmth and friendliness also contribute. Explaining this atmosphere, which is part of her philosophy of the "Innkeeper's Obligation," Mrs. Martin notes, "People like to be treated on a familiar basis. When a customer walks in the door, we approach him or her as a guest in our home. Most people enjoy it when we talk to them, join them for a drink, get to know them and what they like."

    The Brennans insist on knowing their guests. And a stranger to Commander's Palace will certainly not be a stranger for long. Explains Mrs. Martin, "When one of us is working (which is most of the time), we go over the reservation sheet. If none of us knows a person, we go over and introduce ourselves. By the time a customer walks out the door, we know that person and we'll remember him or her the next time he or she comes in." The Brennan family has won every major award the industry has to offer.

Crab and Corn Bisque SOUP

Ingredients:	6 portions	___portions
Crabs, medium, hard-shelled	6	
Water	1½ qt	
Onions, medium, yellow, quartered	2	
Celery, coarsely chopped	6 stalks	
Liquid Crab Boil	2 T	
Green onions, chopped	1½ c	
Butter	½ c	
Flour	to thicken	
Thyme	pinch	
Garlic powder	1 t	
Salt	to taste	
Cayenne pepper	to taste	
Corn (12-oz cans)	2	
Cream, heavy	1 c	
Crabmeat, lump	1 lb	

Put first five ingredients in a heavy saucepan. Bring to a rolling boil, then reduce heat to a simmer. Cook stock for 3 hours. Add water as needed to keep volume at 1 quart.

In a 3-quart saucepan, saute green onions in butter until wilted. Add flour and seasonings; cook until flour begins to stick to pan. Add 1 quart of crab stock and simmer for 15 minutes. Add corn and simmer 15 minutes longer. Pour in cream, stirring well. Gently fold in lump crabmeat, being careful not to break the lumps. Remove from heat and let stand for 30 minutes. Reheat gently so that the lump crabmeat does not break up and the cream does not curdle. Serve immediately.

Notes:

DAN H. MATHEWS, JR. Regional General Manager, ARA Services, Inc., Birmingham, Michigan

From 1973 through 1981, Dan H. Mathews was the corporate food services administrator for the worldwide foodservice activities of the Chrysler Corporation. In this position, he was the corporate liaison with foodservice contractors and directly supervised activities at the world headquarters locations.

Mr. Mathews is a 1966 graduate in hotel, restaurant and institutional management from Michigan State University, a member of the board of directors of the Association for Food Service Management, and an adjunct instructor at Mercy College of Detroit. His early career included positions as operations manager for Marriott In-Flite at Chicago's O'Hare Airport, department head for Host International at Detroit's Metropolitan Airport, a partner in a private restaurant firm, and assistant regional manager for Cardinal Systems.

Supreme of Chicken with Wine in White Sauce
ENTREE

Ingredients:	4 portions	6 portions	___portions
Chicken breast fillets, boneless, skinless, medium	4	6	
Sage, rubbed	¼ t	⅜ t	
Lawry's Seasoned Salt	¼ t	⅜ t	
Lawry's Seasoned Pepper	¼ t	⅜ t	
Water, boiling	1½ c	2¼ c	
Chicken bouillon cube	1	1½	
Parsley flakes	1 t	1½ t	
Onion salt	¼ t	⅜ t	
Celery salt	¼ t	⅜ t	
Garlic powder	dash	dash	
White wine, dry	¾ c	1⅛ c	
White sauce, medium	2 c	3 c	
Green pepper and pimiento, diced	¼ c	⅜ c	
Pastry shells, toast points, or rice	for 4	for 6	
Paprika	dash	dash	
Watercress	garnish	garnish	

Sprinkle chicken breasts with sage and seasoned salt and pepper. Place in baking pan. Dissolve chicken bouillon in boiling water. Add parsley flakes, onion salt, celery salt, and garlic powder; pour over chicken. Add wine. Cover with foil. Bake at 350° for 45 minutes or until tender.

Remove chicken and dice into bite-size pieces. Add to medium white sauce, stirring constantly. Add green pepper and pimiento. Serve over pastry shells, toast points, or rice. Sprinkle with paprika and garnish with watercress.

Notes:

FRANCES E. McGLONE R.D., Director of Food Services and Nutrition Education Department, Oakland Unified School District, Oakland, California

1976   IFMA SILVER PLATE AWARD

Frances McGlone is vitally interested in working to improve child nutrition programs in all schools. She believes that children benefit from the meals served in their school cafeterias through improving their nutritional well-being, which will increase their ability to learn, and through learning good nutritional habits and how to make wise food choices.

Ms. McGlone is actively involved in several professional organizations, including the American Dietetic Association, the American School Food Service Association, and the International Gold and Silver Plate Society.

Cabbage Soup

SOUP

Ingredients:	6 portions	___ portions
Ground beef	1 lb	
Onion, thinly sliced, medium	1	
Celery, thinly sliced	½ c	
Tomatoes, canned, diced	1 lb	
Water	2 c	
Kidney beans, canned	1 lb	
Salt	1 t	
Chili powder	1 t	
Pepper	⅛ t	
Cabbage, thinly sliced	2 c	

Cook the ground beef until brown and crumbly (use either frying pan or microwave oven). Add onion and celery; saute about 5 minutes. Stir in tomatoes, water, beans, and seasonings. Cook until it comes to a boil. Add cabbage, cover, and cook until cabbage is tender (about 3 minutes).

Notes:

Date Dream Dessert

DESSERT

Ingredients:	16–18 portions	___ portions
Graham crackers	30	
Dates	1 lb	
Marshmallows	¾ lb	
Maraschino cherries, chopped	½ c	
Pineapple chunks, canned	½ c	
Walnuts, chopped	1½ c	
Unsweetened evaporated milk	1 c	

Crush graham crackers coarsely. Cut dates, marshmallows, cherries, and pineapple in small pieces. Mix together with chopped walnuts. Slowly add milk to make a moist, malleable mass. Divide the mixture in half, and form into 2 loaves. Wrap each loaf in aluminum foil or waxed paper. Put in freezer for several hours before serving. Slice when hard and serve with ice cream. Store loaves in freezer.

Notes:

Graham Cracker Torte
DESSERT

Ingredients:	6 portions	___portions
Graham crackers, finely ground	1¼ c	
Sugar	1 c	
Walnuts, chopped	¾ c	
Eggs	3	

Mix crackers, sugar, and walnuts. Beat eggs until thick. Add eggs to cracker mixture. Pour into a pie pan (9-inch). Bake in 350° preheated over for 25 minutes. Serve topped with whipped cream or ice cream.

Notes:

Mocha Cream-Filled Cake
DESSERT

Ingredients:	12–16 portions	___portions
Angel food cake, large, round	1	
Vanilla pudding (3-oz pkg)	1	
Coffee, instant	1 T	
Whipping cream	2 c	
Sugar	¼ c	
Nuts, chopped	garnish	

Using a sharp knife, cut center from angel food cake to make a shell. Cut 1¼ inch from sides and to 1¼ inch from bottom. Break removed cake into pieces. Set aside. Prepare vanilla pudding according to package directions. Add instant coffee. Cool. Beat whipping cream with sugar until stiff. Set aside ⅓ of the whipped cream. Fold the rest of the whipped cream into the pudding. Gently fold in the broken cake pieces; fill the cake shell. Spread the reserved whipped cream over the top and sides of the cake. Cake may be garnished with chopped nuts. Chill 4 hours before serving and keep refrigerated at all times.

Notes:

ALAN McLAREN Director of Food Services, Community Hospital of Indianapolis, Indianapolis, Indiana

1976 IFMA SILVER PLATE AWARD

A graduate of the University of Glasgow in Scotland, Mr. McLaren served as a food service officer in the Royal Air Force prior to immigrating to the United States in 1962. Mr. McLaren was formerly vice-president of a food service consulting company specializing in convenience foods systems, prior to which he had been Director of Food Services for the 1,000-bed Albert Einstein Medical Center in Philadelphia, Pennsylvania. He was a charter member of the American Society for Hospital Food Service Administrators, served on the first Board of Directors of that organization, and is a past president of the Hospital Food Directors Association. Mr. McLaren is one of only three hospital food service directors to be named in *Who's Who in Food Service 1974*.

Some of Mr. McLaren's recent efforts in Indianapolis have been directed to the hospital's expansion from 600 to 850 beds. A major part of this expansion is the new dining facilities, incorporating a unique cafeteria that combines the best features of scramble and conventional systems. Mr. McLaren developed this from his own original concept. For the past four years, he has been heavily involved in developing and implementing dietary computer systems. His hospital probably has more varied and extensive computer systems than any other non-University-affiliated hospital. In conjunction with his dietetic staff, he coauthored and edited a diet cookbook *Sunnyside Up—Diet Cooking the Hospital Way*, published in 1977 by Ashley Books, Incorporated. All of the included recipes have been tested and many are incorporated in his menus for patients.

Over the last three years, Mr. McLaren has been a featured speaker at several seminars and workshops sponsored by various organizations on dietary computer systems. One such appearance was as guest lecturer for the masters degree program in Public Health Administration at Indiana University Medical School, and another was at a series of food service seminars at Purdue University.

Scottish Mince 'n Tatties
ENTREE

Ingredients:	4 portions	___portions
Ground beef, lean	1 lb	
Water	½ pt	
Carrots, roughly chopped	½ lb	
Onions, roughly chopped	2 oz	
Celery, roughly chopped	4 oz	
Turnip, roughly chopped	½ lb	
Salt and pepper	to taste	
Cornstarch	1 T	
Gravy browning	1 T	
Seasoned mashed potatoes	1 lb	

Place ground beef and water in a saucepan and bring to a slow boil, stirring to separate meat. Add vegetables and seasoning; cover and simmer for ½ hour. In a dish, stir cornstarch and gravy browning with just enough water to make a smooth paste. Add this to meat mixture, stirring constantly until thoroughly mixed and thickened. Recover and simmer for 5 minutes. Serve over a nest of mashed potatoes for a hearty meal.

This recipe may be prepared ahead for later reheating in oven or microwave. Place meat mixture, when cooked, in a casserole dish and cover with the mashed potatoes.

Notes:

MICHAEL LEWIS MINOR Executive Chef/Vice-President, L. J. Minor Corporation, Cleveland, Ohio

The son of Dr. Lewis Minor, Michael Minor has continued the family tradition of professional excellence and expertise. Mr. Minor was valedictorian of his 1973 class at Greenbriar and served his apprenticeship under Herman Rusch, one of the world's leading culinarians. He then went on to serve as sous chef at the Williamsburg Inn and executive chef at the Deering Milliken Guest House before joining L. J. Minor Corporation.

Michael Minor won a grand prize and a first prize at North Carolina Culinary Shows and the Otto Gentsch Gold Medal from the Greenbriar Hotel, where he apprenticed. He was also a judge for three consecutive years at the U.S. Army Culinary Arts Salon at Fort Lee, Virginia.

Austrian Green Bean Soup

SOUP

Ingredients:	6 portions	___ portions
Butter	6 T	
Onions, small, diced	1 c	
Garlic, medium clove, minced	1	
Flour, all-purpose	¾ c	
Water, hot	2¼ qt	
Minor's Beef Base	3 T	
Pearled barley, medium	2 T	
Green beans, frozen (9-oz pkg), thawed	1	
Mushrooms, slices, drained (4-oz can)	1	
Sour cream	¼ c	

In a heavy 4-quart saucepan, melt butter over medium heat. Add onions and garlic, and saute until tender, but not browned. Blend in flour, stirring over low heat 1 to 2 minutes until bubbly and well blended. Remove from heat. Add hot water gradually, mixing well. Stir in Minor's Beef Base and barley. Bring to a boil. Reduce heat and simmer slowly for 50 minutes. Stir in thawed green beans and mushrooms. Return to simmering and cook for 20–25 minutes longer until beans and barley are tender. Beat 1 cup of hot soup gradually into the sour cream. While stirring the soup, slowly pour in the conditioned sour cream. Serve hot. (Makes 2 qt.)

Notes:

Cream of Tomato Soup

SOUP

Ingredients:	8–10 portions	___portions
Butter	6 T	
Onions, chopped	1 c	
Celery, chopped	½ c	
Flour, all-purpose	¾ c	
Water, hot	2¼ qt	
Minor's Chicken Base	3 T	
Tomato paste (6-oz can)	1	
Sugar	¼ c	
Salt	1 t	
Heavy cream, hot	⅔ c	

In a heavy saucepan, melt butter over medium heat. Add onions and celery, and saute until tender, but not browned. Blend in flour, stirring over low heat 1 to 2 minutes until bubbly and well blended. Remove from heat. Add hot water gradually mixing well. Stir in Minor's Chicken Base, tomato paste, sugar, and salt. Heat to boiling, stirring constantly. Boil and stir 1 minute. Reduce heat and simmer slowly for 10 minutes. Strain soup, discarding the vegetables. Return soup to saucepan. Add hot cream, mixing well. Serve hot. (Makes 2½ qt.)

Notes:

Lobster Thermidor
ENTREE

Ingredients:	4 portions	___portions
Butter	5 T	
Minor's Chicken Supreme Sauce Base (2⅝ oz)	1 jar	
Water, lukewarm	1½ c	
Cream, heavy	1½ c	
Minor's Lobster Base	2 t	
Mushrooms, slices, fresh	2½ c	
Onions or shallots, finely chopped	2 T	
Lobster meat, ½-inch pieces	2 c	
Cocktail sherry, pale, dry	¼ c	
Parmesan cheese, grated	4 T (rounded)	

In a saucepan, melt 2 T of the butter over medium heat. Blend in Minor's Chicken Supreme Sauce Base, using a wire whisk. Add water, heavy cream, and Minor's Lobster Base, mixing well. Heat to boiling, stirring constantly. Boil and stir 1 minute. Remove from heat and set aside.

In a skillet over medium heat, melt 3 T of the butter until bubbly. Add mushrooms and onions or shallots, and saute for 3 to 5 minutes. Add lobster meat and saute 2–3 minutes longer, or until hot. Combine sauteed mixture and juices with reserved cream sauce and dry sherry, mixing well. Divide into 4 buttered individual baking dishes or lobster shells. Sprinkle each serving with a rounded tablespoon of grated Parmesan cheese, and bake in a 400° oven for 10–15 minutes until bubbly hot and lightly browned. Serve hot. (Makes 4½ c.)

Notes:

DEARL MORRIS   Manager of Foodservices, Caterpillar Tractor Company, Peoria, Illinois

1978   IFMA Silver Plate Award

Dearl Morris is Manager of Foodservices for Caterpillar Tractor Company. He provides direction for their worldwide foodservice operation, which includes fifty-two domestic and eighteen foreign units serving over fourteen million customers annually. Mr. Morris is well known and respected throughout the foodservice industry for his forward thinking, his ability, and his working to improve the industry's image and professionalism. He has been a guest speaker and panelist at many industry and university seminars and meetings. He is a past president of the Society for Foodservice Management.

In addition to his many foodservice responsibilities, Mr. Morris has been active in trade associations and civic affairs. He is a former director of the Peoria and Heart of Illinois Restaurant Association and the chairman of their educational committee. He served as co-chairman for the Peoria Area United Way Campaign. He is a past conference leader for the National Alliance of Businessmen.

Ingredients:	40 portions	6 portions	___portions
Flour	12 oz	2 oz	
Paprika	1 oz	dash	
Salt	2 oz	⅛ t	
Liver, frozen, 4-oz slices	40	6	
Shortening (or bacon grease), melted	1½ lb	4 oz	
ONION GRAVY	1 gal	20 oz	
Onions, sliced, dried	4 lb	9½ oz	
Paprika	1½ lb	3½ oz	
Black pepper	2 oz	⅛ t	
Caramel color	4 oz	⅓ t	
Chicken mix	2 lb	5 oz	
Shortening	10 lb	1½ lb	
Flour	10 lb	1½ lb	
Salt	8 oz	1¼ oz	

Baked Liver with Onion Gravy

ENTREE

Mix flour, paprika, and salt together. Dip the frozen liver, one slice at a time, into cold water. Then coat with the flour mixture. Dredge each side through the warm fat and arrange on baking sheets. Bake at 350° until done. Arrange in steamtable pans and cover with Onion Gravy.

Notes:

Ingredients:	142 portions	___portions
American cheese	2 lb	
Paprika	1 oz	
Tomatoes, diced, #10 can	1 can	
Kluski noodles	10 lb	
Ground chuck	15 lb	
Salt	4 oz	
Black pepper	½ oz	
Bay leaves	⅛ oz	
Beef Crumbles TVP	24 oz	
Tomato puree, #10 can	½ can	
Brown gravy	4 gal	

Beef and Noodle Fiesta

ENTREE

Chop the cheese and paprika together and save for topping. Drain the tomatoes, reserving the juice. Cook the noodles until barely done. Cool in cold water and drain. Brown the ground beef, with salt, black pepper and crumbled bay leaves. Add Beef Crumbles TVP and stir. Add the tomato puree, tomato juice, and brown gravy. Simmer 20–30 minutes. Add drained noodles and stir. Put into 2-inch deep steamtable pans. Sprinkle the cheese and then the drained tomatoes on top. Place in 350° oven and heat until bubbling hot and the cheese melts.

Notes:

Braised Beef Stew with Vegetables
ENTREE

Ingredients:	192 portions	6 portions	___portions
Stew meat, diced, ½-inch cut	24 lb	12 oz	
Water (approx.)	24 lb	12 oz	
Salt	8 oz	¼ oz	
Black pepper	½ oz	dash	
Chicken base	1 lb	½ oz	
Caramel color	2 oz	¼ t	
Tomatoes, diced, #10 cans	2	6 oz	
Tomato puree, #10 can	1	3 oz	
Potatoes, frozen, stew cut	12 lb	6 oz	
Celery, large, diced	6 lb	3 oz	
Onions, large, chopped	9 lb	4½ oz	
Carrots, baby, frozen	8 lb	4 oz	
Flour	1½ lb	¾ oz	
Cornstarch	1½ lb	¾ oz	
Peas, frozen	4 lb	2 oz	

Bring meat to a boil in enough water to cover. Add salt, pepper, chicken base, and caramel color. Reduce heat to a simmer. Cover and cook for about 30 minutes. Stir in tomatoes and tomato puree and continue at a simmer until beef is almost done, stirring occasionally (approx. 60 minutes).

Add potatoes, celery, onions, and carrots and continue cooking until vegetables are done but still firm. Add water to cover if needed. Dissolve the flour and cornstarch in 3 qt of cold water. Add frozen peas and flour-cornstarch mixture. Return to simmer and stir until thickened. Serve.

Notes:

Creamed Pork Tips
ENTREE

Ingredients:	80 portions	6 portions	___portions
Pork loin ends, boneless, ½-inch pieces	16¼ lb	20 oz	
Salt	1 oz	⅛ t	
Black pepper	¼ oz	⅛ t	
Flour	1 lb	1½ oz	
Cornstarch	1 lb	1½ oz	
Mushrooms, stems and pieces, canned, including juice	2½ lb	3 oz	
Milk, warm	2½ gal	24 oz	

Add salt and pepper to pork and cook in suitable container until tender. Do not overcook. Mix flour and cornstarch together and dissolve in cold water (1 gal for 80 portions; 9 oz for 6 portions).

When meat is cooked add mushrooms with their juice; next add warm milk. Add flour-cornstarch mixture and continue cooking, stirring constantly, until mixture thickens and bubbles around edges. Adjust seasoning. Serve over biscuits or noodles.

Notes:

OTTO E. MUELLER   Assistant Vice-President (retired), Housing and Food Service Operations, Pennsylvania State University, University Park, Pennsylvania

    1978   Association of College and University Housing Officers Award
    1977   Ivy Award of Distinction

Otto Mueller, Retired Colonel AUS-QMC, followed his 1939 graduation from the University of Wisconsin, Madison, with nine years there in residence hall management, interrupted by four years of World War II military service. He retired from his position at Pennsylvania State University in 1978, after twenty-five years in charge of foodservice and housing operations, serving some 30,000 meals daily. Mr. Mueller's housing and foodservice operation at Penn State generated $28 million dollars in annual revenue. Over the years, he instituted a meal-hours system to cover the entire 7:00 a.m. to 10:00 p.m. range of classroom hours. He designed and implemented several new foodservice facilities on the campus, including one, the Terrace Room, offering a 24-hour "Dial a Menu" system. He was responsible for instituting special meal tickets for graduate students who were not on board contracts, a pizza shop, a take-out service, and a deli operation. It was Mr. Mueller's foresight that led him to set the pace for the fast-food type of service that is commonly available on university campuses throughout the country today.

Otto Mueller is a past president of the National Association of College and University Housing Officers and a member of the American Management Association, American College Personnel Association, and the higher education administration referral service management committee.

Chicken Velvet
ENTREE

Ingredients:	50 portions	___portions
Margarine	1 lb 4 oz	
Flour, all-purpose	10 oz	
Salt	2 T	
Pepper, white	¾ t	
Milk, dried skim	6 oz	
Water, cool	1½ qt	
Chicken stock (or chicken base, 4 oz, and water, 1¼ gal)	1¼ gal	
Half and half cream (*not* nondairy product)	2 c	
Homogenized milk	1¼ qt	
Chicken pieces, chopped	2 lb 8 oz	
Parsley, dried flakes	1 T	

Make a roux with melted margarine, flour, salt, and white pepper. In a steam kettle, combine dried milk with cool water to reconstitute. Add chicken stock or stock made with chicken base and water (if real chicken stock is not available). Heat to 185° (scalding). Slowly add the roux and cook until thickened and completely smooth. Add half and half cream, homogenized milk, and diced chicken pieces, and blend well. Turn off heat and let stand to develop flavor. Reheat just to serving temperature just before serving. *Do not boil.*

Notes:

Mostaccioli
ENTREE

Ingredients:	100 portions	___portions
Water, hot	2 gal	
Salt	4⅔ oz	
Salad oil	½ c	
Mostaccioli Rigati, as purchased	5 lb 4 oz	
Onion, dried, chopped, as purchased	3 oz	
Garlic, dried, chopped, as purchased	¼ t	
Ground beef	10 lb 8 oz	
Celery, diced, ½-inch pieces	1 lb 8 oz	
Mushrooms (#1 can)	1½ can	
Salt	5⅓ T	
Sugar, granulated	5⅓ T	
Pepper, black	1½ t	
Thyme, ground	1½ t	
Oregano, ground	2⅔ T	
Basil, ground	2½ t	
Bay leaves, crushed	5 leaves	
Tomatoes, conc. (#10 can)	1⅓ can	
Water, hot	1½ gal	
Beef base	5 oz	
Tomato paste (#10 can)	2 qt	
Parmesan cheese, grated	12 oz	

Measure 2 gal of water into a steam kettle, add 4⅔ oz of salt and salad oil. Bring to a full rolling boil. Add Mostaccioli Rigati, and boil for 4 minutes. (It should still be *firm*.) Drain. Rinse well in cold water and drain again.

Gather all ingredients before starting. Reconstitute dried onion and garlic. Put ground beef and reconstituted onion and garlic in a large steam kettle, and saute, using *low heat*, until pink color disappears (allow 20–30 minutes). Add celery and mushrooms. Add salt, sugar, black pepper, thyme, oregano, basil, and bay leaves and mix well. Add concentrated tomatoes, hot water, beef base, and tomato paste and stir, while heating, to be sure all ingredients are thoroughly mixed. Bring to a full boil, then reduce heat and simmer slowly for approximately 30 minutes. Add well-drained Mostaccioli Rigati to cooked sauce. Mix well. Dip into 4-inch insert pans (2¾ gal/pan). Top with Parmesan cheese. Bake at 350° for 45 minutes.

Notes:

Ingredients: ___*portions*

Sugar, granulated	54 lb
Cocoa, utility powder	13 lb 8 oz
Vanilla, concentrate	12 lb
Shortening, high-ratio	20 lb 4 oz
Salt, cooking	10 oz
Flour, cake	27 lb
Cinnamon, ground, blended	2 lb
Baking soda	1 lb 6 oz
Buttermilk powder	3 lb 8 oz
Eggs, dried, Sweet'n Lite	9 lb
Water	60 lb

Midnight Cakes

DESSERT

Cream together first 5 ingredients at #1 speed for 1 minute and then #3 speed for 6 minutes. Sift together dry ingredients into creamed mixture; alternate with water in small amounts until all dry ingredients have been worked in at #1 speed, 6–8 minutes. Add balance of water and mix in on #1 speed. Mix at #2 speed for 4 minutes to finish off. Bake in 23 8-lb sheets at 400° for 28–30 minutes, or, bake in 63 round layers at 350° for 40–45 minutes.

Notes:

JAMES A. NASSIKAS President and Managing Partner, The Stanford Court, San Francisco, California

        1974   Ivy Award of Distinction
        1970   Hall of Fame, *Hospitality* magazine

In December 1969, James A. Nassikas resigned from the Hotel Corporation of America, where he was Vice-President of Royal Sonesta Hotels, and assumed the presidency of the Stanford Court Management Company. Mr. Nassikas directed the day-to-day activities of the restoration work and the planning for and supervision of operations at The Stanford Court. He has made innovative contributions, carrying out his basic beliefs of what a hotel should be. Recently, Mr. Nassikas has withdrawn from the day-to-day business of running the hotel in order to devote himself to planning the future of the Stanford Court Management Company and to developing other projects in association with the Royal Street Corporation, a general partner.

Mr. Nassikas's philosophy is reflected in The Stanford Court itself, where he has sought to establish a "total hotel." He explains: "The true birth of a hotel takes place when it begins to assume its own personality and character. A hotel is born at the point where it begins to respond to the operating philosophies and principles from which it was conceptualized. If the operating philosophies and principles are designed to motivate a high standard of acceptance from guests, the hotel will reflect this design in its personality and character." James A. Nassikas believes that The Stanford Court completely fulfills his dream of what a hotel should be.

Mr. Nassikas is a member and/or director of thirty-one industry, civic, and social organizations. He was awarded the Diplome de l'Excellence Européene in Paris.

Ingredients:	20 portions	6 portions	____portions
Artichokes, whole, fresh	2 lb	10 oz	
Chicken stock	4 qt	1 qt 7 oz	
Hazelnuts	4 oz	1¼ oz	
Rice flour	8 oz	2½ oz	
Salt and pepper	to taste	to taste	
Cream, heavy	1 pt	4¾ oz	
Sherry	2 oz	⅔ oz	

Cream of Artichoke Soup with Crushed Hazelnuts
SOUP

Remove all leaves and stems from fresh large artichokes. Clean and scoop out artichokes, keeping bottoms or pedestals only. Poach artichoke bottoms for 1 hour in water. Remove from water. Place artichoke bottoms in chicken stock.

Roast hazelnuts in 250° oven until golden brown (approximately 10 minutes). Crush hazelnuts to a fine consistency. Place in chicken stock with artichoke bottoms. Simmer for ½ hour. Pass all ingredients through a chinacap.

Thicken soup with rice flour. Simmer for ¼ hour. Add salt and pepper. Add heavy cream. Finish with sherry wine to taste.

Notes:

Ingredients:	4 portions	6 portions	____portions
White wine, dry	¾ c	1⅛ c	
Lemon juice	1 t	1½ t	
Shallots, finely minced	2	3	
Butter, sweet, soft	6 T	9 T	
Fish demi-glace	½ c	¾ c	
Dungeness crab legs, freshly cooked	32	48	
Parsley, freshly chopped	1 T	1½ T	
Salt and white pepper	to taste	to taste	

Crab Legs Bercy
ENTREE

Reduce white wine and lemon juice in a saute pan over high heat. Lower heat and add minced shallots. Add soft butter, lump by lump, with care; this is the most sensitive phase in the preparation of a sauce Bercy. Let butter melt, swirling the pan constantly or stirring with a light wire whisk. Do not let butter separate. Add fish demi-glace, continuing to swirl or whisk. Add crab legs and finish with parsley, salt, and white pepper.

Notes:

Saltimbocca alla Romana
ENTREE

Ingredients:	4 portions	6 portions	___portions
Veal loin, white	8 oz	12 oz	
Prosciutto ham, thinly sliced	2 oz	3 oz	
Flour	2 T	3 T	
Butter, clarified	½ c	¾ c	
Olive oil	½ c	¾ c	
Sage leaves, dried	16	24	
White wine, dry	1 c	1½ c	

Slice white veal loin into 2-oz portions of meat. Pound each to ¼-inch thickness with the side of a heavy meat cleaver. Have a paper-thin slice (approx. ¼ oz) of prosciutto ham for each veal scallop. Cover one side of each veal scallop with slice of prosciutto. Turn each veal scallop and dust lightly with flour.

Heat equal amounts of clarified butter and olive oil in a saute pan. When sufficiently hot, but *not* brown, quickly place veal scallops in butter and oil, ham side down. Allow to saute on first side only for about 1 minute. Quickly turn and sprinkle crushed (not too fine) dry sage over the veal. Continue to saute for about 2 minutes. At precisely the point the veal scallops begin to shrink at the edges, add white wine (deglaze). Remove veal scallops to a warm platter. Finish pan juices with additional white wine. Pour juices over the veal and serve.

Notes:

Praline Ice Cream Pie
DESSERT

Ingredients:	6–8 portions	___portions
Brown sugar	4 oz	
Cream, heavy	½ c	
Butter, melted	1 oz	
Pecans, crushed	4 oz	
Vanilla extract	to taste	
Vanilla ice cream	1½ qt	
Meringue	topping	
Pie shell, 9-inch	1	

RUM SAUCE

Butter	3 oz	
Sugar	3 T	
Egg yolks	2	
Lemons, whole	2	
Rum	to taste	

First, prepare praline mixture. Heat brown sugar until it reaches the point where it begins to turn color. Mix with heavy cream and melted butter. Add crushed pecans and flavor with vanilla extract.

Then, whip vanilla ice cream. Mix with the praline mixture until well blended. Place praline ice cream in pie shell and top with meringue, as for lemon meringue pie. Place under broiler briefly, in order to color meringue to give baked appearance.

To make rum sauce, melt butter, add sugar, and blend with two beaten egg yolks over bain-marie. Add juice of two lemons and grate lemon rind into mixture. Blend with rum (Myer's Dark Jamaican Rum) to the desired flavor.

Notes:

ROBERT H. NELSON C.E.C., C.C.E., Chairman of the Board, Capitol Professional Chef's Association, Lansing, Michigan

Robert Nelson recently took a leave of absence from his career as a Certified Executive Chef to be Regional Supervisor for the American Culinary Federation Educational Institute's National Apprenticeship Training Program. Chef Nelson is a member of the American Academy of Chefs, Confrèrie de la Chaine des Rôtisseurs, Royal Order of the Carvers, and the Escoffier Society. He is Treasurer of the American Culinary Federation Educational Institute and a member of the board of trustees of that organization. Chef Nelson is also Regional Director of the American Culinary Federation for Minnesota and Michigan, Treasurer for the Lansing Chapter of the Michigan Restaurant Association, and on the advisory board for the Culinary Arts Program with the Lansing Board of Education.

Chef Nelson's talent and expertise have gained him many awards and prizes. He has won three grand prizes in the Kraft Foods contests, the grand prize at the Michigan Restaurant Association show in 1975, two first prizes at the National Restaurant Association show in 1978, and four first prizes at the 1979 National Hotel and Motel Association show. He also has won the Thomas Jefferson Award and the Escoffier Medal for Culinary Excellence.

Mushrooms à la Chef Robert

ENTREE

Ingredients:	12 portions	6 portions	___portions
Mushrooms, choice, large	24	12	
Onion, chopped	1	½	
Green pepper, chopped	½	¼	
Ground chuck	1 lb	½ lb	
Worcestershire sauce	2 t	1 t	
Black walnuts, chopped	4 T	2 T	
Bread crumbs	4 T	2 T	
Tarragon vinegar	2 T	1 T	
Eggs	2	1	
Butter, clarified	4 T	2 T	

Wash mushrooms and remove stems. Chop onion, green pepper, mushroom stems; run twice through grinder with meat. Mix with Worcestershire sauce, walnuts, bread crumbs, vinegar, and eggs.

Saute the mushroom caps in the clarified butter for a few minutes on both sides. Add the butter from the pan to the meat mixture. Stuff mushroom caps with meat mixture and place on a baking sheet. Drizzle butter on each filled mushroom and broil for 5 minutes, 3 inches below the flame. Serve warm.

Notes:

Bread and Butter Pickles

Ingredients:

Cucumbers, medium, sliced	4 qt
Onions, white, medium, sliced	6
Green peppers, chopped	2
Garlic cloves	3
Salt, coarse-medium	⅓ c
Sugar	4 c
Cider vinegar	3 c
Turmeric	1½ t
Celery seed	1½ t
Mustard seed	2 T

Do not peel cucumbers; slice thin. Add onions, peppers, and garlic cloves (whole). Add salt; cover mixture with 2 traysful of ice cubes. Mix well. Let stand overnight.

Drain cucumber mixture well. Combine remaining ingredients; pour over cucumber mixture. Heat just to a boil. Seal in hot sterilized jars.

Notes:

MARY NIX Director of School Food and Nutrition, Cobb County Public Schools, Marietta, Georgia

1980   IFMA S‌ILVER P‌LATE A‌WARD

The Marietta *Daily Journal* described Mary Nix as a zealous foodservice director who "talks food constantly and gets excited when she opens a can of green beans to test it against a competing food distributor's products." Mrs. Nix exuded enthusiasm for school food service even when she began her career, washing pots and pans at her high school. She maintained her enthusiasm when she worked as a supervisor while attending college and graduate school and feels it to this day, when she plans nutritious, satisfying meals on a very limited budget.

Mrs. Nix attempts to instill her enthusiasm in her managers and staff, emphasizing good food served with genuine concern for each student. She strives for innovative lunches within the federal guidelines for school programs. Her county's long-time policy of student involvement in product testing and menu planning is now mandated by federal regulations.

Mrs. Nix has continually served on committees of both the Georgia and the American School Food Service Associations. She was president of the Georgia chapter in 1977–1978 and was president of ASFSA in 1980–1981.

Ingredients:	6 portions	___portions
Chicken, cooked, cubed	2 c	
Celery, diced	2 c	
Bread cubes, toasted	2 c	
Almonds	2 T	
Salt	½ t	
Onion, grated	2 t	
Mayonnaise	½ c	
Lemon juice	2 T	
Cheese, grated	½ c	
Bread crumbs	¼ c	

Hot Chicken Salad

ENTREE

Combine chicken, celery, toasted bread cubes, almonds, salt, and onion. Add mayonnaise and lemon juice and mix well. Put mixture in greased pan. Combine grated cheese with bread crumbs. Sprinkle over chicken mixture. Bake at 350° for 20 minutes, or until bubbles form around the edge.

Notes:

Ingredients:	6 portions	___portions
Onions, sliced	¾ c	
Butter (or margarine)	½ c	
Squash, cooked, drained	2 c	
Tomatoes, drained, chopped	¾ c	
Cheese, grated	¾ c	
Salt	1 t	
Pepper	dash	
Bread crumbs	½ c	

Squash Medley

VEGETABLE

Saute onions in half of the butter. Combine onions, drained squash, tomatoes, cheese, salt and pepper. Place mixture into greased baking pan. Melt remaining butter and mix with bread crumbs. Top squash mixture with bread crumbs. Bake at 350° for 30 minutes.

Notes:

W. J. O'SULLIVAN M.B.A., Manager, Food Services Department, Ford Motor Company, Dearborn, Michigan

After serving as a major in the United States Air Force, W. J. O'Sullivan joined Ford Motor Company in 1946 in the then newly organized industrial relations office. Since then, he has held various positions with Ford Motor Company in personnel and employee relations at plant, division, and central office levels. He was appointed Manager, Food Services Department, at corporate headquarters in April, 1975. In that capacity, Mr. O'Sullivan is responsible for directing the activities of the central food processing center and of 16 company-operated foodservice units serving approximately 20,000 meals daily. In addition, he has the responsibility of overseeing caterer-operated food services in all Ford Motor Company components throughout the United States.

Mr. O'Sullivan earned his certificate in management development at the University of Chicago in 1957.

Lamb Chops Stroganoff

ENTREE

Ingredients:	8 portions	6 portions	___portions
Lamb chops, thick, fat removed	8	6	
Salt and pepper	to taste	to taste	
Flour	to coat	to coat	
Mace	½ t	⅜ t	
Butter	2 oz	1½ oz	
Brandy	1 oz	¾ oz	
Onions, small, sliced thin	2	1½	
Bacon drippings	to saute	to saute	
Tomato, sliced thin	1	¾ oz	
Dill pickle, chopped fine	1 slice	1 slice	
Lemon rind, grated	1 t	¾ t	
Sour cream	1 c	6 oz	
Madeira	2–3 oz	1½–2¼ oz	
Rice, steamed	4 c	24 oz	

Salt and pepper the lamb chops and dip in flour seasoned with mace. Brown on both sides in butter, add brandy and light. Saute onions in bacon drippings. Add onions to lamb chops, along with tomato, dill pickle, and lemon rind. Over all of this, pour sour cream mixed with madeira. Cover skillet and simmer over low heat until done, medium rare, 10 minutes, or well done, 15 minutes. Serve on steamed rice.

Notes:

Green Rice
VEGETABLE

Ingredients:	6 portions	___portions
Onion, finely chopped	2 T	
Garlic, minced	¼ t	
Olive oil or butter	3 T	
Rice, cooked	1½ c	
Parsley, ground or finely chopped	½ c	
Milk	1 c	
Salt	1 t	
Worcestershire sauce	1 t	
Cheddar cheese, grated	1 c	
Eggs, slightly beaten	2	

Saute chopped onion and minced garlic in olive oil or butter. Measure cooked rice and parsley into a mixing bowl; then add milk, salt, Worcestershire sauce, cheddar cheese, and slightly beaten eggs. Add sauteed onion and garlic; mix thoroughly and pour mixture into buttered baking dish. Bake in a moderate oven (350°) for about 40 minutes.

Notes:

Rice Mangalais with Curry Sauce

VEGETABLE

Ingredients:	10 portions	6 portions	___portions
Onions, finely chopped	2	1¼ oz	
Garlic, clove	1	⅔	
Rice, uncooked	1½ c	7¼ oz	
Curry powder	2 t	1¼ t	
Currants	¼ lb	2½ oz	
Almonds, chopped	¼ lb	2½ oz	
Chicken broth	3½ c	16¾ oz	
Salt and pepper	to taste	to taste	

CURRY SAUCE

Curry powder	2 t	1¼ t	
Onions, chopped	3	1¾	
Ham, diced	1 c	4¾ oz	
Apples, diced	2	1¼	
Flour	2 T	3⅔ t	
Chicken broth	1½ qt	14½ oz	

Braise onions; add garlic and rice. Cook for 1 minute. Stir in curry powder, currants, almonds, and chicken broth. Add salt and pepper. Bake in moderate oven for 18 minutes.

To make Curry Sauce, mix all ingredients together. Cook for ½ hour and strain and season to taste. Serve with Rice Mangalais.

Notes:

Lemon Cheese Cake
DESSERT

Ingredients:	6–9 portions	___ portions
CRUST		
Zwieback, finely crushed	1 box	
Sugar, granulated	1 c	
Butter, melted	6 T	
Cinnamon	1 t	
FILLING		
Cottage cheese, dry	2 c	
Egg yolks, beaten	4	
Sugar	1 c	
Salt	¼ t	
Lemon juice	3 T	
Lemon rind, grated	1 lemon	
Gelatin	2 env	
Water	½ c	
Whipping cream	1 c	
Vanilla	½ t	
Egg whites	4	
Sugar	¼ c	

For crust, mix finely crushed zwieback, granulated sugar, melted butter, and cinnamon. Press firmly into the bottom and sides of a well-buttered spring form (6½- to 7-inch pan, 3 inches deep).

For filling, rub dry cottage cheese through a sieve; add beaten egg yolks, sugar, salt, lemon juice, and grated lemon rind. Cook mixture in double boiler until thoroughly heated. Don't overcook. Dissolve gelatin in water; add to lemon mixture. Whip whipping cream flavored with vanilla; beat egg whites sweetened with sugar. Fold into cooled filling. Pour into crust. Chill in refrigerator for 6 hours.

Notes:

RAYMOND B. PEDDERSEN   C.F.E., F.H.C.F.A., Director of Dietetics, LDS Hospital, Salt Lake City, Utah

1980   IFMA S󠀠ilver P󠀠late A󠀠ward
1980   FM Gold/The Editors Choice, *Food Management* magazine

Ray Peddersen believes that being in the hospital is bad enough and that the food should not add to a patient's misery. In his sixteen years in hospital food service, he has devoted himself to the task of improving on cost efficiency, menu planning, food preparation and delivery systems.

In 1970, Mr. Peddersen brought the airline flight concept of meals to Long Island Jewish/Hillside Medical Center, converting the all-scratch preparation kitchen there to a convenience/portion control operation for over half of the entrees. At LDS Hospital, he developed an aseptic cook/chill system, by which a twenty-day supply of food can be prepared, stored at temperatures just above freezing, and then rethermalized when needed. The system will effect major savings in labor costs.

For his contributions, Mr. Peddersen was named a Fellow by the American Society of Hospital Food Service Administrators in 1979. In 1978, he was the first Utah citizen to be designated a Certified Food Executive by the International Food Service Executives Association. He is the author of *Increasing Productivity in Foodservice* (1973), *Specs: The Comprehensive Foodservice Purchasing and Specification Manual* (1977), and *Hotel and Foodservice Purchasing* (1980).

Beef Burgundy
ENTREE

Ingredients:	100 portions	___portions
Beef, tenderloin tips	33 lb	
Salt	¼ c	
Garlic powder	1½ t	
Onion salt	3 T	
Pepper, black	2½ t	
Thyme	2 T	
Beef stock	1¾ gal	
Cornstarch	2 c	
Burgundy	1 qt	
Meat drippings		
Tomatoes, canned, diced	3 lb 14 oz	
Onions, quartered	1 lb 10 oz	

Sprinkle meat with salt, garlic powder, onion salt, black pepper, and thyme. Brown in fry skillet. Remove meat. Mix enough beef stock with cornstarch to make a smooth paste. Heat liquid to boiling; add cornstarch paste, stirring constantly until thick. Add burgundy and meat drippings. Simmer for 30 minutes. Combine meat, sauce, tomatoes, and onions in fry skillet and simmer 1 hour. Serve over noodles.

Notes:

Lasagna

ENTREE

Ingredients:	288 portions	___portions
Ground chuck	25 lb	
Onions, finely chopped	10 lb	
Garlic cloves, minced	10	
Tomatoes, canned	30 lb	
Tomato paste	15 lb	
Salt	1 c	
Worcestershire sauce	1 c	
Sugar	1 c	
Thyme	2½ t	
Rosemary	2½ t	
Oregano	2½ t	
Noodles, lasagna	15 lb	
Cottage cheese, dry curd (or drained)	25 lb	
Eggs	25	
Parsley, chopped	2 c	
Cheese, cheddar	10 lb	
Cheese, mozzarella	9 lb	
Cheese, Parmesan	3 c	

Brown meat with onions and garlic in tilting fry skillet. Pour off grease. Puree tomatoes, tomato paste, and spices in blender. Add to meat mixture and simmer 1½ hours, stirring occasionally.

Cook lasagna noodles in salted boiling water until barely tender. Drain. Mix cottage cheese, eggs, and parsley. Grind or grate cheddar, mozzarella, and Parmesan cheeses. Place 1 qt of meat sauce in a pan (12 × 20 × 2 inches). Cover with 2 layers of noodles, 3 c of cottage cheese mixture, grated cheeses, then noodles, meat sauce, cottage cheese mixture, and grated cheeses. Top with ½ c of Parmesan cheese. Bake at 350° for 30–40 minutes. Cut pans 3 × 8 for serving.

Notes:

Escalloped Potatoes
VEGETABLE

Ingredients:	70 portions	___portions
Potatoes, raw, sliced	2 gal	
White sauce, medium	3 gal	
Margarine, melted	½ c	
Bread crumbs	3 c	

Put sliced raw potatoes into pans (12 × 20 inches). Place in steamer and cook 20 minutes. Make white sauce of medium consistency. Pour white sauce over potatoes. Combine melted margarine with bread crumbs, then sprinkle on top of potatoes. Bake 30–45 minutes in oven 350°.

Notes:

G. WILLIAM PEFFERS   Director of Dietary Services, Ingalls Memorial Hospital, Harvey, Illinois

1974 Ivy Award of Distinction
1970 President, American Society for Hospital Food Service Administrators (ASHFSA)

Bill Peffers is a graduate of Michigan State University with a major in hotel administration. His experience includes six years in hotel and restaurant management, some of which was at the Americana in New York; nineteen years in hospital food service management, a major part of which was at Michael Reese Medical Center in Chicago; and five years with the firm of Harris Kerr Forster as a management advisory services consultant in Chicago and Cincinnati.

"Pepikalua" Hawaiian Beef Marinade
SAUCE

Ingredients: ___portions

Ingredient	Amount
Salad oil	1 pt
Kikkoman Soy Sauce	2 oz
Worcestershire sauce	2 oz
White wine	1 pt
Soup stock (beef or chicken)	1½ pt
Ginger root, 2 inches long	3 pieces
Garlic clove, whole, peeled and separated	1

Mix all ingredients. The total volume from the above quantities will be almost a half-gallon. Depending upon the pan sizes used for marinating, this volume will be enough for from 12 to 15 pounds of beef.

Notes:

Shangri-la Sauce
SAUCE

Ingredients: ___portions

Ingredient	Amount
Apricots, pureed (#10 can)	½ can
Mustard, dry, mixed with a little water until smooth	2 T
Catsup (to color)	¼ c
Soy sauce	1 t
Salt	to taste
Honey	6 T

Mix all ingredients. This sauce is excellent for variety in place of cocktail sauce for chilled shrimp, lobster, and crabmeat.

Notes:

Smothered Pheasant à la G.W.P.
ENTREE

Ingredients:

Pheasant(s)
Water, cold
Salt
Flour
Vegetable oil
Salt and pepper
Wine or water (2 oz for each bird)

Prepreparation from the frozen state: If the pheasants are frozen, it is recommended that they be placed in a bath of cold salt water for about 4 hours.

Prepreparation for fresh birds: It is recommended that fresh birds, after they are drawn, be placed in cold salt water overnight.

Take off the legs and thighs. Take off the back (a cleaver will help). Cut the wishbone portion away from the breast. Slice off one boneless portion of breast meat; leave the other half of the breast attached to the bone. (The use of the back portion, which has very little meat, is optional.)

The cut portions of pheasant should be fairly wet when floured generously. Fill a skillet with about ⅛ inch of vegetable oil. Heat the vegetable oil; when the oil is at a high temperature, reduce heat (do not boil). Place the floured portions of pheasant in the skillet. It is recommended that the legs and thighs be placed in the skillet first. When all portions are browning in the skillet, add salt and pepper.

Lightly brown on one side and then turn the portions. (The main key to keeping the meat tender is in this cooking process; the temperature should be kept very low and one should not expect to achieve a heavily browned result. It is better to underbrown the pheasant. One should not expect to produce a dark brown gravy from this browning process.)

Place the browned portions of pheasant in a roasting pan with a lid that fits fairly tightly. For each pheasant, pour 2 oz of wine or water in the roasting pan. Place covered roasting pan in a preheated 325° oven for approximately 1 hour. Baste the pheasant twice during this roasting period. Remove the lid of the roasting pan and finish off in the oven at the above temperature for approximately 30 minutes. If there is to be a delay before eating, the pheasants may be held in the oven at a keep warm temperature (approximately 200°) with the roasting pan lid on.

Notes:

MICHAEL S. PINKERT President, Mental Health Management, Inc., 1010 Wisconsin Avenue, Washington, D.C.

Michael Pinkert was with the firm of Gordon A. Friesen, International, from 1968 to 1973, when the first "Ready Foods Systems" were developed and installed in hospitals. Mr. Pinkert worked closely with the researchers at Cornell University and a San Francisco foodservice consultant to develop methods of fast freezing, storage, and microwaving that would permit patients to be served a wide range of entrees at times that were convenient for them. As a result of these developmental activities, Michael Pinkert and Paul Hysen authored a series of articles in *Canadian Hospital Journal* on various topics related to "Ready Foods Systems." Mr. Pinkert also has lectured widely on the latest advances in hospital foodservice systems. Internationally, he worked on one of the largest "Ready Foods Systems" ever designed (for the 2,400-bed University of Cologne Medical Center in Cologne, West Germany).

Mr. Pinkert is the author of *The Ready Foods System for Health Care Facilities*, which won the 1973 Hospital Management Systems Society literary award.

Waffles Grand Marnier

Ingredients:	6 portions	___portions
Flour, unbleached, white	1 c	
Flour, soy	½ c	
Baking powder	2 t	
Salt	½ t	
Sugar	1 T	
Wheat germ (optional)	¼ c	
Egg yolks	3	
Butter, melted and cooled	4 T	
Milk	1½ c	
Egg whites, beaten until stiff	3	

GRAND MARNIER BUTTER SAUCE

Orange marmalade	2 T	
Egg yolks	4	
Orange peel, grated	2 t	
Grand Marnier	2 T	
Butter, melted	¼ lb	

Mix together flours, baking powder, salt, sugar, and wheat germ, if desired. Mix together egg yolks, butter, and milk; fold into flour mixture. Fold egg whites into batter. Bake in waffle iron until brown. Be careful not to dry them out by overbaking.

To make Grand Marnier Butter Sauce, put orange marmalade, egg yolks, orange peel, and Grand Marnier in blender and mix. Add melted butter by droplets until mixture is creamy and slightly thick.

Notes:

HARRY H. POPE   President, H. A. Pope and Sons, Inc., St. Louis, Missouri

1959   IFMA Gold Plate Award

Harry H. Pope's firm, H. A. Pope and Sons, Inc., of St. Louis, operates seven public cafeterias, two luxury dining rooms, two "food fairs," nine employee cafeterias, five executive dining rooms, a dining room of a retirement residence, and many franchise operations in the United States. It has interests in European restaurants and is the controlling stockholder in a large nationwide chain.

A second-generation restaurateur, Mr. Pope has been active in the restaurant business for forty-nine years. He is the author of *Increasing Productivity in Food Service* (1973). He is well known for his work in the fields of menu pricing, cost analysis, time study, psychological testing, and employee training.

Ingredients:	8 portions	___ portions
Egg whites, large	3	
Cream of tartar	⅛ t	
Brown sugar, packed	½ c	
Sugar, granulated	½ c	
Vanilla	½ t	
Almond extract	¼ t	
Graham cracker crumbs	¾ c	
Pecan pieces	½ c	
Shortening, to grease pan		
Banana, peeled	1	
Whipped cream	3 c	
Maraschino cherries	2	
Toasted almonds (or pecan pieces)	to garnish	

Nut Torte
DESSERT

Have egg whites at room temperature. Place egg whites and cream of tartar in a mixer bowl. Turn mixer to high speed and mix until egg whites form soft peaks. Sift brown sugar and granulated sugar together. Add sugar gradually to the beaten egg whites, being sure to beat each addition of sugar into the egg whites. It is important to add sugar slowly. After all the sugar has been added, *continue beating* mixture approximately 5 minutes, or until egg whites are glossy and in peaks. Add vanilla and almond extract and mix thoroughly. Remove mixing bowl from machine.

Combine graham cracker crumbs and pecan pieces. Sprinkle ¼ of graham cracker crumbs and pecan pieces over beaten egg white mixture and fold in gently. Gradually add remaining crumbs and pecan pieces, folding in after each addition. Grease cake pan heavily with shortening. Put batter into pan. Preheat oven to 300° and bake torte for approximately 30 minutes. Top of torte will be light in color when baked. Leave torte in pan to cool.

Preparation of Torte. Cut banana into ⅛-inch slices. Place layer of sliced bananas on top of torte. With pastry tube, decorate top and sides of torte with whipped cream. Cut each maraschino cherry into 4 pieces. Arrange 8 pieces of cherry and toasted almonds around the edge of the torte (in the whipped cream). Keep decorated torte in refrigerator.

Notes:

LAWRENCE S. PROCOPIO C.F.E., D.O.D.G., Owner/Chef, Palms Restaurant, East Providence, Rhode Island

1973   Certified Food Executive (C.F.E.)
1973   Dignified Order of the Dinner Gong (D.O.D.G.)

Larry Procopio has been in the food business for thirty-two years, working as chef and manager of his family's restaurant, the Palms Restaurant, in East Providence, Rhode Island.

Mr. Procopio has served as an officer of the Rhode Island chapter of IFSEA for twenty-eight years and has been president for fourteen of those years. He is currently a member of the Culinary Advisory Committee of the Cumberland School Department; a member of the Advisory Council of the Cooperative Vocational Education Program (culinary arts) at the William M. Davies Jr. Technical High School; and a liaison officer between the Johnson and Wales student branch of the International Food Service Executives Association and its parent, the Rhode Island branch. He is an advisory board member of Creative Cuisine, Rhode Island Heart Association.

Ingredients:	1 portion	6 portions	___portions
Chicken, half	1	6	
Onions, chopped	2 oz	12 oz	
Garlic, granulated	5 pinches	1 t	
Oregano	2 pinches	½ t	
Bay leaf	1	4	
Parsley flakes	1 pinch	¼ t	
Salt and pepper	to taste	to taste	
Tomatoes, crushed, canned, 8-oz	1 can	6 cans	

Chicken Cacciatora alla "Palms"
ENTREE

Cut up chicken into small pieces. Put all above ingredients in a skillet (preferably cast-iron). Simmer until meat separates from the bone. This may be served with a pasta dish or potato and a salad.

Notes:

Ingredients:	1 portion	6 portions	___portions
Clams, littlenecks (out of shells)	1 c	6 c	
Olive oil	4 oz	24 oz	
Salt and pepper	pinch	¼ t	
Garlic, granulated	4 pinches	½ t	
Parsley flakes	pinch	¼ t	
Spaghetti, uncooked	¼ lb	1–1½ lb	

White Clam Sauce with Spaghetti
ENTREE

Saute clams slowly with olive oil and seasonings in a small saucepan. Meanwhile, bring salted water to a boil, drop in spaghetti, and cook to desired doneness, then drain. Put spaghetti on a platter and pour the clam sauce over it.

Notes:

RUBY P. PUCKETT R.D., M.A., Director, Food and Nutrition Services, Shands Teaching Hospital and Clinics, Inc., Gainesville, Florida

    1980   Ivy Award of Distinction
    1978   IFMA Silver Plate Award
    1972   Outstanding Dietitian in Florida

"People are important!" No one sentence more accurately describes the philosophy under which Ruby P. Puckett has served the foodservice industry. Since her graduation from Auburn University, she has had the determination and the tenacity to change food service from the image of "kitchen help" to a viable industry. She believes in the necessity of focusing on the people being served: "They must feel as important as they are."

Ms. Puckett has proved that education is the key to obtaining the image food service deserves. This includes the education of personnel both within and outside of the industry. Over 7,000 people have completed her correspondence courses. The course titles are *Food Service Supervisor*, *Dietetic Assistant*, and *Preceptor's Manual*. She has also authored the *Shands Diet Manual* and three education tapes and workbooks for the American Dietetic Association. She is a coauthor of *Basic Guide to Normal Nutrition and Diet Modification* and, with Robert Neville, of *Training the Food Service Employee* and *Teacher's Guide for Training the Food Service Employee*.

Ms. Puckett has worked extensively to bring about improvements within the dietetic profession. Her philosophy is that hospital patients should be served foods they are familiar with. She thinks food comforts people, serves as a reward, and gives a warm feeling to any gathering. She often asks, "Would you eat foods prepared by someone you don't trust?"

Southern Gumbo SOUP

Ingredients:	10 portions	6 portions	___ portions
Butter (or margarine or lard)	¼ c	1¼ oz	
Flour	2 T	3⅔ t	
Garlic cloves, minced	2	1¼	
Onions, white, cut in rings	2	1¼	
Green pepper, large, cut into strips	1	⅔	
Tomato chunks with juice	2½ c	12 oz	
Okra, fresh or frozen	1 lb	9⅔ oz	
Tomato paste (6-oz can)	1	3⅔ oz	
Beef bouillon cubes	4	2½	
Worcestershire sauce	4 t	2½ t	
Chili powder	½–¾ t	¼–½ t	
Basil	⅛ t	1/10 t	
Cloves, ground	⅛ t	1/10 t	
Bay leaves, medium size	2	1¼	
Salt	1¼ T	2¼ t	
Chicken	1½–2 lb	1–1½ lb	
Water	3 c	14½ oz	
Rice, cooked	4 c	19¼ oz	
Parsley, fresh	¼ c	1¼ oz	
Shrimp, raw, deveined, shelled	1½ lb	1 lb	
Lobster or crab, raw	½ lb	⅓ lb	

In heavy kettle or dutch oven (use this type pan *only*), melt butter (or margarine or lard) over low heat. Stir in flour, and cook over low heat until brown. Stir very frequently using a wooden spoon. (This roux is the basis of the gumbo and takes patience—cook slowly.) Add garlic, onions, green pepper; cook slowly until tender. (Stir gently—do not crush vegetables.) Add tomato chunks, okra, tomato paste, bouillon cubes, Worcestershire sauce, chili powder, basil, cloves, bay leaves, and salt. Simmer *uncovered*, for 45 minutes to an hour. Stir gently to avoid sticking or burned spots. Remove from heat; cool and cover. Refrigerate.

Boil chicken in water until completely cooked. Cool. Refrigerate.

Remove chicken from refrigerator. Remove skin and meat from bones. Add shrimp, lobster or crab, and chicken to gumbo mixture. Simmer covered for 5 minutes, or until shrimp and lobster or crab are pink and tender.

Cook rice according to directions on package. Snip the fresh parsley. Lightly mix snipped parsley with hot rice. Serve gumbo in shallow plates or dinner-size bowls. Hot parsley rice is served either on top of gumbo or to the side of the plate.

Notes:

Homemade Praline-Pecan Ice Cream

DESSERT

Ingredients:	12–15 portions	___portions
Milk, whole	1½ c	
Sugar	½–¾ c	
Flour	2 T	
Salt	⅛ t	
Eggs, whole	4	
Butter	¼ c	
Pecans, broken	1 c	
Salt	¼ t	
Vanilla extract	1½ t	
Cream, heavy	½ c	
Milk, condensed	1 can	
Praline candy, broken into pieces	½ lb	

In a double boiler, scald milk. Mix sugar, flour, and salt. Stir in enough scalded milk (approximately ⅓ c) to make a smooth paste. Stir this paste into rest of milk in double boiler. Stir with a wooden spoon until thickened. Cover and cook 10 minutes. Remove from heat. Beat eggs slightly. Stir eggs into the milk mixture. Return to double boiler and cook 1 minute. Cool.

In a heavy skillet, melt butter. Saute broken pecans until golden. Add salt. Cool.

Add vanilla, cream, condensed milk, pecans, and praline candy to milk-egg mixture. Freeze in a 4-qt crank freezer until crank is difficult to turn. (Use 8 parts ice to 1 part rock salt.)

Ice cream may be ripened or served immediately. Serve in meringue glacée; top with pecans, whipped cream, fudge sauce, or cherry.

Notes:

Meringue Glacée
DESSERT

Ingredients:	18–24 portions	6 portions	___portions
Egg whites, large	6	2	
Salt	⅛ t	dash	
Sugar, granulated	2 c	5⅓ oz	
Vanilla	1 t	⅓ t	
Vinegar	1 t	⅓ t	

Make meringue a day or two in advance. Add salt to egg whites. Set electric mixer control on high. Beat egg whites and salt until stiff enough to hold shape. Turn mixer to low speed. Add approximately 2 T of sugar at a time, beating for an additional 2 minutes after each addition. Preheat oven to 275°. Add vanilla and vinegar to meringue. Beat at high speed for 10 minutes. Butter a cookie sheet. Drop heaping spoonfuls onto cookie sheet. Using base of spoon, shape meringue into shells. Bake at 275° for 45 minutes. Reduce heat to 250° and bake 15 minutes more, or until ivory color and delicately firm. Remove to rack; cool. Cover cooled shells lightly with waxed paper or foil and store in covered container until needed.

To serve, fill the meringue shells with ice cream, fruit, and whipped cream.

Notes:

GERALD RAMSEY Director of Food Services, Southern Methodist Univesity, Dallas, Texas

1972	IVY AWARD OF DISTINCTION
1971	Executive Director's Award for Exceptional Service to Youth, American School Food Service Association
1967	IFMA GOLD PLATE AWARD
1964	President, National Association of College and University Food Service (NACUFS)
1963	President, American School Food Service Association (ASFSA)
1962	Trendmaker Award, *Foodservice* magazine

Mr. Ramsey has been Director of Food Service at Southern Methodist University since 1950. In 1977, the students there awarded him the "M" Award. He is the author of a cookbook titled *Morning, Noon and Night*.

In the fall of 1966, Mr. Ramsey was selected by the State Department as a member of a team to assist the Jordanian government in establishing a feeding program for its national schools. This team was under the sponsorship of the Agency for International Development's Food for Peace Program.

Spanish Sauce for Shrimp

SAUCE

Ingredients:	16 portions	___portions
Cooking oil	1½ c	
Ham scraps, cubed	1 c	
Onion, chopped	1 c	
Garlic cloves, finely chopped	4	
Celery, julienned	1 c	
Green pepper, julienned	1 c	
Flour	½ c	
Thyme	½ t	
Oregano	½ t	
Gumbo filé	1 t	
White wine	1 c	
Chicken stock	2 c	
Celery salt	1 T	
Tomatoes, fresh or solid pack	2 c	
Tomato puree	1 c	
Tabasco	⅛ t	
Bay leaf	1	
Parsley, fresh, chopped	garnish	

Heat oil in heavy kettle. Add ham scraps; saute until lightly browned. Add onion and garlic, and continue cooking until lightly browned. Add celery and green pepper, and mix well. Saute for 5 more minutes. Add flour, thyme, oregano, and gumbo filé, and allow to smother for 3 minutes. Add wine, stock, celery salt, tomatoes, tomato puree, Tabasco, and bay leaf. Cook 30 minutes on low heat. Add to cooked shrimp as needed. Serve over rice. Garnish with parsley.

Notes:

CLINTON L. RAPPOLE Ph.D., Associate Dean, Hilton College of Hotel and Restaurant Management, University of Houston, Houston, Texas

Dr. Clinton Rappole grew up in the resort business in northern New York state on the St. Lawrence River. He received a B.A. from Colgate University in 1962 and B.S., M.S., and Ph.D. degrees from Cornell University. His doctoral dissertation researched the "Feasibility of On-Premise Production of Frozen Entrees Under Institutional Conditions." It was abstracted for the Society for the Advancement of Food Service Research. He taught at Cornell University, as a lecturer and then as an assistant professor. In 1972, he accepted a position as an assistant professor at the University of Houston, and later became an associate professor and then an associate dean.

Dr. Rappole's major areas of specialization are hotel management, foodservice systems, frozen foods, and sanitation. He has participated extensively in workshops and seminars, both domestically and overseas, on sanitation, frozen foods, and food cost control. He has written several publications on these subjects and has often reviewed books and courses on them for various publishers and organizations.

While at the University of Houston, Dr. Rappole was involved in research for NASA in the development of a foodservice system for the space shuttle crews. Also, he was the principal investigator for the Hilton College of Hotel and Restaurant Management in a project to develop a 350-room hotel in the city of Lake Charles. He has been a frequent consultant to the food and hotel industries, consulting for such companies as Inter-Continental Hotels, H. J. Heinz, Mrs. Smith's Pies, Medenco, Inc., and Keydril, a drilling company.

Dr. Rappole was president of the Cornell Club of Houston in 1974–1975. He is a member of the Society for the Advancement of Food Service Research, the Institute of Food Technologists, the Texas Hotel and Motel Association, and the Industry/Education Advisory Board for Wiley College and El Centro College.

Carrots Provençal
VEGETABLE

Ingredients:	45 portions	6 portions	___portions
Carrots, julienned, E.P.	15 lb	2 lb	
Onions, minced	1½ lb	3¼ oz	
Margarine	2 lb	4¼ oz	
Water	3 qt	2 c	
Salt	to taste	to taste	
Parsley, chopped	¼ c	¼ oz	

Place a third of the carrots and a third of the onions in a saute pan. Add a third of the margarine and a third of the water. Cover and steam for 20 minutes. Remove cover and continue cooking until done, stirring constantly (10 minutes). Repeat twice more to cook all carrots and onions. Season to taste. Garnish with parsley.

Notes:

Raisin Streusel Pie
DESSERT

Ingredients:	64 portions	___ portions
Raisins	1 lb 5 oz	
Water	5¼ qt	
Cornstarch	1½ oz	
Water	2 c	
Sugar	1 lb 5 oz	
Salt	1½ T	
Lemons, finely ground	2	

PASTRY

Flour, all-purpose	4 lb	
Flour, cake	4 lb	
Lard (or vegetable shortening)	5 lb 8 oz	
Salt	6 oz	
Water, cold	1 qt	

STREUSEL TOPPING

Flour	1 lb	
Sugar	1 lb 10 oz	
Powdered milk	2 oz	
Salt	1 t	
Butter (or margarine)	10 oz	
Pecans, chopped	6 oz	

Combine raisins and 5¼ qt of water, bring to a boil in a steam-jacketed kettle. Combine cornstarch and 2 c of water to make a suspension. Whip cornstarch into raisin mixture, cook until clear. Add sugar and bring back to a boil, add salt and lemons. Cool.

For pastry, weigh 3 lb of all-purpose flour and cake flour and place in mixing bowl. Weigh shortening and place on top of flour. Combine salt and water. Mix 1 lb of all-purpose flour with salt and water until blended. Using pastry blender at first speed, cut shortening into flour. The flour and shortening should be in lumps rather than a pastry mass. Add water-flour mixture and mix until blended. Do not overmix. Place pastry on tray. Let dough rest for 15 to 20 minutes before rolling, or refrigerate until needed. Roll out into 9-inch pie shells. (When substituting vegetable shortening for lard, use 6 lb instead of 5 lb 8 oz.)

For topping, combine flour, sugar, powdered milk, and salt. Rub in shortening; add pecans.

Place 1 qt of filling in each unbaked pie shell. Place streusel topping on raisin filling. Bake at 425° for 30–40 minutes or until crust is baked and top is browned.

Notes:

KARL A. RATZSCH, JR.   President, Karl Ratzsch's Restaurant and Fox & Hounds Restaurant, Milwaukee, Wisconsin

1952–1982	Holiday Award
1976	Wisconsin Restaurateur of the Year
1974	IVY AWARD OF DISTINCTION

Few celebrities leave Milwaukee without a visit to Karl Ratzsch's Restaurant. The guest book is a veritable who's who: Helen Hayes, Jack Dempsey, Richard Nixon, Gene Autrey, Stan Musial, Marlene Dietrich, Victor Borge, Julie Harris, etc. When Lucille Ball was in Milwaukee for eight days, she stopped in at Ratzsch's eight times and ordered pork shanks and beer each time. Skating star Sonja Henie came in regularly after her ice show and asked for champagne, rye bread, and steak à la tartare (chopped raw filet mignon) every night. Senator and Mrs. John F. Kennedy dined at Ratzsch's during the Wisconsin presidential primary campaign of 1960. The future president was diplomatic—he selected Wisconsin pike.

But although Ratzsch's has served presidents and kings, it is also a favorite with secretaries and shoppers for a hearty but modestly priced lunch. The restaurant's most popular foods evolved from peasant dishes. Sauerbraten, the best seller, dates from before the invention of refrigeration. To preserve beef, German housewives soaked it in vinegar and brine. When it came time to braise the meat, those thrifty women wasted nothing. They used the brine, sweetening it with spices and sugar to make it more palatable. Ratzsch's accomplishes the same thing today by adding ginger snaps to the brine.

Mr. Ratzsch is a past president of the Wisconsin Restaurant Association. He is a member and/or director of twenty-eight industry, civic, and social organizations.

Karl Ratzsch's Lentil Soup

SOUP

Ingredients:	6 portions	___portions
Onions	½ c	
Celery	½ c	
Carrots	½ c	
Shortening	2 T	
Lentils	2 c	
Ham stock	3 c	
Bacon, diced	¼ lb	
Flour	2 t	

Saute onions, carrots, and celery in shortening. Add vegetables and lentils to the ham stock and boil until tender, then simmer. While this is simmering, take a separate pan and saute diced bacon. Strain. Add flour to the bacon drippings and heat until there is a roux effect. Add this roux to the simmering soup to attain the desired consistency.

Notes:

Karl Ratzsch's Braised Lamb Shanks Gemüse
ENTREE

Ingredients:	4 portions	6 portions	___portions
Lamb shanks, ¾–1 lb each	4	6	
Onions, diced	1 c	1½ c	
Celery, diced	1 c	1½ c	
Carrots, diced	1 c	1½ c	
Red wine and beef stock, equal parts	to cover	to cover	
Peas	1 c	1½ c	
Green beans	1 c	1½ c	
Flour and water	to thicken	to thicken	
Kitchen Bouquet	to taste	to taste	
Salt	to taste	to taste	
Bouquet garni			
Bay leaves	2	3	
Garlic cloves, mashed	2	3	
Peppercorns	12	18	
Summer savory,	¼ t	⅜ t	
Thyme	¼ t	⅜ t	
Marjoram	¼ t	⅜ t	

Saute lamb shanks until well browned. Place in dutch oven with bouquet garni (in cheesecloth bag), onions, carrots, celery, and enough wine and stock to cover. Braise in oven at 375°, covered, until lamb shanks are tender, about 2½ hours. In the last ½ hour of cooking, add peas and beans and remove bouquet garni. Blend in flour and water mixture (1 T of flour with ¼ c of water for each cup of liquid) to thicken. Add Kitchen Bouquet to create desired brownness and salt to taste.

Notes:

DOUGLAS H. RICHIE (Retired) Director of Food Service, California State College at Long Beach, Long Beach, California

1978 President, National Association of College and University Food Services (NACUFS)

Doug Richie has experience both with food service companies and in independent operation for a university. He believes in an ecumenical approach to food service that identifies the common element of professionalism. During his twenty years at California State College at Long Beach, Mr. Richie has coordinated the fourfold expansion of the program. He also pioneered the implementation of a shopping center concept in the student union.

Mr. Richie has taught classes in foodservice management to university students for eight years. He believes strongly in the employment of students in food service and has facilitated the training and advancement of dozens of young people. Dedication to food quality is a priority for Doug Richie. His belief in the virtues of preparing food from scratch underlies his primary management goals. He has received the Distinguished Service Award of the National Association of College and University Food Services.

Lima Bean and Bacon Soup

SOUP

Ingredients:	50 portions	6 portions	___portions
Lima beans, dried	3 lb	6 oz	
Stock, ham or beef	48 lb	6 lb	
Bacon ends, diced	1 lb	2 oz	
Fat, ham or bacon	8 oz	1 oz	
Onions, diced	1 lb	2 oz	
Celery, diced	1 lb	2 oz	
Garlic clove, crushed	1	⅛	
Green peppers, diced	½ lb	1 oz	
Carrots, diced	½ lb	1 oz	
Flour	1 lb	2 oz	
Catsup	1 lb 12 oz	3 oz	
Pepper, white	1 t	⅛ t	
Marjoram	1 t	⅛ t	
Chili powder	1 t	⅛ t	
Worcestershire sauce	2 oz	¼ oz	
Salt	to taste	to taste	

Soak beans overnight. Drain and bring to a boil in stock; simmer until beans are tender, about 2 hours. Saute bacon in fat; add vegetables and stir until well blended. Slowly stir in bean stock and flour. Stir in beans, catsup, and seasonings. Bring to a boil and simmer for 30 minutes. Season to taste with salt. Serve garnished with crisp bacon pieces.

Notes:

Health Sandwich No. 3
ENTREE

Ingredients:	48 portions	6 portions	___portions
Mustard	1 c	⅛ c	
Mayonnaise	1 c	⅛ c	
Bread slices, whole wheat (or other)			
open	48	6	
closed	96	12	
Green peppers, sliced	1 qt	¼ c	
Tomatoes, sliced	8	1½	
Muenster cheese, slices (½-oz each)	48	6	
Alfalfa sprouts	1 qt	¼ c	
Eggs, hard-cooked, sliced	24	3	

Mix mustard with mayonnaise and spread bread slices with mixture. Top slices with pepper, tomato, cheese, sprouts, and egg slices. Top with second slice of bread, if desired.

Notes:

WILLY O. ROSSEL   Executive Chef/Director of Food Planning, Braniff Airways, Inc., Dallas, Texas

    1964   President, American Culinary Federation
    1964   Gold Medal, World Culinary Olympics (U.S. Team Captain)
    1951   Gold Medal, World Culinary Olympics (Swiss Team Member)

Chef Rossel, a former president of the American Culinary Federation, twice Gold Medal winner at the World Culinary Olympics in Frankfurt, recipient of the French Medal in the Pan American Culinary Show and of highest individual honors in the Grand Prix du Salon of the Salon Culinaire, has a rich background.

Chef Rossel pioneered in the airline foodservice planning field, joining Braniff Airways, Inc., in 1965 and serving for fifteen years as Executive Chef of Braniff International. His experience in the hotel industry prior to that time included the direction of specialty restaurants, private clubs, and banquet planning, as well as the coordination of all foodservice operations of the several major hotels in which he served as Executive Chef—Sheraton Hotel in Dallas, Hotel Manhattan and the Hampshire House in New York City, Caribe Hilton in Puerto Rico, and the Tower Isle Hotel in Jamaica. He was directly responsible for designing and opening the food facilities of the Sheraton International Hotels in Venezuela, Puerto Rico, Houston, and Boston.

Whether the job at hand is negotiating contracts for food preparation, creating operational manuals and buying guides, planning budgets or analyses of budget variances, discerning the special needs of new operations, or finding the ongoing difficulties inherent in present operations, Chef Rossel brings a fresh eye and a new approach that could only emanate from his great creativity and experience.

Crabmeat Lorenzo
HORS D'OEUVRES

Ingredients:	24 portions	6 portions	___portions
Onion, minced	1 t	¼ t	
Butter, melted	1 T	¾ t	
Sherry, dry	2 T	1½ t	
Salt	½ t	⅛ t	
Pepper	⅛ t	dash	
Crabmeat, cooked	½ lb	⅛ lb	
Tart shells, baked, 2-inch	24	6	
Hollandaise sauce	to top	to top	
Parmesan cheese, grated	to top	to top	
Ripe olives	garnish	garnish	

Saute onion in butter until tender. Remove from heat. Stir sherry, salt, and pepper into onion mixture. Toss crabmeat lightly with onion mixture. Spoon mixture into tart shells. Top each tart with a small amount of hollandaise sauce. Sprinkle Parmesan cheese over hollandaise sauce. Broil 3–4 inches from source of heat about 2 minutes, or until very lightly browned. Garnish with ripe olive wedges, if desired.

Notes:

Sopa de Calabaza Fria
SOUP

Ingredients:	6 portions	___portions
Spanish pumpkin, medium (about 3 lb)	1	
Chicken stock (or 5 bouillon cubes and water)	1½ qt	
Salt	1 t	
Monosodium glutamate	1 t	
Sugar	1 t	
White pepper	dash	
Curry powder	¼ t	
Nutmeg ("tip of knife"), ground	pinch	
Saffron (optional)	pinch	
Cream, light	1 pt	
Cream, heavy	1 c	
Croutons, toasted	to garnish	

Wash pumpkin. Cut in half. Remove seeds and pulp. Cut each half into 4 slices and then into 2-inch cubes. Heat chicken stock to boiling in a saucepan. Add pumpkin. When stock returns to boil, cover saucepan, reduce heat, and simmer 25 minutes. Drain pumpkin. While pumpkin is still warm, cut off skin. Put pumpkin in blender (or electric mixer) and puree. (If you use an electric mixer, put pulp through a strainer for a puree.) This should give you about 2 c of puree.

In a saucepan, mix pumpkin puree, salt, monosodium glutamate, sugar, pepper, curry powder, nutmeg, and saffron. Add 1 c of light cream. Bring pumpkin mixture to a simmer and cook 2–3 minutes, stirring constantly to prevent scorching. Remove from heat. Cool to room temperature. Chill in refrigerator.

When ready to serve, blend in 1 c of chilled light cream and ½ c of heavy cream. (Consistency should be comparable to vichyssoise.) Whip remaining ½ c of heavy cream. Serve soup in chilled bowls or cups. Top each with 1 heaping t of whipped cream. Garnish with toasted croutons.

Notes:

Crepes Carioca
DESSERT

Ingredients:	6 portions	____portions
Flour	3 c	
Sugar	½ c	
Salt	pinch	
Vanilla extract	1 t	
Eggs	8	
Egg yolks	4	
Milk	3 c	
Cream	½ c	
Butter, melted	2 oz	
CHOCOLATE SAUCE		
Half and half	1 qt	
Sugar	5 oz	
Chocolate	2 oz	
Egg yolks	6	
Cornstarch	1 oz	
Vanilla	dash	
Walnut ice cream		
Fresh cream		
Grand Marnier		
Walnuts, chopped		

The crepe batter should be made a little in advance and allowed to stand for a time before use.

Prepare very thin pancakes, 2½–3 inches in diameter, with the batter.

Cook chocolate sauce as you would a custard. When cool, add some liquid cream to make it smooth and shiny.

Place in each pancake a bar-shaped portion of walnut ice cream. Fold or roll the crepe over the ice cream. Cover the crepe, half with hot chocolate sauce (on one side diagonally) and the other half with fresh cream flavored with Grand Marnier. At the center where both sauces meet, sprinkle chopped walnuts.

Notes:

Guava con Queso
DESSERT

Ingredients:	6 portions	___portions
Guavas, 14-oz cans	2	
Cream cheese	8 oz	
Cream, heavy	2 T	
Sugar	1 t	
Salt	dash	
Orange peel, grated	⅛ t	
Lemon peel, grated	⅛ t	
Orange juice, fresh	1 T	
Lemon juice, fresh	1 T	
Pistachio nuts, chopped (or cashews or pecans)	2 oz	
Sesame seed crackers		

Chill guavas in refrigerator. Put cream cheese in bowl of electric mixer and let stand at room temperature at least 1 hour to soften. Cream well. Add heavy cream, sugar, and salt; beat thoroughly. Add orange and lemon peel. Beat. Slowly beat in orange juice. Then slowly beat in lemon juice. Beat in 1 oz of nuts, reserving remainder for garnish.

Allow two guava shells per serving. Put drained guava shells into small individual serving dishes and top each guava shell with 1 T of cream cheese mixture. Either drop filling from spoon or put cream cheese mixture into pastry tube or cake decorator and squeeze into guava shell. Top with nuts. Serve with sesame seed crackers.

(If you use a cake decorator, use all of the nuts as topping; don't put any into the cream cheese mixture, as nuts may get caught in decorator.) If you prepare guava shells ahead of time, put serving dishes on a tray, cover with foil, and refrigerate until serving time.

Notes:

DON ROTH Owner, Don Roth's Blackhawk Restaurant, Chicago, Illinois

>1978 IFMA GOLDEN PLATE AWARD
>1971 IVY AWARD OF DISTINCTION

Don Roth joined his father in the family business in Chicago a few years after graduating from the University of Illinois. Before entering the restaurant field, he was affiliated with MCA, the country's largest theatrical booking agents, and with Benton and Bowles Advertising Agency in New York City. During World War II, he was an officer in the Marine Corps, assigned to administration mess management.

Until 1952, the Blackhawk Restaurant was the home of many big-name orchestras, such as Coon-Sanders, Hal Kemp, Kay Kyser, Bob Crosby, Les Brown, Ozzie Nelson, and many others; they broadcast nightly to a nationwide radio audience. When the era of big bands faded, Mr. Roth quickly remodeled his restaurant and introduced the roast beef cart, an open-hearth grill, and the famous spinning salad bowl.

In 1978, Don Roth was the first recipient of the Chicago Foodservice Marketing Club's Hall of Fame Award. He is currently a member of the Board of Directors and Executive Committee of the National Restaurant Association. He was the chairman of the NRA convention in Chicago in 1976 and 1977. He is a past chairman of the Chicago and Illinois Restaurant Association. He is currently the chairman of Chicago's Fine Dining Association and an honorary member of the Board of Trustees of the Culinary Institute of America.

Within the past few years, Mr. Roth has added two new restaurants to his family business—one in Wheeling, a suburb of Chicago, and the newest Blackhawk, across from the Water Tower on the near north side of Chicago.

Blackhawk Salad
APPETIZER

Ingredients:	4 portions	___portions
Cream cheese, softened	3 oz	
Blue cheese, crumbled	3 oz	
Water	5–6 T	
Egg	1	
Lemon juice	1 T + 1½ t	
Vegetable oil	1 c	
Egg, hard-cooked, chopped	1	
Vinegar, red wine	¼ c	
Mustard, sharp, prepared	¼ t	
Paprika	¾ t	
Salt	¾ t	
Garlic powder	¼ t	
Pepper, white	¼ t	
Sugar	1 T	
Chives, snipped	2 T	
Worcestershire sauce	1½ t	
Salad and sandwich sauce	2 T	
Salad greens	8 c	
Pepper, freshly ground	to taste	
Anchovy fillets	8	

 Beat cheeses together until smooth. Beat in water, 1 T at a time, until mixture is of pouring consistency; reserve.
 Place egg, lemon juice, and ¼ c of oil in blender container; cover. Blend on medium speed for 15 seconds. Increase to high speed; add remaining oil very slowly. Turn off blender occasionally and clean sides of container with rubber spatula. Add vinegar, mustard, seasonings, sugar, chives, Worcestershire sauce, and salad and sandwich sauce to blender container; cover. Blend on high speed until smooth. Place salad greens in a bowl. Pour enough dressing over greens to coat. Sprinkle salad with chopped egg. Toss gently 3 times. Sprinkle with freshly ground pepper. Add 2–3 T of reserved cheese mixture. (Remaining dressing and cheese mixture can be covered and stored in refrigerator for up to 2 weeks.) Toss gently 3 times. Garnish with anchovies.

Notes:

Blackhawk au Jus for Prime Ribs of Beef
SAUCE

Ingredients:

Prime rib, oven prepared (short rib, excess fat and back bone removed)	
Celery	as needed
Tomatoes	as needed
Carrots	as needed
Onions	as needed
Salt and pepper	to taste
Caramel color	few drops

The secret of a good au jus is to combine the natural juices of good-quality beef with the flavors obtained from fresh vegetables, such as celery, tomatoes, carrots, and onions. Only the highest grade ground pepper and salt should be added for seasoning—no other spices are needed.

Put beef roast in a roasting pan with fat side up. Rub a little salt and pepper on both sides of the meat. Add vegetables and attach meat thermometer. Roast at 500° for 1 hour, reduce to 300° for 1¾ hours. Occasionally add a little water and baste the meat. When roast is done, let it "set" at room temperature from 30 to 60 minutes, depending on the size. Cool the juice and skim off excess fat. Add a few drops of caramel color to get a more attractive color.

If the roast is too small to yield a sufficient amount of juice, get some beef rib bones and a few veal bones from your butcher. Have them chopped into small pieces. Put them in a separate roasting pan, add some vegetables, pepper, and salt and simmer for 2 or 2½ hours, or until bones are dark brown. Pour off juice (remove most of the fat) and add to the juice obtained from the roast.

Notes:

Ingredients:
Prime short ribs, excess fat and back
   bone removed
Rock salt, damp

Roast Prime Ribs of Beef

ENTREE

   Cover ribs completely with damp rock salt. Put ribs in 500° oven for 1 hour, then reduce thermostat to 300° to lower temperature to 350°. Roast for an additional 1¾ hours. (Set timer to ring after 1 hour, and then reset to ring again 1 hour and 45 minutes later.)

Notes:

Ingredients:	8 portions	___portions
Salt pork, finely ground	2½ oz	
Onion, chopped	1½ oz	
Spinach, frozen, finely ground	1½ lb	
Salt and pepper	to taste	
Cream sauce	½ pt	

Creamed Spinach

VEGETABLE

   Saute salt pork until brown. Add chopped onion and saute 20–30 minutes until brown. Add spinach, salt, and pepper, let come to a boil, stirring occasionally. Add cream sauce and cook about 35 minutes, stirring frequently.

Notes:

WINSTON J. SCHULER Win Schuler's, Inc., Marshall, Michigan

>   1971   IFMA GOLD PLATE AWARD
>   1971   IVY AWARD OF DISTINCTION

   Win Schuler studied at the University of Michigan and received his degree from Albion College. He then spent four years in upper Michigan on the shores of Lake Superior in a town called Wakefield, teaching history and political science and coaching the athletic teams. He returned to his home town of Marshall to assist his father in running the forty-room Royal Hotel, acquired ten years earlier. In a few years, his father turned the responsibility for the hotel and its restaurant over to Win. During the ensuing twenty-five years, in addition to running the family business, he officiated at football and basketball games at colleges and high schools throughout the Midwest. His greatest pleasure has been the development of the family group of restaurants in Michigan.

   After developing the original Win Schuler's in Marshall, he acquired an obscure restaurant in Jackson and transformed it into a fine dining establishment. Five years later, he purchased a piece of property in St. Joseph and expanded that. Today, Win Schuler's restaurant business embraces nine different units, including a Marriott Inn. In addition, he developed a product called "Bar-Scheeze," which is marketed nationally. Mr. Schuler is proud of the list of chairmanships he has held. He has also been the recipient of many awards.

Swiss Onion Soup

SOUP

Ingredients:	12 portions	___ portions
Onions, thinly sliced	2 lb	
Butter	½ c	
Paprika	2 t	
Beef stock	6 c	
Vegetable oil	½ c	
Flour	¾ c	
Celery salt	¾ t	
Salt and pepper	to taste	
Bread, slices	12	
Parmesan cheese	½ c	
Dark beer	8 oz	

Cook onions in butter until soft. Stir in 1½ t of paprika, then add beef stock and bring to a boil. Make a roux by browning the vegetable oil and stirring in the flour. Stir the roux, celery salt, and salt and pepper into the soup. Simmer at least 2 hours.

Shortly before serving, sprinkle the slices of bread liberally with Parmesan cheese and paprika and toast them in the oven. Add the dark beer to the soup, bring it back to serving temperature, and then remove from heat. Pour soup into bowls, add a slice of toast to each, and sprinkle with additional Parmesan cheese.

Notes:

TED L. SMITH Coordinator of Food Services, Michigan State University, East Lansing, Michigan

1980 IFMA Silver Plate Award

At Michigan State University, Ted Smith in his position of Coordinator of Food Services sets a shining example of food service at its finest. Many of Ted Smith's employees are also students in the Hotel, Restaurant, and Institutional Management program. Mr. Smith provides his managers and supervisors with current, accurate, and detailed information to help them in meeting the goals they set. That information covers food costs for all segments of the university food service, menu planning, and management and general operating procedures.

Employee training programs and expansion of career opportunities are major priorities for Mr. Smith. There are working laboratories in the residence hall kitchens that are used for a course in foodservice systems management. Also, cooks and production supervisors attend periodic refresher courses.

In addition to publishing articles on food service, Mr. Smith has served as an officer of the National Association of College and University Food Services and as a member of several other associations.

Spinach Lasagna
ENTREE

Ingredients:	6 portions	___portions
Lasagna noodles, uncooked	4½ oz	
Mozzarella, shredded	2½ oz	
Sharp cheddar cheese	2½ oz	
Bread crumbs	⅛ c	
Parmesan cheese	⅛ c	
Cottage cheese	7 oz	
Spinach, frozen, chopped	6 oz	
SAUCE		
Margarine	½ oz	
Onions, chopped	2 oz	
Tomato pieces (#10 can)	1½ lb	
Tomato puree	1½ lb	
Water	⅛ c	
Salt	1 t	
Pepper, black	dash	
Garlic powder	⅛ t	
Sugar, granulated	¾ t	

Cook noodles and drain. To make sauce, saute onions in margarine. Add tomato pieces, tomato puree, water, salt, pepper, garlic powder, and sugar. Simmer. Mix together mozzarella and cheddar cheese. Mix together bread crumbs and Parmesan cheese.

Layer in a casserole dish: cooked noodles (half), sauce (half), mixed cheeses, cottage cheese, chopped spinach, cooked noodles (half), sauce (half), and mixed crumbs and cheese. Bake.

Notes:

LLOYD AND LES STEPHENSON Stephenson's Restaurants, Inc., The Old Apple Farm, Kansas City, Missouri

1972 Ivy Award of Distinction

Lloyd and Les Stephenson, both past presidents of the Missouri Restaurant Association, tell the story of their business: "In 1870, when Highway 40 was a mud road, the Stephenson fruit and vegetable farm had its beginning. From a one-room stone building, our grandparents sold homegrown produce to folks between Lee's Summit and Independence. Old timers say the little building was regarded as the half-way point between these two towns. In 1935, Norman, our brother, joined father in the orchard business. Since then, the orchard acreage has spread from Lee's Summit to locations in Blue Springs, Grain Valley, and Sibley. From these orchards come our fresh apples, peaches, berries, and the sweet cider which we serve all year long. Fresh produce from these orchards can also be bought, in season, at Norman's stand next to the restaurant.

"Like most early Missouri settlers, our grandparents smoked meats, made apple butter, and canned their own fruits and vegetables. And so, on April 16, 1946, when we opened our restaurant in the original stone building, it seemed natural to call it The Apple Farm. We had ten booths then and served only thirty-eight people the first day. Then, as now, we served old-fashioned hickory-smoked meats, homemade apple butter, preserves, and relishes—all prepared in our kitchens in the unique manner which our grandparents had taught us. Gradually, during seven remodelings, the original stone building has been engulfed. It remains, however, as part of the restaurant's superstructure.

"In 1977, due to popular demand, we decided to open two new restaurants, since our original restaurant had been expanded to its capacity. One of the new restaurants is located eight miles south of the Kansas City International Airport in Platte Woods, Missouri. The other new restaurant is located in Jane, Missouri, on Highway 71."

Escalloped Sweet Potatoes

VEGETABLE

Ingredients:	6 portions	___portions
Sweet potatoes, medium, cooked, peeled, halved	3	
Orange, unpeeled, thinly sliced	1	
Apple, unpeeled, thinly sliced	1	
Peach, fresh, peeled and sliced	1	
SYRUP		
Water	½ c	
Honey	2 T	
Orange juice	2 T	
Pineapple juice	2 T	
Brown sugar	2 T	
Butter	1 T	
TOPPING		
Bread crumbs	3 T	
Brown sugar	2 T	
Butter	1 T	
Marshmallows, large	6	
Maraschino cherries, halved	3	

Put sweet potato halves into an 8- or 9-inch square pan. Cover with fruit. Bring syrup ingredients to a boil. Pour over potatoes. Make a crumbly mixture of bread crumbs, brown sugar, and butter. Sprinkle over potatoes. Bake at 350° for 20 minutes. Put a marshmallow in center of each potato. Bake 10 minutes more, or until marshmallows are browned. Garnish with cherry halves.

Notes:

LOUIS I. SZATHMARY II Ph.D., Owner, The Bakery Restaurant, Louis Szathmary Associates, Chicago, Illinois

1973 IVY AWARD OF DISTINCTION

Chef Louis Szathmary's home base is "Szathmaryland," a complex of renovated residences that includes The Bakery Restaurant, a honeycomb of supply and test kitchens, offices, and apartments, and a private food library-museum with 18,000 books and 15,000 prints and artifacts. From there, the rotund, mustachioed Chef Louis smoothly wades through the crowded schedule of public and private happenings that reflects his diversified background.

He was educated as a journalist and psychologist in his native Hungary. During his much-traveled life, he has been an an actor, soldier, marriage counselor, prisoner of war, lecturer, writer, chef, and a sort of "foodfather" to scores of blood and adopted relatives and Old World compatriots.

While overseeing The Bakery, a restaurant consistently selected among the most popular in Chicago, he also operates Louis Szathmary Associates, a food systems design and management consulting firm with some of the best-known names in American commerce as clients. Within recent years he has published *The Chef's Secret Cookbook*, fifteen volumes of *Cookery Americana*, *American Gastronomy*, *The Chef's New Secret Cookbook*, and, most recently, *The Bakery Restaurant Cookbook*. He writes a syndicated weekly food column and reports on restaurants from all over the world in *Travel/Holiday*.

Cream of Kohlrabi Soup

SOUP

Ingredients:	8 portions	___portions
Kohlrabi, fresh	1–1½ lb	
Butter	4 T	
Onion, finely minced	½ c	
Sugar	1 T	
Carrot	1	
Parsley root	1	
Peppercorns	4–5	
Bay leaf	½	
Salt	to taste	
Chicken broth (10-oz cans)	2	
Water	20 oz	
Parsley, flatleaf, coarsely chopped	½ c	
Flour	3 T	
Cornstarch	3 T	
Milk	1 pt	
Sour cream (or heavy cream)	1 c	

Wash and peel kohlrabi. Cut into ½-inch cubes. In a heavy pot, melt the butter and saute the onion until translucent. Add the sugar and kohlrabi. Cover and cook over medium heat for 2–3 minutes. Turn the heat to low and simmer for 15–20 minutes. Scrape, wash, and chop the carrot and parsley root. The pieces should be a little smaller than the kohlrabi pieces. Add to the kohlrabi along with the peppercorns, bay leaf, and very little salt. Cover and simmer again for 15–20 minutes.

Add the two cans of chicken broth and two cans of water, along with half of the chopped parsley. Bring to a boil. Dissolve the flour and cornstarch in the milk. Stirring the soup constantly with a large spoon, pour in the milk mixture. Turn the heat to low, cover, and simmer for another 20–25 minutes. Correct the seasoning by adding more salt, if it is needed.

Combine the remaining chopped parsley with the sour cream (or heavy cream). Pour this into a soup tureen and ladle the soup over it. If you like a thicker soup, simply add more flour and cornstarch, mixing it first with a little cold water or cold milk.

Chef's secret: If you have time, instead of using canned broth and water, make the soup with 1 lb of veal bones cooked in 6–8 c of water with a little salt, black pepper, and bay leaf.

Notes:

Sauce Louis

SAUCE

Ingredients:	4 portions	___portions
Eggs	2	
Mustard, prepared	3 T	
Brown sugar, light	3 T	
Salt	½ t	
White pepper, ground	⅛ t	
Lemon juice	1 lemon	
Vinegar	1 t	
Sour cream (or half and half, soured)	1 pt	

Blend eggs, mustard, brown sugar, salt, white pepper, lemon juice, and vinegar in a medium-size bowl, stirring them vigorously together with a wire whip. Gently fold in the sour cream. Keep refrigerated.

Chef's secret: This is probably the simplest, quickest, and yet most elegant sauce. It can be made in 20 seconds, without cooking or even getting near the stove. All the ingredients except the sour cream should be blended vigorously with a wire whip or in an electric mixer at the highest speed. But the sour cream must be gently folded into the sauce with a rubber spatula. If commercial sour cream is beaten, it will become runny and will separate, and you will not get the proper silky texture and consistency. Try it with yogurt!

Notes:

JAY TREADWELL Director, Food Services, United States Senate, Washington, D.C.

1978 IFMA Silver Plate Award

Jay Treadwell, a native of New York, attended various schools there, then graduated from Deerfield Academy in 1956. He received his B.S. degree in 1961 from the Cornell School of Hotel Administration. While there, he was a member of Ye Hosts, a scholastic honorary and hotel sales management association.

Mr. Treadwell received his commission as an officer in the United States Navy and ran the Officers' Club at the naval air station at Los Alamitos, California, until 1963. He then joined Pan Am World Airways, holding a number of positions from Supervisor of Food and Beverage Control to Senior Director of In-flight Services. In 1975, he left Pan Am to become Director of Food Services for the thirteen United States Senate restaurants. Mr. Treadwell has been successful in virtually eliminating a more than a quarter of a million dollar deficit in three years while drastically improving the service standards. He has made the Senate complex what *Institutions* (February 15, 1973) called ". . . the closest thing we have to a National Restaurant."

Cold Cucumber Soup

SOUP

Ingredients:	6 portions	___portions
Cucumbers, fresh	2 lb	
Onion, large	1	
Salt and pepper	to taste	
Butter, unsalted	4 oz	
Chicken broth	1 can	
Cream, light	3 pt	
Cream of celery soup	1 can	

Blend all ingredients thoroughly in a blender. Refrigerate until very cold.

Notes:

Paupiette de Coeur de Filet with Shallot Sauce
ENTREE

Ingredients:	12 portions	6 portions	___portions
Onion, small, chopped	1	½	
Spinach, fresh, chopped	1 pkg	½ pkg	
Garlic clove, crushed	¼	⅛	
Butter	½ lb	¼ lb	
Ground chuck	1 lb	½ lb	
White cream sauce (roux and cream)	¼ c	⅛ c	
Parsley, dry	1 t	½ t	
Sherry wine	to taste	to taste	
Oregano	to taste	to taste	
Salt and pepper	to taste	to taste	
Beef tenderloin	4 lb	2 lb	

SHALLOT SAUCE

Shallots, chopped	2	1	
Mushroom caps	12	6	
Butter	3 T	4½ t	
Consommé	1 c	½ c	
Cornstarch	½ t	¼ t	
Red wine	1 oz	½ oz	

Saute onion, crushed garlic, and chopped spinach in butter. Add ground beef and brown. Slowly add warmed white cream sauce, stirring constantly. Add parsley, sherry, oregano, salt, and pepper to taste.

Slice raw, peeled tenderloin on the bias (45 degress) ¼-inch thick. Roll a portion of ground beef mixture inside each slice and hold together with a toothpick. Place on preheated grill or roasting pan and roast for 10 minutes at 425°.

For sauce, saute chopped shallots and mushrooms caps in butter. Remove mushrooms and save. Add consommé to sauteed shallots. Heat and stir until warm. Dissolve cornstarch in a little water and add to the consommé mixture, stirring until thickened. Add red wine.

Place a mushroom cap on each plate with tenderloin and add Shallot Sauce as desired.

Notes:

MILTON VALLEN Director of Food Services, Moss Rehabilitation Hospital, Philadelphia, Pennsylvania

1978–80   International President, IFSEA

Milton Vallen's operation is 95 percent convenience, including the therapeutic menus. Foods are purchased in bulk and taken cold to the various floors, where individual servings are heated in microwave ovens.

Mr. Vallen has been and is presently International President of the IFSEA. He has been a member of this association for over twenty years, was one of its first certified members, and is a life member. Mr. Vallen is also a member of the Hospital Food Directors and of the Dignified Order of the Dinner Gong. He has been involved in the foodservice industry for over thirty-five years, working in all facets from the front to the back of the house, including industrial, institutional, and restaurant food service.

Spareribs à la Vallen
ENTREE

Ingredients:	3 portions	6 portions	___portions
Pork spareribs	3–5 lb	6–10 lb	
Kikkoman Soy Sauce	2 c	4 c	
Mustard, dry	1 t	2 t	
Scallions, medium-size bunches, finely chopped	2	4	
Garlic cloves, flattened	3	6	
Honey or marmalade (orange or apricot)	to baste	to baste	

Wash the spareribs, and blot dry. Mix the rest of the ingredients except honey or marmalade and place in a pan. Add the spareribs; marinate overnight, turning several times.

Remove spareribs from marinade (save marinade) and place on oven rack. Bake at 350° about 1 hour, turning over several times and basting with marinade. About 5 minutes prior to serving, remove rack from oven and place in broiler. Brush spareribs with honey or marmalade (orange or apricot) and broil for a few minutes until crisp.

Notes:

JANE YOUNG WALLACE Editor-in-Chief, *Restaurants & Institutions* magazine, Chicago, Illinois

Jane Young Wallace is editor-in-chief of *Restaurants & Institutions* magazine, the leading publication serving the foodservice field. This twice-monthly publication has a circulation of 105,000. Since joining the staff in 1958, Ms. Wallace has been production editor, food editor, and managing editor, as well as editor-in-chief. Ms. Wallace received the Jesse Neal Award for best editorial in the business press in 1970, 1971, 1973, 1976, and 1977. (The Jesse Neal Award is comparable to the Pulitzer Prize for newspapers.)

In addition to serving as editor-in-chief of *Restaurants & Institutions*, Ms. Wallace is also editorial director of *Service World International*, a magazine for those engaged in food service and lodging in the international market; *Foodservice Distributor Salesman*, a tabloid newspaper for those who distribute food and supplies to the foodservice market; and *Equipment Specialist*, a tabloid newspaper specializing in equipment and supplies for the foodservice and lodging industry.

Ms. Wallace is active in many industry associations and has served as president of the Institutional Food Editors Council. She has also served on various state and federal committees concerned with personnel utilization and education for the foodservice industry. She is the author of the "Restaurant" listing for *World Book Encyclopedia*, as well as editor of several foodservice recipe books and textbooks.

Ms. Wallace received both her B.S. and M.S. degrees in journalism from Northwestern University. Ms. Wallace, her husband Don, and their two children, Bob and Julie, live in Barrington, Illinois.

Easy Beef Stroganoff
ENTREE

Ingredients:	4 portions	___portions
Onion, chopped	½	
Butter	1 T	
Beef, sirloin strips or chunks	1½ lb	
Beef bouillon crystals	1 t	
Water, hot	¼ c	
White wine	¾ c	
Mushrooms, sliced, 4-oz jar (include liquid)	1	
Flour	1 T	
Chives, fresh or freeze dried	to taste	
Dill, fresh (or dry, if not available)	to taste	
Sour cream	1 c	

Saute onion in butter. Add beef and saute until brown. Mix beef bouillon crystals in hot water and add ¼ c of white wine. Add mushrooms, including liquid, to meat. Add bouillon-wine mixture to meat. Thicken with flour and simmer about 10 minutes. Add chives and dill to taste, and rest of wine as needed.

Just before serving, add sour cream (nondairy product will also work). Heat and serve with rice, noodles, or wild rice. A tossed salad or green beans amandine is a good accompaniment. The plate should be garnished with a bright fruit garnish. The dessert is usually an ice cream or sherbet with a complementary fruit and a liqueur topping.

Notes:

FRANK GEORGE WANGEMAN Senior Vice-President, Hilton Hotels Corporation, and Executive Vice-President/General Manager, Hotel Waldorf-Astoria Corporation, New York, New York

Frank Wangeman's early training took place at such famous European hotels as the Lausanne Palace, the George V, the Ritz, and the Hyde Park Hotel. He joined the Waldorf-Astoria in 1954, becoming assistant manager at the age of twenty-three. In 1943, he joined Hilton as operating manager of the Plaza Hotel.

Mr. Wangeman is a founding member of the board of Hilton Hotels International and contributed to the start and development of Hilton hotels around the world. He established prizes so that top students could receive further training at Hilton hotels. He gives lectures at both the Harvard and Columbia business schools and is a member of many organizations and the recipient of numerous awards.

Ingredients:

Blue trout, alive
Vinegar

COURT BOUILLON VII

Salt water
Vinegar
Carrots
Onions, sliced
Parsley
Thyme
Bay leaf
Salt and pepper
Parsley, fresh

*River Trout
(Truites de
Rivière)*
ENTREE

For this dish, the trout must be not only absolutely fresh but actually alive. Ten minutes before serving, take the fish out of the water, kill them with a blow on the head, and clean them. Sprinkle them with vinegar, then plunge them into court bouillon containing a high proportion of vinegar. Cook as rapidly as possible, allowing 7–8 minutes for fish weighing about 5 oz each.

Drain the trout; arrange on a napkin-covered dish and garnish them with fresh parsley. Serve melted butter or hollandaise sauce separately.

Notes:

PAUL CRAIG WEISMAN Director of Food Services, University of Washington Hospital, Seattle, Washington

1978 President, American Society for Hospital Food Services Administrators (ASHFSA)

Paul Weisman, a graduate of the Cornell School of Hotel and Restaurant Administration, has been primarily affiliated with industrial and institutional food management. In twenty-eight years of professional endeavor, Mr. Weisman has spent twenty-three years involved directly in the organization, supervision, and management of foodservice systems and five years involved in business accounting and automation. For the past eighteen years Mr. Weisman has been associated with the University of Washington Hospital as a food service administrator.

During his association with this hospital, Mr. Weisman has served as the area representative for the formation of the Puget Sound chapter of Hospital Food Service Administrators, a personal membership society affiliated with the American Hospital Association. Following the formation of the Puget Sound chapter, Mr. Weisman served as its president in 1969. Mr. Weisman is also a member of the American Dietetic Association and a past president of the Greater Seattle Dietetic Association.

Kippered Salmon Salad Plate

APPETIZER

Ingredients:	48 portions	6 portions	___portions
Lettuce, iceberg, shredded	12 heads	1½ heads	
Kippered salmon	8 lb	1 lb	
Eggs, hard-cooked	6 doz	9	
Tomatoes, sliced	4 lb	8 oz	
Cucumbers, sliced	2 lb	4 oz	
Radish roses	96	12	
Olives ripe	144	18	
Carrot curls	48 curls	6	
Three-bean salad, marinated	3 qt	12 oz	
Lemon wedges	48	6	
Parsley, fresh	garnish	garnish	

Arrange lettuce leaves on plates. Pile with shredded lettuce. Place 2⅔ oz of salmon, 1½ eggs (wedges), 2 tomato slices, 2 cucumber slices, 2 radishes, 3 olives, 1 carrot curl, ¼ c of bean salad, and 1 lemon wedge on each plate. Serve garnished with parsley.

Notes:

Pancit Guisado
ENTREE

Ingredients:	45 portions	6 portions	___portions
Pork strips	3½ lb	7½ oz	
Garlic cloves, chopped	12	1½	
Oil	½ c	1 oz	
Celery, sliced	3 lb	6½ oz	
Mushrooms, sliced	1 lb	2¼ oz	
Carrots, sliced	2 lb	4¼ oz	
Onions, sliced	2 lb	4¼ oz	
Shrimp, frozen	1½ lb	3¼ oz	
Soy sauce	1 c	1 oz	
Chinese noodles	4 lb	8½ oz	
MSG	2 T	1 t	
Salt	to taste	to taste	

Combine pork strips, garlic, and oil. Fry until pork is tender. Add celery, mushrooms, carrots, onions, shrimp, and soy sauce. Mix and simmer about 5 minutes.

Bring the pork stock to a boil. Add Chinese noodles, breaking into 2-inch pieces. Cook until tender. Combine with pork mixture. Season with MSG and salt.

Notes:

CHARLES H. WILSON Director of University Food Service, University of Northern Colorado, Greeley, Colorado

As a member of the board of directors and as director of training of the National Association of College and University Food Services, Charles H. Wilson designed the first NACUFS national training program. He was ready for this task, having been born into a restaurant family and having spent four years as a teacher after his graduation from Michigan State University. He began work as a full-time chef's helper at age thirteen and worked in hotels, restaurants, and yacht clubs until his college graduation.

Mr. Wilson was a high school industrial education teacher for four years, then returned to food service to help plan Michigan State University's food processing center. After that, he moved on to become food service director at the National College of Education in 1976 and at the University of Northern Colorado in 1977.

Krautburgers
ENTREE

Ingredients:	15 portions	___portions
Ground beef	3 lb	
Onions, chopped	1 c	
Cabbage, shredded	2⅓ lb	
Salt and pepper	to taste	
Onion salt	to taste	
Puff paste crust (18 × 26 × ¼ inch), unbaked	1	

Brown ground beef in a large stock pot. Add chopped onions and shredded cabbage. Cook until cabbage is tender. (A small amount of water may be needed so that cabbage steams.) Season.

Cut crust into 15 equal squares. Place approximately 1 c of filling on each square. Bring corners together and seal. Place sealed side down on greased baking sheet. Lightly brush each roll with melted margarine or cooking oil. Bake in a moderate oven at 350° until golden brown, approximately 25–30 minutes. *Serve hot.*

Notes:

Plantation Spareribs
ENTREE

Ingredients:	64 portions	___portions
Molasses	1 gal	
Mustard, prepared	3 qt	
Vinegar	3 qt	
Worcestershire sauce	1 qt	
Salt	2⅔ T	
Tabasco	2⅔ T	
Pork spareribs	64 lb	

Blend molasses into mustard. Stir in the vinegar, Worcestershire sauce, salt, and Tabasco. Bring to a boil.

Place spareribs, with meaty side down, in shallow pans. Roast at 450° for 30 minutes. Remove pan from oven; drain off excess fat. Turn ribs so that meaty side is up. Reduce oven temperature to 350°, roast till tender, about another 1 hour. During the last 30 minutes of roasting, baste often with molasses mixture.

Notes:

TED WRIGHT Vice-President and Managing Director, The Cloister Hotel, Sea Island, Georgia

1977 IVY AWARD OF DISTINCTION

Ted Wright feels that the industry places entirely too much emphasis on the profit generated by each operation and that there is not enough dedication to true hospitality in innkeeping.

The Cloister Hotel is the perfect example of old-fashioned hospitality. It continues to follow the traditions of the full American plan: assigned tables in the dining room, evening turn-down service, strict dress codes, and a constant emphasis on employee attitudes. The Cloister has been awarded the Mobil 5-Star Award three times in recent years. Mr. Wright demands excellence throughout the facilities he directs, especially in food service for resort guests. He is a leader in setting new standards for hotels and in introducing new guest services. His food operations are characterized by their high quality and the outstanding service by the staffs.

Mr. Wright is a member of the resort committee of the American Hotel and Motel Association, a director of the Georgia Hospitality and Travel Association, and a past president and director of the Arizona Hotel and Motel Association and the Houston Hotel and Motel Association.

Veal Cloister
ENTREE

Ingredients:	4 portions	6 portions	___portions
Veal steaks, centercut, boneless, ⅓-inch thick, 6 oz	4	6	
Salt	to taste	to taste	
White pepper	to taste	to taste	
Flour	to coat	to coat	
Butter	to saute	to saute	
White chicken meat, cooked, diced	1½ c	2¼ c	
Mushrooms, chopped, cooked	¾ c	1⅛ c	
Basic white sauce, thick, well-seasoned	1 c	1½ c	
Tomatoes, fresh, thin slices	12 slices	18 slices	
Mushroom caps, large	4	6	
Hollandaise sauce	2 c	3 c	

Season the veal steaks lightly with salt and white pepper, dip in flour, and saute in drawn butter until half done (3–4 minutes). Place side by side on a baking sheet.

Combine chicken meat, chopped mushrooms, and white sauce in a bowl. Spread this mixture over the steaks. Cover each steak from end to end, with 3 slices of tomato. Place one mushroom cap on the center of each steak, pressing it down lightly. Cover steaks with hollandaise sauce and bake in moderately hot oven (375°) for 5 minutes, or until golden brown.

Notes:

HERMAN E. ZACCARELLI C.S.C., Director, Restaurant, Hotel, and Institutional Management Institute, Purdue University, West Lafayette, Indiana

1980 Honorary Member, American Academy of Chefs
1979 Achievement Award for Food Service Education, American Culinary Federation

Brother Herman E. Zaccarelli is a native of New Castle, Pennsylvania. A prolific and very popular writer, Brother Herman has published over one hundred foodservice articles and seven books. He is the author of the *Retirement Food and Nutritional Manual*. This manual, the first of its kind, has been prepared for mature adults, especially those on restricted diets. Brother Herman has served as a consulting editor for the second edition of the *American Culinary Federation Manual for Culinarians*, and presently is Management Systems Editor of *Chef Institutional Magazine*.

A member of the Congregation of Holy Cross for over twenty-seven years, Brother Herman has had a pervasive and humanitarian impact on the foodservice industry. In 1958, he became Director of Food Service at Stonehill College. He has earned an international following during his seventeen years as Founder and Director of the International Food Research and Education Center in North Easton, Massachusetts.

Brother Herman has, at various times, served on the faculties of the University of Puerto Rico, Lansing College, and the School of Hotel, Restaurant, and Institutional Management, University of Minnesota at Crookston. In the fall of 1976, he was selected by the Educational Institute of the American Hotel and Motel Association as a faculty member of a team to present supervisory development training programs in the far eastern countries of Nepal, Sri Lanka, and Pakistan. In July 1978, Purdue University appointed Brother Herman as the first director of its Restaurant, Hotel, and Institutional Management Institute. He also serves as a consultant to many health care facilities in the United States. He has recently authored a booklet, *Guidelines for Employing Food Management Companies*, for administrators of health care and educational institutions.

Brother Herman is a recipient of the coveted Theodore W. Minah Distinguished Service Award. *Foodservice* magazine has named Brother Herman as one of the "Ten Most Notable People in the Foodservice Industry."

Ingredients:	48 portions	___portions
Lime Jello	3½ c	
Water, hot (140–160°)	3½ qt	
Mayonnaise (or mayonnaise and sour cream, equal parts)	3 c	
Avocados, diced	2¼ qt	
Lime or lemon juice	1½ c	
Salt	1½ T	
Onion, finely grated	1 T	

Avocado Lime Salad

APPETIZER

    Dissolve Jello in hot water; cool. Gradually add mayonnaise, blending with a wire whip. Chill until slightly thickened.

    Combine remaining ingredients. Let stand 15 minutes to marinate; then fold into Jello. Pour into shallow pans or individual molds. Chill until firm. Cut into squares or unmold. Serve on crisp greens and garnish with tomato wedges, if desired.

Notes:

Ingredients:	120 portions	___portions
Beets, diced, with juice (#10 can)	6	
Water and beet juice, hot (140–160°)	8½ gal	
Orange or lemon Jello	2¼ gal	
Salt	1 c	
Vinegar	3¾ qt	
Celery, diced	3¾ gal	
Horseradish, prepared	2½ c	
Onion, grated	2½ c	

Cardinal Salad

APPETIZER

    Drain beets, measuring juice. Add hot water to beet juice to make required amount of liquid. Dissolve Jello and salt in hot liquid. Add vinegar. Chill until slightly thickened.

    Fold beets, celery, horseradish, and onion into Jello. Pour into containers. Chill until firm.

Notes:

Apricot–Sour Cream Pie
DESSERT

Ingredients:	48 portions	___portions
Apricot halves, canned	1 qt	
Water and apricot syrup, hot (140–160°)	3 qt	
Apricot Jello	1 pkg	
Sugar	¼ c	
Sour cream (or yogurt, plain or vanilla)	2 qt	
Pie shells, 9-inch, baked, cooled (or graham cracker crumb crusts)	6	
Dream Whip	garnish	

Drain apricots, reserving syrup. Add hot water to syrup to make required amount of liquid. Dissolve Jello and sugar in hot liquid. Chill until slightly thickened.

Blend in sour cream. Dice the apricots and stir in. Pour into pie shells, allowing 1 qt of filling for each. Chill until set. Garnish with Dream Whip topping and additional sliced apricots, if desired.

Apricot–Sour Cream Tarts: Prepare Apricot–Sour Cream Pie as directed, but omitting pie shells. Spoon filling into 72 baked and cooled, 3-inch tart shells, allowing ⅓ c of filling for each.

Apricot–Sour Cream Dessert: Prepare Apricot–Sour Cream Pie as directed, but omitting pie shells. Spoon filling into 48 individual dessert dishes, allowing ½ c of filling for each.

Notes:

Butter Pecan Dream Pie
DESSERT

Ingredients:	32 portions	___portions
Milk, cold	2¼ qt	
Butter pecan or vanilla ice cream, softened	1½ qt	
Jello Butter Pecan Instant Pudding and Pie Filling	1 pkg	
Pie shells, 9-inch, baked, cooled (or graham cracker crumb crusts)	5	
Dream Whip	to top	
Pecan halves	garnish	

PRALINE CRUMB MIXTURE

Coconut, flaked	1½ c	
Pecans, chopped	1 c	
Brown sugar, firmly packed	1 c	
Butter or margarine	½ c	

Blend milk with ice cream in a 12-qt mixer bowl. Add Jello mix and beat as directed on package for pie filling. Pour immediately into pie shells, allowing about 3 c of filling for each. Chill until set, about 3 hours. Garnish with Dream Whip and pecan halves, if desired.

Butter Pecan Dream Tarts or Dessert: Prepare Butter Pecan Dream Pie as directed, but omitting pie shells. Ladle into 48 baked and cooled, 3-inch tart shells, allowing ⅓ c of filling for each. Sprinkle each with 1 T of Praline Crumb Mixture. Or pour filling into a 12 × 20 × 2½-inch pan. Chill and cut into squares.

To make Praline Crumb Mixture, combine coconut, pecans, brown sugar, and butter or margarine in skillet. Cook and stir over medium heat until butter is melted and mixture begins to brown slightly, or about 5 minutes. Spread evenly on buttered baking sheet. Cool, then break into crumbs.

Notes:

Chinese-Style Relish

Ingredients:	60 portions	___portions
Bean sprouts	2 qt	
Lemon Jello	1 pkg	
Salt	4 t	
Water, hot (140–160°)	1 gal	
Onion, grated	½ c	
Vinegar	½ c	
Sherry wine	½ c	
Water chestnuts, sliced	2 c	
Green pepper, diced	2 c	

Soak bean sprouts in enough boiling water to cover for at least 15 minutes. Drain; cut or snip with scissors into shorter lengths.

Dissolve Jello and salt in hot water. Add onion, vinegar, and sherry. Chill until slightly thickened. Stir in bean sprouts, water chestnuts, and diced green pepper. Pour into individual molds or two 12 × 10 × 2½-inch pans. Chill until firm. Unmold or cut into squares. Serve with meat or poultry.

Notes:

Curried Fruit Relish

Ingredients:	72 portions	___portions
Curry powder, mild	¼ c	
Brown sugar, firmly packed	½ c	
Salt	2 t	
Water	1 gal	
Lemon Jello	1 pkg	
Peaches, sliced, frozen, thawed	2½ lb	
Bananas, large, sliced	4	
Maraschino cherries, halved	24	
Chutney, finely chopped	½ c	

Combine curry powder, brown sugar, salt, and 2 qt of the water in a saucepan. Bring to a boil; reduce heat and simmer 5 minutes. Remove from heat, add Jello and stir until dissolved. Add remaining water and stir. Chill until thickened.

Stir in fruits and chutney. Pour into individual molds or two 12 × 10 × 2½-inch pans. Chill until firm. Unmold or cut into squares. Serve with meats or poultry. (Specks of curry powder will be evident.)

Notes:

Peach-Wine Relish

Ingredients:	54 portions	___portions
Peaches, frozen, sliced, thawed	2½ lb	
Sugar	1 qt	
Water	1½ qt	
Vinegar	2 c	
Cloves, whole	2 t (48)	
Cinnamon sticks	4	
Peach Jello	1 pkg	
Water and peach syrup	1 qt	
Sauterne wine	3 c	

Drain peaches, reserving syrup. Add water to syrup to make 1 qt. Combine sugar, water, vinegar, and spices in saucepan. Bring to a boil; reduce heat and simmer 10 minutes. Strain. Dissolve Jello in hot syrup. Add measured liquid and wine. Chill until slightly thickened. Stir in peaches. Pour into individual molds or two 12 × 10 × 2½-inch pans. Chill until firm. Unmold or cut into squares. Serve with meats or poultry. (For frozen peaches, you may substitute 16 fresh peaches, peeled, pitted, and sliced, and 1 qt water.)

Notes:

APPENDIX

Table of Equivalents

1 cube butter	= 4 ounces or ½ cup	1 pound whole eggs	= 2 cups or 9–11 eggs
1 cup butter	= ½ pound or 8 ounces	1 cup egg white	= 8–10 egg whites
1 cup shortening	= ½ pound	1 cup egg yolks	= 10–11 egg yolks
1 ounce chocolate	= 1 square	1 ounce plain gelatin	= 4 tablespoons
1 pound cheese	= 4 cups shredded cheese	1 pound macaroni	= 4 cups raw or 9 cups cooked
1 cup cocoa	= 4 ounces	1 cup mayonnaise	= 8 ounces
1 cup sifted all-purpose flour	= 4 ounces	1 pound noodles	= 6 cups raw or 9 cups cooked
1 cup brown sugar	= 5 ounces	1 pound oatmeal	= 6 cups raw or 4 quarts cooked
1 cup granulated sugar	= 8 ounces	1 pound chopped onions	= 2–3 cups
1 cup powdered sugar	= 5 ounces	1 pound peanut butter	= 1¾ cups
1 cup rice	= 8 ounces or 3–3½ cups cooked	1 pound raisins	= 3 cups or 4 cups after cooking
1 cup cornstarch	= 4 ounces	1 pound prunes	= 2½ cups or 3–4 cups after cooking
1 cup cornmeal	= 5 ounces	1 pound spaghetti	= 5 cups or 10 cups after cooking
2 tablespoons baking powder	= 1 ounce	1 pound tapioca	= 3 cups or 7½ cups after cooking
1 pound bread, broken	= 2½ quarts	20 salt crackers	= 1 cup crumbs
1 cup coconut	= 3 ounces	12 graham crackers	= 1 cup crumbs
1 pound cracker crumbs	= 5–6 cups	1 slice bread	= ½ cup cubes or 3 tablespoons bread crumbs

Source: James R. Myers, *Commercial Kitchens*, 6th ed. (Arlington, Va.: American Gas Association, 1979), p. 307. Used by permission of copyright holder—American Gas Association.

Approximate Ingredient Substitutions

Ingredient	Approximate equivalent	Ingredient	Approximate equivalent
Thickening agents:		*Chocolate and cocoa:*	
1 oz flour	= 3½ whole eggs (5½ oz) = 7 egg yolks (5 oz) = 1⅓ oz quick-cooking tapioca = ¾ oz cornstarch = ¾ oz bread crumbs	1 oz or 1 square chocolate	= 3 T cocoa plus 1 T fat
		Milk:	
		1 c sour milk	= 1 c sweet milk plus 1 T lemon juice or vinegar
1 T flour	= ½ T cornstarch = 2 T quick-cooking tapioca	*Cream:*	
		1 c cream, thin (18–20%)	= ⅞ c milk plus 3 T butter
Shortening agents:		1 c cream, heavy (36–40%)	= ¾ c milk plus ⅓ c butter
1 lb butter	= 1 lb margarine = ⅞ lb hydrogenated shortening plus 1 t salt = ⅞ lb oil (1⅜ c) plus 1 t salt	*Flour:*	
		1 c all-purpose flour	= 1 c plus 2 T cake flour = ⅞ c corn meal = 1 c graham flour = 1 c rye flour = 1¼ c bran = 1½ c bread crumbs = 1 c rolled oats
Leavening agents:		*Seasoning:*	
1 t baking powder	= ¼ t soda (plus ⅝ t cream of tartar, ½ c sour milk, ½ T vinegar used with 7½ T sweet milk or ¼ to ½ c molasses to neutralize the alkalinity of the soda) = 2 egg whites	1 medium onion	= 1 T instant minced onion
1 small pkg. active dry yeast	= 1 cake compressed yeast		
1 oz dry yeast	= 2 oz compressed yeast		

Note: To substitute sour milk or buttermilk for sweet milk, add ½ t soda and decrease baking powder by 2 t per cup of milk. To sour reconstituted dry milk, add 1 c cultured buttermilk to 1 gal reconstituted dry milk.

Source: James R. Myers, *Commercial Kitchens*, 6th ed. (Arlington, Va.: American Gas Association, 1979), p. 308. Used by permission of copyright holder—American Gas Association.

The following table is designed to help change fractional parts of pounds, cups, gallons, etc., to accurate weights or measures. For example, reading from left to right in the second line, the table shows that ⅞ of 1 cup is 1 cup less 2 T, ⅞ of 1 quart is 3½ cups, ⅞ of 1 pound is 14 ounces.

Fractional Equivalents

Fraction	Tablespoon	Cup	Pint	Quart	Gallon	Pound
1	3 t	18 T	2 c	2 pt	4 qt	16 oz
⅞	2½ t	1 c − 2 T	1¾ c	3½ c	3 qt 1 pt	14 oz
¾	2¼ t	12 T	1½ c	3 c	3 qt	12 oz
⅔	2 t	10 T 2 t	1⅓ c	2⅔ c	2 qt 2⅔ c	10⅔ oz
⅝	2 t (scant)	10 T	1¼ c	2½ c	2 qt 1 pt	10 oz
½	1½ t	8 T	1 c	2 c	2 qt	8 oz
⅜	1⅛ t	6 T	¾ c	1½ c	1 qt 1 pt	6 oz
⅓	1 t	5 T 1 t	⅔ c	1⅓ c	1 qt 1⅓ c	5⅓ oz
¼	¾ t	4 T	½ c	1 c	1 qt	4 oz
⅛	½ t (scant)	2 T	¼ c	½ c	1 pt	2 oz
1/16	¼ t (scant)	1 T	2 T	¼ c	1 c	1 oz

Source: James R. Myers, *Commercial Kitchens*, 6th ed. (Arlington, Va.: American Gas Association, 1979), p. 307. Used by permission of copyright holder—American Gas Association.

Common Container Sizes

Industry term	Approximate net weight or fluid measure	Approximate yield (cups)
6 oz.	6 oz.	¾
8 oz.	8 oz.	1
Picnic	10½–12 oz.	1¼
12 oz.	12 oz.	1½
No. 300	14–16 oz. (14 oz.–1 lb.)	1¾
No. 303	16–17 oz. (1 lb.–1 lb. 1 oz.)	2
No. 2	20 oz. (1 lb. 4 oz.)	2½
No. 2½	27–29 oz. (1 lb. 11 oz.–1 lb. 13 oz.)	3½
32 oz.	32 oz.	4
No. 3 cyl. or 46 fl. oz.	51 oz. (3 lb. 3 oz.) or 46 fl. oz. (1 qt. 14 fl. oz.)	5¾
No. 10	6½ lb.–7 lb. 5 oz.	12–13

Source: Raymond B. Peddersen, *Foodservice and Hotel Purchasing*, p. 137. Also published by CBI Publishing Company, Inc. (Boston: 1980).

Reconstitution Guide (Approximate yields from 1 lb dried or dehydrated product)

Dried or dehydrated product	Yield
Onions	10 lb fresh as purchased or 8 lb peeled
Peppers	7 lb 4 oz fresh as purchased or 6 lb trimmed
Potatoes	7 lb fresh as purchased or 5 lb 4 oz peeled and pared
Peas or beans	2 lb 5 oz cooked product
Rice/noodles/macaroni	3 lb 4 oz cooked product

Source: James R. Myers, *Commercial Kitchens*, 6th ed. (Arlington, Va.: American Gas Association, 1979), p. 307. Used by permission of copyright holder—American Gas Association.

Preheat Guide (average times)

Type of appliance	Time required
Griddle	10 to 15 minutes
Grooved griddle	30 minutes
Solid top range	10 to 30 minutes
Open top range	no preheat
Range oven	20 to 30 minutes
Deck oven	45 to 60 minutes
Convection oven	20 to 30 minutes
Fryer	10 to 12 minutes
Tilting fry pan	5 to 7 minutes
Compartment steamer	10 to 12 minutes
Steam jacketed kettle	10 to 20 minutes
Over-fired infrared broiler	1 minute (15 to 20 minutes for grid marking)
Radiant broiler	15 to 20 minutes
Under-fired or open hearth broiler	20 minutes

Source: James R. Myers, *Commercial Kitchens*, 6th ed. (Arlington, Va.: American Gas Association, 1979), p. 225. Used by permission of copyright holder—American Gas Association.

Timetable for Braising Meats

Cut	Average weight or thickness	Approximate cooking time
Beef:		
Pot roast	3–5 lb	3–4 hr
Pot roast	5–15 lb	3–5 hr
Swiss steak	1–2½ in	2–3 hr
Round or flank steak	½ in (pounded)	45 min–1 hr
Stuffed steak	½–¾ in	1½ hr
Short ribs	2 × 2 × 2-in pieces	1½–2 hr
Fricasse	1–2 in pieces	2–3 hr
Birds	½ × 2 × 4-in pieces	1½–2 hr
Lamb:		
Breast, stuffed	2–3 lb	1½–2 hr
Breast, rolled	1½–2 lb	1½–2 hr
Shanks	½ lb each	1–1½ hr
Neck slices	½–¾ in	1–1½ hr
Riblets	¾ × 2½ × 3-in pieces	2–2½ hr
Pork:		
Chops or steaks	¾–1 in thick	45 min–1 hr
Spareribs	2–3 lb	1½ hr
Veal:		
Breast, stuffed	3–4 lb	1½–2 hr
Breast, rolled	2–3 lb	2–3 hr
Cutlets	½ × 3 × 5½-in pieces	45 min–1 hr
Steaks or chops	½–¾ in	45 min–1 hr
Birds	½ × 2 × 4-in pieces	45 min–1 hr

Source: James R. Myers, *Commercial Kitchens*, 6th ed. (Arlington, Va.: American Gas Association, 1979), p. 312. Used by permission of copyright holder—American Gas Association.

Timetable for Simmering Meats (cooking in liquid)

Cut	Average size or average weight (lb)	Approximate time (min/lb)	Time total (hrs)
Large cuts:			
Fresh beef	4–8	40–50	3–5
Corned beef	6–8	40–50	4–6
Fresh pork	Weight desired	30	
Smoked whole ham	12–16	18–20	4–5
Smoked half ham	6–8	25	2½–3½
Smoked picnic ham	4–8	35–45	3–4½
Stew cuts:			
Beef	1–2 in cubes		2–3
Lamb or veal	1–2 in cubes		1½–2

Source: James R. Myers, *Commercial Kitchens*, 6th ed. (Arlington, Va.: American Gas Association, 1979), p. 312. Used by permission of copyright holder—American Gas Association.

Timetable for Broiling Meats

Cut	Approximate thickness in inches	Approximate cooking time (minutes) Rare	Medium	Well-done
Rib, club, T-bone, porterhouse tenderloin, or individual serving of sirloin beef steak	1 1½ 2	15 25 35	20 35 50	30 — —
Sirloin beef steak (whole sirloin)	1 1½ 2	20–30 30–40 40–55	30–40 40–50 50–65	— — —
Ground beef patties	1	15	20	—
Shoulder, rib, loin, and sirloin lamb chops or steaks	1 1½ 2	— — —	12–15 17–20 20–25	— — —
Ground lamb patties	1	—	20	10–12
Smoked ham slice	½ 1	— —	— —	16–20 —
Bacon	—	—	—	4–5

Note: For broilers cooking meat on one side at a time. Do not broil veal or fresh pork.

Source: James R. Myers, *Commercial Kitchens*, 6th ed. (Arlington, Va.: American Gas Association, 1979), p. 96. Used by permission of copyright holder—American Gas Association.

Temperature and Timetable for Roasting Meat

Cut	Approximate weight (lb)	Interior temperature (°F)	Time (minutes/lb)	Total cooking time (hrs)
Standing 7-rib roast				
Rare	23	125	11	4
Medium	23	140	12	4½
Well	23	150	13	5
Lamb				
Leg	6½–7½	180	30–35	3–4
Rolled shoulder	3–4	180	40–45	2½–3
Pork, fresh				
Ham (leg)	10–12	185	30–35	8
Loin, bone in	12–15	185	16	3–4
Loin, rolled	7–8	185	11	4
Shoulder, rolled	4–6	185	35–40	3–3½
Pork, cured				
Ham, whole	10–14	180	15–18	3½
Shoulder butt	2–4	170	30–35	1–2

Oven temperatures: 300°F for all meats except fresh pork—350°F.

Source: James R. Myers, *Commercial Kitchens*, 6th ed. (Arlington, Va.: American Gas Association, 1979), p. 312. Used by permission of copyright holder—American Gas Association.

Deep Fat Frying Temperatures

Food	Temperature (°F) High input fryer	Temperature (°F) Standard fryer
Potatoes:		
Saratoga chips	320–340	325–360
French fried (blanching)	275–325	325–370
French fried (browning)	325–350	350–400
Shoestring or julienne	325–335	325–350
Waffle	330–340	350–375
Souffle (blanching)	290–320	300–340
Souffle (puffing)	350–425	350–425
Fish:		
Small (as perch, smelts)	325–335	350–375
Fillets, whitefish, etc.	325–335	350–375
Fish cakes, croquettes, or other cooked mixtures	330–350	360–390
Oysters, clams, scallops	330–350	330–390
Sliced halibut	330–340	380
Meat and fowl:		
Spring chickens and other fowl	320–335	325–370
Veal cutlets	325–335	350–375
Frankfurters	325	325
Croquettes	335–350	380
Nuts:		
Almonds	350	250
Cashews	285	285
Blanched peanuts	285	325
Spanish peanuts	290	350
Other food:		
Doughnuts, crullers	360–400	360–400
Fried cakes	360–400	370–400
Fritters	335–350	350–380
Chinese noodles	335–350	375–390
Onion rings	325–340	325–350

Note: Properly fried foods should have all of these five characteristics: (1) an attractive brown color; (2) a crisp crust; (3) a thoroughly cooked interior; (4) a dry, not greasy, appearance; and (5) a flavor that is characteristic of the original food.

Source: James R. Myers, *Commercial Kitchens*, 6th ed. (Arlington, Va.: American Gas Association, 1979), p. 41. Used by permission of copyright holder—American Gas Association.

Timetable for Cooking Vegetables

Vegetable	Boiling[1] (minutes)	Steaming in thermostatic compartment-type steamer[1,2] (minutes)	Steaming in self-generating high pressure cooker[3] (minutes)	Baking (minutes)
Artichokes	25–40	10	—	30–60
Asparagus, tips	5–20	5–12	3–5	—
Beans, lima	15–25	15–20	3–5	—
Beans, string	15–30	15–25	3–5	—
Beets, fresh, whole	30–45	30–60	25–35	40–60
Broccoli, split, heavy stalks	10–15	8–12	4–6	—
Brussels sprouts	10–20	10–16	4–6	—
Cabbage, quartered	10–15	6–14	5–7	—
Carrots, sliced or diced	10–25	12–25	5–8	30–40
Cauliflower, flowerets	8–15	8–10	5–6	—
Celery	15–18	10–17	—	—
Collards	10–20	—	—	—
Corn, on cob	5–15	4–8	4–6	—
Okra, sliced	10–15	8–12	—	—
Onions, medium	15–25	12–15	5–8	40–50
Peas	8–20	6–10	1–2	—
Potatoes, whole, small	25–40	12–20	—	45–60
Potatoes, quartered	20–25	15–30	12–15	—
Spinach	3–10	5–7	3–5	—
Squash, summer	10–20	8–12	1–2	30
Tomatoes	7–15	—	1–2	15–30

Fresh vegetables are assumed for this table. Considerable variation from the above occurs depending on the variety, size, maturity, storage time, temperature, and amount in the cooking equipment.

[1]Free vented steamers require about 25 percent more time.

[2]Frozen vegetables require up to 40 percent less time than fresh vegetables.

[3]In general the higher figures are for frozen vegetables. Equipment manufacturers' recommendations should be checked; variation does exist.

Source: James R. Myers, *Commercial Kitchen*, 6th ed. (Arlington Va.: American Gas Association, 1979), p. 97. Used by permission of the copyright holder—American Gas Association.

Incorrect Oven Temperatures

Baked item	Oven temperature too high	Oven temperature too low
Muffins	Coarse grain, small volume, unevenly browned, cracked top, peaks in crust, hard crust, crust too brown	Poor texture, pale crust, small volume, soggy or compact interior
Popovers	Hard, small volume, crust too brown, irregular shape	Tough, fail to "pop," soggy, pale crust
Biscuits	Hard crust, small volume, crust too brown	Pale crust, irregular shape
Yeast bread	Small volume, crust too brown, compact texture	Thick crust, pale crust, dark crumb, sour taste, coarse or uneven grain
Sponge-type cake	Thick hard crust, cracked crust, tough or coarse crumb, small volume	Dryness, shrinkage, coarse grain, sticky crust, poor volume
Butter cake	Peaked, cracks on top, heavy or compact texture	Sticky crust, falls to a hollow in center, crumbly, grayish color in white cake, coarse texture
Pastry	Too brown	Poor shape, pale color

Source: James R. Myers, *Commercial Kitchens*, 6th ed. (Arlington, Va.: American Gas Association, 1979), p. 24. Used by permission of copyright holder—American Gas Association.

Temperature Conversion Chart

°F	°C	°F	°C
0	−17.8	20	−6.6
32	0.0	40	4.4
45	7.2	50	9.9
60	15.5	70	21.0
80	28.6	90	32.1
100	37.7	212	100.0
250	121.0	300	148.7
350	176.4	400	204.2

Note: Conversion formulas are °C = .555(°F − 32) and °F = (1.8 × °C) + 32.

Source: James R. Myers, *Commercial Kitchens*, 6th ed. (Arlington, Va.: American Gas Association, 1979), p. 312. Used by permission of copyright holder—American Gas Association.

Spice Chart

Spice	Forms available
Allspice	Whole allspice, Ground allspice
Anise	Anise seed, Ground anise
Basil	Basil leaves
Bay leaves	Bay leaves, Ground bay leaves
Caraway	Caraway seed, Ground caraway seed
Cardamom	Whole cardamom, Ground cardamom seed
Celery	Celery seed, Ground celery seed
Chervil	Chervil leaves
Chives	Chopped chives (dehydrated or freeze-dried)
Cinnamon	Stick cinnamon, Ground cinnamon
Cloves	Whole cloves, Ground cloves
Cumin	Cumin seed, Ground cumin seed
Dill	Dill seed, Ground dill seed
Dill Weed	Dill weed
Fennel	Fennel seed, Ground fennel seed
Garlic	Instant minced garlic, Instant garlic powder
Ginger	Whole ginger, Ground ginger
Mace	Whole mace, Ground mace
Marjoram	Marjoram leaves, Ground marjoram
Mustard	Mustard seed, Powdered mustard
Nutmeg	Whole nutmeg, Ground nutmeg
Onion	Instant minced onion (or chopped onion), Instant onion powder (or granulated onion)
Oregano	Oregano leaves, Ground oregano
Paprika	Ground paprika
Pepper, black	Whole black pepper, Ground black pepper, coarse, Ground black pepper
Pepper, red	Whole red pepper, Crushed red pepper, Ground red pepper, Ground cayenne
Pepper, white	Whole white pepper, Ground white pepper
Poppy	Poppy seed
Rosemary	Rosemary leaves, Ground rosemary
Saffron	Saffron
Sage	Sage leaves, Rubbed sage, Ground sage,
Savory	Savory leaves, Ground savory
Sesame	Sesame seed
Shallots	Chopped (freeze-dried)
Tarragon	Tarragon leaves
Thyme	Thyme leaves, Ground thyme
Turmeric	Ground turmeric

Spice blends

Apple pie spice	Curry powder	Onion salt
Barbecue spice	Garlic salt	Poultry seasoning
Celery salt	Herb seasoning	Pumpkin pie spice
Chili powder	Italian seasoning	Seasoned or flavor salt
Cinnamon sugar	Mixed pickling spice	Shrimp spice or crab boil

Flakes

Celery flakes	Mixed vegetable flakes	Parsley flakes
Mint flakes	Onion flakes	Sweet pepper flakes

Source: American Spice Trade Association.

U.S. Grade Standards for Nuts

Kind of nut	Grade	Description of quality
In the shell:		
Almonds	U.S. No. 1	Best quality.
Brazil nuts	U.S. No. 1	Best quality.
English walnuts	U.S. No. 1	Best quality.
Filberts	U.S. No. 1	Best quality.
Pecans	U.S. No. 1	Best quality.
Mixed nuts (almonds, brazils, filberts, pecans, and English walnuts)	U.S. Extra Fancy U.S. Fancy	Best quality and largest sizes. At least 10 percent but not over 40 percent of each kind in the mixture.
Shelled, raw:		
Almonds	U.S. Fancy	Best quality.
	U.S. Extra No. 1	Almost the best—permits a few doubles and broken pieces.
	U.S. No. 1	Very good quality—permits more doubles and broken pieces.
English walnuts	U.S. No. 1	Best quality.
Pecans	U.S. No. 1	Best quality.
Peanut butter	U.S. Grade A	Best quality.

Source: Raymond B. Peddersen, *Foodservice and Hotel Purchasing*, p. 528. Also published by CBI Publishing Company, Inc. (Boston: 1980).

Portion Yields of Cereals, Mixes, and Bakery Products

Product	Unit	Portion size (cooked)	No. of portions
Corn grits	1 lb	¾ c	16.4
Macaroni	1 lb	¾ c	12.0
Noodles	1 lb	¾ c	10.7
Rice	1 lb	¾ c	11.3
Rolled oats	1 lb	¾ c	15.3
Spaghetti	1 lb	¾ c	12.1
Bran flakes	14 oz	1¼ oz	11.2
Corn flakes	12 oz	1 oz	12.0
Cake mixes	5 lb	6 sq in	75–100
Frosting mixes	5 lb	6 sq in	125–130
Biscuit mixes	5 lb	2 in	100
Raisin bread	2 lb	1 slice	36
Rye bread	1½ lb	1 slice	28
White bread	1½ lb	⅝-in slice	24

Source: Raymond B. Peddersen, *Foodservice and Hotel Purchasing*, p. 562. Also published by CBI Publishing Company, Inc. (Boston: 1980).

Can Equivalents

Can Number	____		Can Number (No.)				
	300	303	2	2½	3 cyl	10	12 (gal)
300	1.000	.901	.751	.511	.294	.139	.110
303	1.111	1.000	.822	.566	.347	.154	.122
2	1.350	1.216	1.000	.689	.397	.187	.148
2½	1.957	1.765	1.452	1.000	.577	.272	.215
3 cyl	3.401	3.061	2.517	1.735	1.000	.472	.373
10	7.194	6.488	5.355	3.673	2.120	1.000	.791
12 (gal)	9.102	8.203	6.744	4.646	2.680	1.264	1.000

Case Equivalents

Can Number		Can Number (No.)		
	303	2	2½	10
24/300	.90	.74	.51	.556
24/303	1.00	.82	.57	.616
24/2	1.22	1.00	.69	.748
24/2½	1.77	1.45	1.00	1.088
12/3 cyl	1.53	1.26	.87	.944
6/10	1.62	1.33	.92	

Source: National Canners Association. To convert: Multiply figure in the first column (horizontal) by the figure in desired vertical column *or* divide the figure in the desired vertical column by the desired size in the horizontal column.

Milk Equivalents

Fluid	Concentrate + water
1 quart skim	3¾ oz (¾ cup) dry powdered + 3¾ cups water
1 quart skim	3¾ oz (1½ cups) instant + ¾ cup water
1 quart whole	4 oz (⅞ cup) dry whole + ¾ cup water
1 quart whole	1 lb 2 oz (2 cups) evaporated + 2 cups water
1 gallon skim	15 oz (3 cups) dry powdered + 3¾ quarts water
1 gallon skim	15 oz (6 cups) instant dry + 3¾ quarts water
1 gallon whole	1 lb (3½ cups) dry whole + 3¾ quarts water
1 gallon whole	2 quarts (4 lb 7 oz) evaporated + 2 quarts water

Source: James R. Myers, *Commercial Kitchens*, 6th ed. (Arlington, Va.: American Gas Association, 1979), p. 308. Used by permission of copyright holder—American Gas Association.

Canned Fruit Weight Chart (no. 10 can except where indicated)

Item	Grade	Av. drained weight (oz) per can	Av. label weight (oz) per can
Apple sauce	Fancy	108	108
Apples	Solid pack	96	96
Apricots, halves	Fancy, choice, standard	66	108
Apricots, whole	Fancy, choice, standard	63	110
Blueberries	Water pack	65	102
Blackberries	Water pack	80	106
Boysenberries	Water pack	60	108
Cherries, red, sweet, pitted	Pie	74	110
Cherries, dark, sweet	Fancy	70	110
Cherries, Royal Anne	Fancy	70	110
Cranberry sauce	Fancy	117	117
Figs, Kadota	Fancy, choice, standard	66	108
Fruit cocktail	Fancy, choice	71	108
Fruits for salad	Fancy	64½	108
Grapefruit segments (#5 tin)	Fancy	29¾	50
Peaches, free, halves	Fancy	67¼	108
Peaches, free, slices	Fancy	65⅕	108
Peaches, yellow cling, halves and slices	Fancy	66	108
Peaches, yellow cling, halves and slices	Choice	68	108
Peaches, yellow cling, halves and slices	Standard	70	106
Peaches, yellow cling, halves and slices	Pie, solid pack	92	106
Pears, halves	Fancy	63½	110
Pears, halves	Choice	64	108
Pears, halves	Standard	65	106
Pineapple, slices	Fancy, choice	61½	108
Pineapple, tidbits	Standard	62½	107
Pineapple, crushed	Fancy	68	109
Pineapple, tidbits	Fancy	66	108
Plums, green gage	Fancy	60	110
Plums, prune	Fancy, choice, standard	60	110
Prunes, dried	Fancy, choice	70	110
Pumpkin	Solid pack	106	106

Source: James R. Myers, *Commercial Kitchens*, 6th ed. (Arlington, Va.: American Gas Association, 1979), p. 309. Used by permission of copyright holder—American Gas Association.

Approximate % Yields of Fresh Fruits

Fruit	% yield
Applesauce	87
Apples, sliced	63
Bananas, sliced	68
Cantaloupe, diced	50
Grapefruit, juice	44
Grapefruit, segments	47
Grapes, seedless	94
Honeydew melon, sliced	60
Lemons, juice	43
Oranges, juice	50
Oranges, sections	70
Peaches, sliced	76
Pears, sliced	78
Pineapple, cubed	52
Raspberries	97
Rhubarb, trimmed	103
Strawberries	87
Watermelon	46

Source: James R. Myers, *Commercial Kitchens*, 6th ed. (Arlington, Va.: American Gas Association, 1979), p. 309. Used by permission of copyright holder—American Gas Association.

Approximate % Yields of Vegetables

Vegetable	% yield of Fresh	% yield of Frozen	% yield of Canned
Asparagus	49	80	61
Beans, snap, green, or wax	84	91	62
Beets, without tops	76	—	65
Broccoli	62	85	—
Brussels sprouts	77	96	—
Cabbage	79	—	—
Carrots, without tops	82	96	66
Celery	70	—	—
Corn	37	97	66
Cucumbers	73	—	—
Lettuce, head	74	—	—
Mushrooms	67	—	66
Peas	—	96	64
Potatoes	80	100	71
Spinach	72	80	61
Squash, summer	83	67	69
Squash, winter	58	92	100
Tomatoes, medium	91	—	100

Source: James R. Myers, *Commercial Kitchens*, 6th ed. (Arlington, Va.: American Gas Association, 1979), p. 310. Used by permission of copyright holder—American Gas Association.

Canned Vegetable Weight Chart (No. 10 cans only, Fancy grade unless otherwise specified)

Vegetable	Minimum Drained Weight
Beans, green or wax:	
Whole beans	61 oz
French style	63 oz
Long cut	63 oz
Short cut	65 oz
Beans, lima:	
Green	72 oz
Green and white	72 oz
Beets:	
Whole Beets	73 oz
Sliced	71 oz
Diced	72 oz
Shoestring	68 oz
Carrots:	
Whole Carrots	67 oz
Sliced	67 oz
Diced	72 oz
Shoestring	67 oz
Corn:	
Corn, whole kernel	72 oz
Okra:	
Cut okra	64 oz

Peas:
  No minimum drained weight. Canned peas shall be considered standard in fill if the container is so filled that when the peas and liquid are removed from the container and then returned, the leveled peas, fifteen seconds after they are so returned, completely fill the container.

Potatoes:	
Irish potatoes	75 oz
Sweet potatoes	75 oz
Sauerkraut	80 oz
Spinach	60 oz
Tomatoes:	
Fancy Solid Pack	72¼ oz
Extra Standard (Choice)	63¼ oz
Standard	54¾ oz

  Tomato puree is made from the pulp of tomatoes, from which all skins, cores, and seeds have been removed. Heavy, or 1.07°, puree contains 12 to 25 percent tomato solids. Medium, or 1.06°, puree contains 10.7 to 12 percent tomato solids. Light, or 1.045°, puree contains 8.37 to 10.7 percent tomato solids.

Source: James R. Myers, *Commercial Kitchens*, 6th ed. (Arlington, Va.: American Gas Association, 1979), p. 310. Used by permission of copyright holder—American Gas Association.

Sizes and Weights of Fresh Eggs

1. JUMBO—30 ounces per dozen, minimum weight. Come in outsize cartons.
2. EXTRA LARGE—27 ounces per dozen, minimum weight.
3. LARGE—24 ounces per dozen, minimum weight. Most common size—fine for single serving.
4. MEDIUM—21 ounces per dozen, minimum weight. Fine size for general use.
5. SMALL—18 ounces per dozen, minimum weight. Plentiful in late summer and fall. Sometimes called "pullet" eggs.
6. PEEWEE—15 ounces per dozen, minimum weight. Come in special small cartons. Fine size for serving small children.

Source: James R. Myers, *Commercial Kitchens*, 6th ed. (Arlington, Va.: American Gas Association, 1979), p. 310. Used by permission of copyright holder—American Gas Association.

Egg Products Needed to Replace a Specific Number of Whole Eggs, Egg Yolks, or Egg Whites

Product	Amount of product to use	Shell egg equivalent
Frozen (thawed)		
Whole	3 T	1 egg
Whole	2¼ c	12 eggs
Yolks	1⅓ T	1 egg
Yolks	1 c	12 eggs
Whites	2 T	1 egg
Whites	1½ c	12 eggs
Dried (sifted)		
Whole	2½ T + 2½ T water	1 egg
Whole	2 c + 2 c water	12 eggs
Yolks	2 T + 2 t water	1 egg
Yolks	1½ c + ½ c water	12 eggs
Whites	2 t + 2 T water	1 egg
Whites	½ c + 1½ c water	12 eggs

Source: James R. Myers, *Commercial Kitchens*, 6th ed. (Arlington, Va.: American Gas Association, 1979), p. 310. Used by permission of copyright holder—American Gas Association.

Pan Sizes to Fit 19⅞ × 11⅞ Openings (often called 200 openings)

Depth	Capacity					
	Full Size	⅔ Size	⅓ Size	¼ Size	⅙ Size	½ Size
2.5 in	240	216	96	80	44	136
4 in	464	320	140	108	64	208
6 in	704	464	212	152	88	352
8 in	992	—	—	—	—	—

Note: Capacity given in fluid ounces. Divide ounce capacity by portion size desired to obtain total number of portions. Example: desired chili portion = 8 ounces; 6-in deep full size pan capacity = 704 fluid ounces; therefore, total number of portions in pan = 86.

Source: James R. Myers, *Commercial Kitchens*, 6th ed. (Arlington, Va.: American Gas Association, 1979), p. 308. Used by permission of copyright holder—American Gas Association.

Dippers and Ladles

Dipper	Measure	Weight	Ladle	Measure
30	2 T +	1–1½ ounces	1 oz	⅛ c
24	2⅔ T +	1½–1¾ ounces	2 oz	¼ c
20	3 T +	1¾–2 ounces	4 oz	½ c
16	4 T (¼ c)	2–2¼ ounces	6 oz	¾ c
12	5 T + (⅓ c)	2½–3 ounces	8 oz	1 c
10	6 T +	3–4 ounces		
8	8 T (½ c)	4–5 ounces		
6	10 T +	6 ounces		

Note: These measurements are based on level fill of dippers and ladles. If a heaping dipper or ladle is used, the measure and weight are closer to that of the next larger dipper or ladle. Dipper numbers are equal to portions per quart.

Source: James R. Myers, *Commercial Kitchens*, 6th ed. (Arlington, Va.: American Gas Association, 1979), p. 308. Used by permission of copyright holder—American Gas Association.